D0758413

Parenting by Men Who Batter

INTERPERSONAL VIOLENCE

Series Editors

Claire Renzetti, PhD
Jeffrey L. Edleson, PhD

Parenting by Men Who Batter

New Directions for Assessment and Intervention

Edited by

Jeffrey L. Edleson

Oliver J. Williams

OXFORD
UNIVERSITY PRESS

2007

OXFORD
UNIVERSITY PRESS

Oxford University Press, Inc., publishes works that further
Oxford University's objective of excellence
in research, scholarship, and education.

Oxford   New York
Auckland   Cape Town   Dar es Salaam   Hong Kong   Karachi
Kuala Lumpur   Madrid   Melbourne   Mexico City   Nairobi
New Delhi   Shanghai   Taipei   Toronto

With offices in
Argentina   Austria   Brazil   Chile   Czech Republic   France   Greece
Guatemala   Hungary   Italy   Japan   Poland   Portugal   Singapore
South Korea   Switzerland   Thailand   Turkey   Ukraine   Vietnam

Copyright © 2007 by Oxford University Press

Published by Oxford University Press, Inc.
198 Madison Avenue, New York, New York 10016

www.oup.com

Oxford is a registered trademark of Oxford University Press

Library of Congress Cataloging-in-Publication Data
Parenting by men who batter : new directions for assessment and intervention /
Jeffrey L. Edleson and Oliver J. Williams [eds.].
    p. cm.
Includes bibliographical references and index.
ISBN-13 978-0-19-530903-4
ISBN 0-19-530903-0
1. Family violence.   2. Abusive men—Counseling of.   3. Parenting.   I. Edleson,
Jeffrey L.   II. Williams, Oliver J.
HV6626.P365 2007
362.82'92—dc22   2006010265

9 8 7 6 5 4 3 2 1

Printed in the United States of America
on acid-free paper

This book is dedicated to the memory of

Sheila Wellstone
Susan Schechter
Ann L. Kranz
Diane Reese
Linda Saltzman
B. B. Robbie Rossman
Kathy Sternberg

Seven women who dedicated their lives and professional careers to ending domestic violence

To the loving memory of our fathers
LeRoy Edleson and Oliver F. Williams

And to our wives and children:
Sudha Shetty, Nevin, Daniel, Neil, and Eli
Sonia Davila-Williams and Sam

This book would not exist without the generous support of
the David and Lucile Packard Foundation
and Lucy Salicido Carter, our program officer at the
Foundation

Contents

1   Introduction: Involving Men Who Batter in Their
Children's Lives   3
Jeffrey L. Edleson and Oliver J. Williams

2   Shared Parenting After Abuse: Battered Mothers' Perspectives
on Parenting After Dissolution of a Relationship   19
Carolyn Y. Tubbs and Oliver J. Williams

        Box: Fathers' Voices on Parenting and Violence   32
Tricia Bent-Goodley and Oliver J. Williams

3   Assessing the Best Interests of the Child: Visitation and
Custody in Cases of Domestic Violence   45
Peter G. Jaffe and Claire V. Crooks

4   Deciding on Fathers' Involvement in Their Children's
Treatment After Domestic Violence   65
*Betsy McAlister Groves, Patricia Van Horn,
and Alicia F. Lieberman*

5   A Conceptual Framework for Fathering Intervention
With Men Who Batter   85
Einat Peled and Guy Perel

6   Guidelines for Intervention With Abusive Fathers   102
*Katreena L. Scott, Karen J. Francis, Claire V. Crooks,
Michelle Paddon, and David A. Wolfe*

7   Working With Fathers in Batterer Intervention Programs:
Lessons From the Fathering After Violence Project   118
Juan Carlos Areán and Lonna Davis

8   Latino Fathers in Recovery   131
        Ricardo Carrillo and Jerry Tello

9   Evaluating Parenting Programs for Men Who Batter:
        Current Considerations and Controversies   137
        Cris M. Sullivan

About the Contributors   149

Index   157

Parenting by Men Who Batter

1

Introduction

Involving Men Who Batter in Their Children's Lives

Jeffrey L. Edleson
Oliver J. Williams

This book is the result of years of work by many dedicated individuals and organizations concerned first and foremost with the safety of children and adults in families where domestic violence is occurring. It is also the result of our collective understanding that many women will continue to have contact with the men who have battered them as a result of these men's parenting of their shared children. Ironically, as will be stated repeatedly in this book, many mothers and children desire a connection with these violent men as long as it can be a safe one for all involved.

This book is more specifically the result of a two-day meeting held in San Francisco, California, in February 2004 with generous support from the David and Lucile Packard Foundation and the enthusiastic encouragement of our program officer, Lucy Salcido Carter. The meeting was attended by a diverse group of practitioners, policymakers, and researchers from three countries. The authors represented in this book prepared and circulated their papers in advance of the San Francisco meeting, briefly presented them at the meeting, and then discussed them at length with those in attendance. The papers were later revised into the chapters in this book. Those in attendance but not represented as authors included David J. Mathews and Aaron Milgrom of the Domestic Abuse Project; Anne Menard of the National Domestic Violence Resource Network; Alan Fox of San Francisco's Safe Start Initiative; Leiana Kinnicutt, Lynne Lee, and James Lang of the Family Violence Prevention Fund; Derrick M. Gordon of the Yale University School of Medicine; Johnny Rice II from the Center for Fathers, Families, and Workforce Development; and Jennifer Hardesty of the University of Illinois at Urbana-Champaign.

The meeting was a lively exchange that raised many thorny issues on which there was not always agreement. Some of the issues raised included:

- What do we know about the contact that mothers desire their children to have with fathers who have been violent?
- What sorts of contact with their children are desired by men who batter?

- What kinds of contact do children desire with these men?
- How safe is it to arrange contact between a man who has battered his female partner and his child?
- What criteria beyond safety should be used to determine if violent men should have contact with their children?
- What is the most appropriate forum in which to encourage such contact?
- Will court officers substitute fathering programs for batterer-intervention programs and, if so, what are the consequences in terms of safety and accountability for batterers?
- What are the goals of our work with these violent men who are also fathers?
- Are our goals solely focused on the best interest of the children and their battered mothers, or should they also include the needs of nuclear or extended families and communities?
- When men are involved, do we encourage respectful coparenting, parallel parenting, or another model of decision making for the children?
- What are the content and the most appropriate format in which to achieve these goals?
- What are the roles of the courts and the criminal justice system in responding to a violent man's involvement with his children?

The results of our discussions were new ways of thinking about these questions, as reflected in the chapters that follow.

About This Book

The authors represented in this book are accomplished individuals from research, policy, and practice domains who are struggling to understand the impact of domestic violence on children's lives, to find their way through the thicket of issues raised, and to come to some sense of best practices for when and how to encourage safe contact and engagement between children and their violent fathers.

The chapters in this book are consciously organized to be grounded at the start in the voices of mothers and fathers and at the end with a more abstract discussion of how we might know if we have achieved successful outcomes in parenting programs for men who batter. In between, there are deep discussions of how to assess and evaluate the parenting of violent men and how to intervene to encourage change. First, we start the book with the voices of mothers in Tubbs and Williams's chapter and include companion boxes highlighting the voices of fathers which were gathered by Bent-Goodley and Williams. After listening to these voices, Jaffe and Crooks in Chapter 3 and Groves and her colleagues Van Horn and Lieberman in Chapter 4 struggle with the criteria for deciding how the courts and practitioners must assess and decide on the appropriateness of mandating contact or including fathers in children's treatment.

Then the content shifts to how we are to work on parenting skills with men who batter. In Chapter 5, Peled and Perel provide a conceptual framework that has guided their work with Israeli fathers, and they reflect on the practice "dualities" that force them to balance competing goals when working on parenting skills with men who batter women. In Chapter 6, Scott and her colleagues draw on their experience in Canada to lay out a series of accountability guidelines that they believe are required for working with fathers who have engaged in adult domestic violence. In Chapter 7, Areán and Davis describe the Family Violence Prevention Fund's efforts in Boston, Massachusetts, to develop tools for providing fatherhood content in traditional batterer-intervention groups. In Chapter 8, Carrillo and Tello describe their pioneering work with Latino men in California who batter, and they discuss their efforts to reconnect these men to positive concepts of parenting and manhood which are indigenous to Latino culture. Finally, in Chapter 9, Sullivan works through the criteria that we should consider when judging the success of efforts in working on parenting with men who batter.

We cannot state emphatically enough that what is discussed in this book are promising practices and strategies, not empirically supported practices. The field has a long way to go before empirical support is established for any of these practices or strategies. We see this book as further developing the national discussion begun by Bancroft and Silverman (2002), and we expect that it will be followed by the publication of many empirical evaluations of emerging parenting programs for men who batter. We hope the chapters in this book will generate more discussion about how to decide what level of contact, if any, individual violent men should have with their children and how we are to intervene with these fathers when we have decided to do so. We hope that you find the ideas expressed in this book exciting and that they generate new initiatives in your communities.

The context of existing research knowledge and social movements for father involvement within which the programs and strategies described in this book are emerging is of critical importance. We take the remaining pages of this chapter to frame this book within a larger context by providing a definition of the term *men who batter*; a brief overview of the social context of emerging movements in North America to engage with violent fathers; and a selected review of what little research there is on the parenting behaviors of men who batter their intimate partners.

Men Who Batter

Throughout this book, we refer to *men who batter*. Over the years, those working to prevent domestic violence have refined their definitions of the term *battering*. Jaffe and Crooks (2007) state that although perpetrators of domestic violence are often indiscriminately labeled as batterers or men who batter, we would argue that these terms should be reserved for individuals who demonstrate a pattern of abusive behaviors over time, that are designed to control, dominate, humiliate, or terrorize their victims. Conversely, individuals who perpetrate minor, isolated incidents of violence that are not part of a pattern of behavior over time are perpetrators or individuals involved in an incident of abusive behavior. The terms batterer or men who batter would not be accurate in these circumstances. (p. 46)

Jaffe and Crooks's position reflects an emerging consensus among those working to prevent domestic violence. It is similar to the position taken by Osthoff (2002) when she argues that

counting violent acts does not give us enough information to determine whether someone is a batterer or an ongoing victim of battering. To ascertain if battering is occurring and who is doing it, one needs to know a lot about the people in the relationship and the dynamics, especially the power dynamics, of the relationship itself. (p. 1524)

Osthoff continues: "Battering involves a systematic pattern of using violence, the threat of violence, and other coercive behaviors and tactics, to exert power, to induce fear, and to control another person" (pp. 1526–1527).

This is the definition of battering that we will use throughout this book. We assume that the fathers we seek to help are men who have been engaged in a systematic pattern of violence and abuse against their partners and that their children will have been exposed to this violence and the resulting fear and control on repeated occasions and to varying degrees.

The Social Movements to Involve Fathers

The growing movement in North America to engage fathers and to maximize their participation in their children's daily lives is a critical factor to understand when thinking about parenting by men who batter. Work on their parenting with men who batter women will be developed in the context of these larger social currents, ultimately aiming for father engagement and inclusion. Generally speaking, the emerging fatherhood movement, with the exception of (perhaps) fathers' rights advocates and their organizations, is unknown to many researchers, practitioners, and advocates in the field of domestic-violence prevention.

Fatherhood advocates are increasingly sounding the alarm concerning children being raised in households without fathers. They argue that there is a crisis in America due to the economic, physical, and emotional disconnections between fathers and their children (Blankenhorn, 1995; Popenoe, 1996; Whitehead, 1993). As early as 1994, former Vice President Albert Gore Jr.

held a national summit in Nashville, Tennessee, on the role of fathers in the lives of their children. The Clinton and G. W. Bush administrations both asked federal agencies to examine national policies that posed barriers to men's involvement in the lives of their children.

A growing number of fatherhood groups has emerged in order to address the needs of fathers who neither live with nor have custody of their children but who want to be involved and supportive in their children's lives. Together, these groups are often referred to as the "fatherhood movement," but the term "movement" implies a cohesive effort by groups with similar makeup and a common goal. The so-called fatherhood movement is more accurately characterized as a confluence of activity by various types of fathers' groups, men's groups, individual fathers, and other kinds of groups, organizations, and government agencies with overlapping agendas but also with significantly different agendas, objectives, and methods (see Williams, Boggess, & Carter, 2001). The calls for fathers' involvement now come from many quarters: advocates for poor families, men's and fatherhood groups, governmental agencies, and individual men who feel alienated from their families.

While many fatherhood advocates proclaim that the presence of a father in the home is a protective factor for women and children against poverty, child abuse, and intimate partner violence (Pardue & Rector, 2004), there are many other researchers who question the fact that fatherhood at all cost should be the goal. Both the type of fathers and the types of homes and environments that men, women, and children live in must be critiqued in order to determine the extent to which families and children may benefit. These researchers suggest that it is not a forgone conclusion that all families benefit from the presence of a father, and they argue that the research that suggests this is simplistic because it does not include a deeper analysis of populations and factors which would more fully explain the impact of intersecting issues such as separation, divorce, abuse, and child and family well-being (Catlett & Artis, 2004). Despite these questions, the G. W. Bush administration has set aside many millions of dollars a year in the federal budget to encourage not only responsible fatherhood but also marriage promotion in governmental programs that include public and faith-based initiatives (Catlett & Artis, 2004; Parke, 2004).

What follows is a description of the various elements that make up the current social movements to include fathers in their children's lives. Three major groupings are identified: (1) father-involvement programs; (2) responsible-fatherhood groups; and (3) fathers' rights groups. Some in the field may disagree with these labels due to the fact that there are overlapping terms and shared philosophies. The intention is to provide a general overview of the major ideas representing these elements of the fatherhood movements.

Father-Involvement Programs

Father-involvement projects and organizations are designed to help fathers find employment and to reorder their lives so that they will be able to meet the financial, emotional, and physical responsibilities of raising their children. To describe people who conduct or participate in father-involvement program activities as members of a cohesive fatherhood group would be inaccurate. Rather, father-involvement activities are more often centered in fatherhood programs sponsored by nonprofit, community-based organizations in low-income, high-unemployment communities.

Low-income fathers who participate in these programs are engaged in employment-training and peer-group support programs or, when needed, substance-abuse treatment. But, generally speaking, these men do not become members of a fatherhood group or organization. The fatherhood organizations provide services to help respond to the special need of this segment of men. It should also be noted that although such programs have been targeted for fathers, some of them also provide similar services for female coparents, when requested.

Supporters of father involvement often encourage positive outcomes for all family members: fathers, children, and mothers. But they are primarily focused on helping fathers become more involved in their children's lives in a range of positive ways, including financial and emotional support. These fatherhood programs are not necessarily promoting marriage or gender-based divisions of labor. They are, however, concerned about the social-welfare and social-policy issues facing poor families and, specifically, about unmarried fathers and their children, particularly children whose families receive welfare assistance.

Responsible-Fatherhood Groups

The word "responsible" signals the basic moral tenor of many responsible-fatherhood organizations. They call for men not only to be involved with their children but to assume moral responsibility as fathers and husbands. Fathers represented within these groups may be men from any socioeconomic level. Researchers, analysts, and scholars in this field have collaborated and developed national organizations to send their message. Two of the most visible responsible-fatherhood organizations are the Institute for American Values and the National Fatherhood Initiative. Representatives of these groups suggest that one of the most devastating outcomes of divorce is the loss of fathers from children's homes. According to Blankenhorn (1995), founder and president of the Institute for American Values and author of *Fatherless America,* after divorce, children are left fatherless when the biological father no longer lives in the house and the mother has custody. Blankenhorn (1995) has described this situation as follows: "he [the father] still stops by, but he does not stay. He is on the outside looking in. No longer the man of the house, he has been largely defathered. He is a father once removed. He has become a visitor" (p. 148).

Responsible fatherhood organizations contend that the absence of fathers in families and the inadequacy of the parenting in "female-headed" households have led to dysfunctional families and a dysfunctional society. According to Ballard (1995), of the National Congress for Fathers and Families, "more than any other single factor, the absence of biological fathers is the leading cause of many of our nation's problems. Crime, drug problems, teen violence, inner-city strife, and juvenile delinquency are cited among the results of fatherless homes. The compelling implication of these findings is clear: "one parent is simply not enough" (see http://www.ncfc.netcmplt.txt).

Another organization, the National Fatherhood Initiative (NFI), was established in 1994 to create a social movement to combat father absence and promote responsible fatherhood. NFI's organizers view father absence as a chief cause of negative outcomes for children, and they believe that unless society reinforces responsible fatherhood, increasing father-absences will result in serious social consequences. Their mission is to improve the well-being of children by increasing the proportion of children who have committed responsible fathers in their lives (see http://www.fatherhood.org/history.asp).

Father involvement and responsible fatherhood groups are not the most visible advocates of fatherhood. Indeed, when most people think about a movement of fathers they often think of fathers' rights advocates.

Fathers' Rights Groups

Since the early 1960s, divorced, primarily middle-class fathers have made concerted efforts to demand "rights" for themselves (Vaux, 1997). Many of these fathers feel pushed out of their children's lives by the court system and by their children's mothers. Fathers' rights organizations are composed mostly of men who are divorced from their children's mothers. Some of the shared experiences and frustrations of these noncustodial fathers have led them to organize to discuss common issues and to challenge what they perceive as unfair or uninformed systems. They often exchange information with each other and those outside their organizations by way of the Internet.

The perception of an especially angry contingent of this group is that women and the court system have conspired together against fathers. This part of the movement actually represents a collection of membership groups, since fathers' rights groups are often founded and administered by individual leaders. Many fathers' rights groups are drawn to various high-profile divorce lawyers who write how-to books and provide seminars to explain and educate noncustodial fathers about matrimonial law (Baskerville, 1999). Finally, there are a few larger, more influential, and well-known fathers' rights organizations toward which smaller groups gravitate such as the Alliance for Non-Custodial Parents' Rights and the American Coalition for Fathers and Children. The small organizations tend to comprise the constituency and consumers of the information provided by larger, more visible organizations. Collectively, they are working toward a common goal of preserving (or restoring) what they view as fathers' rights. These are the stereotypical fathers' rights groups. When people outside the movement think about this issue, it is usually with the characteristics of these organizations in mind. Part of the reason that these men and their groups are so vocal and visible is that they are more likely to have the resources to be heard.

Fatherhood Movements and Domestic Violence

How do these three groupings of fatherhood advocates view violence between intimate partners? There are distinctions among these groups concerning their willingness to acknowledge and respond to male violence. For example, most father-involvement supporters strongly and sincerely denounce individual acts of violence. However, their inclination is to explain violence as a result of and a reaction to a man's own feeling of powerlessness and ineffectiveness as an individual. They tend to expend the bulk of their resources and efforts in addressing a father's social and personal problems as a priority. They say that the most effective way to improve a man's family life and to stop the violence is to help him change his life and overcome those feelings of powerlessness: get him a job and a good reputation in the community, and then the violence will stop.

Responsible-father groups, on the other hand, acknowledge that domestic violence happens but often suggest that blame should be placed on society and on the move away from traditional family values. These groups argue that because of men's biological makeup, they are naturally aggressive and uncivilized (Blankenhorn, 1995), and that women and children pacify and tame them. However, they say that when the family breaks down or when society allows men to dissociate themselves from families, and men are thus no longer expected to be accountable for the welfare of a family, they revert to a more savage (and violent) state.

Responsible-fatherhood advocates acknowledge that there is domestic violence and that abused women should be protected. In fact, they admit that some of their policy suggestions would create an environment that would put abused women at more risk, and they believe that those women and their children should be protected. However, they rarely address how to accomplish both sets of goals at once. And, as mentioned earlier, they promote the notion that marriages create an inherently safer environment for women and children.

Finally, fathers' rights and men's rights groups tend to be angry at the child's mother and at the system. Many in these groups deny that domestic violence against women is prevalent enough to warrant a concerted effort to deal with it. In fact, some fathers' rights groups contend that men are the victims of domestic violence at least as often as women. Members of these groups often imply that charges of violence perpetrated by men against women are fabricated or exaggerated to intimidate men and to strip them of their rights as fathers.

There is clearly a range of different ideas and opinions among these movements regarding the causes and consequences of domestic violence.

Within this context it is critical that we also explore the issue of parenting and domestic violence, our current knowledge concerning fathering, and where the gaps are within and between these two areas. The following section of this chapter reviews the current state of knowledge.

The Scarcity of Research on Fathering and Domestic Violence

Surprisingly little research has been conducted on parenting by men who batter, though there is a great deal more research on the mental health and parenting of battered mothers (Edleson, Mbilinyi, & Shetty, 2003). This gendered imbalance has itself become the focus of discussion and debate, with repeated calls for more attention to the impact of the batterers' parenting on their children (Peled 2000; Sternberg, 1997; Sullivan, Juras, Bybee, Nguyen, & Allen, 2000).

Parenting Styles of Perpetrators

What little information does exist on the parenting of men who batter reveals that they are likely to parent differently than other fathers. Holden and Ritchie (1991), for example, compared the parenting skills of 37 violent fathers, as described by their shelter-resident women partners, to the parenting skill of 37 nonviolent fathers, as described by their women partners. Violent fathers were reported to be less likely to be involved with their children or to have used positive child-rearing practices when compared to their nonviolent counterparts. Men who batter were more likely to have used negative child-rearing practices, such as spankings, when compared to the other fathers. In a later reanalysis of the same data, Holden, Stein, Ritchie, Harris, & Jouriles (1998) found that men who batter were also more often angry with their children compared to nonviolent fathers.

Children are also frequently involved in adult domestic-violence incidents. Many battered mothers report that their abusers purposefully involve children in violent events. Our own research—involving anonymous telephone interviews with 114 battered mothers in four U.S. cities (Mbilinyi, Edleson, Beeman, & Hagemiester, in press)—has shown that over one third of the children (37.8%) were accidentally hurt at least sometime during an adult domestic-violence incident and that over one quarter of the children (26.1%) were intentionally hurt at least sometime during these incidents. Almost one half of the mothers (48.6%) reported that they were at least sometimes intentionally hurt when they intervened to protect their children from abuse. Almost one half of the perpetrators (48.6%) were also reported to have used their children frequently to very frequently as a tool or pawn to get at the mother indirectly. In addition, almost four in ten of the battered mothers (38.7%) reported that their perpetrator frequently or very frequently hurt them as punishment for children's acts, and more than one in five mothers (22.5%) reported that the perpetrator frequently or very frequently blamed them for the perpetrators' own excessive punishment of the children. Our findings do indicate very high involvement of children in domestic violence incidents in this sample.

Men's Interference in Women's Parenting

The available research on battered mothers indicates that they experience significantly greater levels of stress when compared to nonbattered mothers (Holden & Ritchie, 1991; Holden, et al., 1998; Levendosky & Graham-Bermann, 1998). Bancroft and Silverman (2002) argue that men who batter systematically undermine and interfere with battered mothers' parenting in multiple ways, often continuing into the postseparation period. Available research supports this contention. For example, Holden, et al. (1998) found that battered mothers, when compared to other mothers, more often altered their parenting practices in the presence of the abusive male. Mothers reported that this change in parenting was made to minimize the men's irritability. A survey of 95 battered mothers Levendosky, Lynch, and Graham-Bermann (2000) indicated that abusive partners undermined these mothers' authority with their children, making effective parenting more difficult. In an earlier qualitative study of one child-support and education group program, Peled and Edleson (1995) found that fathers also often pressured their children not to attend counseling when mothers were seeking help for their children.

Postseparation Violence by Men Who Batter

It is often also assumed that once separation or divorce has occurred, a man's violence ceases. The available data on postseparation violence shows otherwise. Domestic violence appears frequently to continue after a couple has physically separated (Hardesty, 2002; Jaffe, Lemon, & Poisson, 2002). Leighton (1989) found that one quarter of the 235 Canadian women he interviewed reported threats by a perpetrator during child visitations. In a more recent report, Fleury, Sullivan, and Bybee (2000) found that over one third (36%) of the 135 battered women they studied were reassaulted during separation from their perpetrators. Their study sample included only those women who had resided in a battered women's shelter and were still separated from their violent partners 10 weeks after shelter exit. One half of the new assaults occurred within 10 weeks after exiting the shelter, but another 8% of the reassaults occurred for the first time since separation in the period of 18–24 months after ending the relationship. Key variables that predicted repeat assaults included prior assaults and threats from the perpetrator, the perpetrator's proximity to his victim, and his prior accusations of her sexual infidelity.

On a more optimistic note, the research on violence and on the types of men who batter also reveals that these men and their behaviors vary a great deal, with almost 80% stopping their violence toward their partners after having completed an intervention program (see Gondolf, 2002, 2004).

Impact of a Violent Man's Behavior on the Child

Many assume that a violent man's behavior toward his adult victim does not represent a risk to children in the home. If the studies reviewed above do not raise doubts about this assumption, the results of 25 years of research clearly refute it. Over 30 studies of the link between physical child abuse and domestic violence show a 41% median co-occurrence in families studied when a conservative definition of child abuse was used (Appel & Holden, 1998). The majority of these studies found a co-occurrence between 30% and 60% of the time (Edleson, 1999a).

The data on co-occurring maltreatment come from a wide range of studies in the United States and other countries. For example, child-fatality reviews in Oregon and Massachusetts found between 41% and 43% of the murdered children's mothers were also victims of adult domestic violence (Felix & McCarthy, 1994; Oregon Child Welfare Partnership, 1996). The National Family Violence Survey of 1985 revealed that 50% of the fathers who beat their wives three or more times in the year of the study had also physically abused their children three or more times that same year (Straus & Gelles, 1990). And a range of other studies based on child-protection records, hospital records, and interviews with battered mothers in shelters indicates similar levels of co-occurring violence in homes. In a study of at-risk mothers participating in a home-visiting program, McGuigan & Pratt (2001) found that child maltreatment was confirmed in 155 of the 2,544 families in the sample. Of these 155 families, 38% (59 families) also had confirmed domestic violence. A closer analysis of the 59 families with both confirmed domestic violence and child maltreatment revealed that in 78% (46) of the families, domestic violence preceded child maltreatment. The wide variation in the degree of co-occurrence among all available studies is most likely the result of the samples used in each study, with some of the lowest co-occurrence rates found in studies drawing participants from the general community, and the highest drawing their samples from social-service agencies.

As Appel and Holden (1998) have also pointed out, co-occurring violence may develop in many different ways. Often it is the perpetrating male who beats both the woman and child, but it may also be that the male beats the woman, who then abuses the child, or that both parents abuse the child.

While somewhere close to one half of children of domestic-violence victims are likely to be physically abused, there is also growing concern for those children who are exposed to domestic violence but are not themselves the victims of physical or sexual abuse. A number of authors have produced reviews of the literature on childhood exposure and its limitations (see Edleson, 1999b; Fantuzzo & Mohr, 1999; Holtzworth-Munroe, Smutzler, & Sandin, 1997; Margolin, 1998; Rossman, Hughes, & Rosenberg, 2001). Overall, existing studies reveal that, on average, children exposed to adult domestic violence exhibit more difficulties than those not so exposed. These difficulties can be grouped into the two major categories associated with recent exposure: (1) behavioral and emotional functioning and (2) cognitive functioning and attitudes. For example, several studies have reported that children exposed to domestic violence exhibit more aggressive and antisocial behaviors (externalized behaviors) as well as fearful and inhibited behaviors (internalized behaviors) when compared to nonexposed children (Fantuzzo, et al., 1991; Hughes, 1988; Hughes, Parkinson, & Vargo, 1989). Exposed children also showed lower social competence than did other children (Adamson & Thompson, 1998) and were found to show higher-than-average anxiety, depression, trauma symptoms, and temperament problems than children who were not exposed to violence at home (Hughes, 1988; Maker, Kemmelmeier, & Peterson, 1998; Sternberg, et al., 1993). In addition, a number of studies have measured the association between cognitive-development problems and exposure to adult domestic violence. While academic abilities were not found to differ between children exposed to domestic violence and other children in one study (Mathias, Mertin, & Murray, 1995), another found increased violence exposure associated with lower cognitive functioning (Rossman, 1998).

The relationship of the child to the violent adult appears to influence how a child is affected. A study of 80 shelter-resident mothers and 80 of their children revealed that an abusive male's relationship to a child directly affects the child's well-being without being mediated by the mother's level of mental health (Sullivan, et al., 2000). Violence perpetrated by a biological father or stepfather was found to have a greater impact on a child than the violence of nonfather figures (e.g., partners or ex-partners who played a minimal role in the child's life). Children whose fathers or stepfathers were the abusers showed lower scores on self-competency measures when compared to the other children. (It is important to note that the self-competency of children in this sample was within the normal range for their age group.) The researchers concluded that "there may be something especially painful in the experience of witnessing one's own father abuse one's mother" (Sullivan, et al., 2000, p. 598). In particular, stepfathers of children in this shelter-based population seemed to be more emotionally abusive to their children and more feared by them when compared to biological fathers and unrelated male partners in the home. As the authors state, this study perhaps raises more questions than it resolves. For instance, questions regarding the interaction among child physical abuse, exposure, and the male caregiver's relationship with the child were not addressed.

Fathers Through Their Children's Eyes

At this point, one might have a fairly negative view of men who batter and of their parenting behavior. In fact, the views of family members have been found to vary substantially (Sternberg, Lamb, & Dawud-Noursi, 1998). It is not uncommon to hear a battered women and/or her child individually express a desire to remain in a relationship with the perpetrator if his violence ends, as can be seen in Tubbs and Williams's next chapter in this book.

Peled (2000) suggests that children view their abusive fathers in two contradictory ways, as the "good, loved father" and as the "bad, abusive father," but these children seldom maintain both views simultaneously. Peled's (1998) earlier qualitative research found that children implement strategies to minimize the negative view of their fathers, which creates complex emotions when it comes to making choices involving their parents. Most children in her study—14 preadolescents associated with an outpatient domestic-violence program—found ways to see their fathers in a positive light despite their negative feelings about the fathers' violence. In a related study of 110 Israeli children, Sternberg et al. (1993) found that children exposed to domestic violence more often rated the perpetrating parent negatively than they did their nonabusive parent, especially when compared to ratings of children from homes with no violence. These same children were no different than comparison children in assigning positive attributes to both parents. Interestingly, boys more than girls in this study viewed the perpetrating parent in both more positive and more negative ways. The authors suggest that fathers may be "more emotionally salient to their sons than to their daughters" (Sternberg, et al., 1994, p. 788). Alternatively, these findings may suggest gender differences in how boys and girls attach meaning to parents' behavior.

Overall, this literature indicates that perpetrators of domestic violence often continue their abuse of the adult victim and make targets of the children in their homes through threats and violence toward them. This behavior negatively affects children in the home in a number of ways, such as through harsh parenting and by involving the children in violent events. Children may continue to hold positive views of both parents despite the violence, but they also differentiate between the perpetrator and victim by more often assigning negative qualities to the perpetrator. An understanding of these dynamics must form a foundation on which to make recommendations for father contact and to design programs that encourage father involvement with their children.

Conclusion

We have reviewed the growing movements to involve fathers in their children's lives and the little research available on the parenting by men who batter. It is within this context of scarce research and the many swirling currents of the emerging fatherhood movements across North America that this book attempts to bring fresh voices to the table. As stated earlier in this chapter, what is discussed in this book are promising practices and strategies, not empirically supported practices. We hope these emerging practices help you generate new policies, practices, and program evaluations that will improve the safety and well-being of the families with whom you work.

References

Adamson, J. L., & Thompson, R. A. (1998). Coping with interparental verbal conflict by children exposed to spouse abuse and children from nonviolent homes. *Journal of Family Violence, 13,* 213–232.

Appel, A. E., & Holden, G. W. (1998). The co-occurrence of spouse and physical child abuse: A review and appraisal. *Journal of Family Psychology, 12,* 578–599.

Ballard, T. (1995). National Congress for Fathers and Children. Retrieved from http://www.ncfc.net.cmplt.txt

Bancroft, L., & Silverman, J. (2002). *The batterer as parent.* Thousand Oaks, CA: Sage.

Baskerville, S. (1999, May 15). Why is Daddy in Jail? *Washington Times,* p. 12.

Blankenhorn, D. (1995). *Fatherless America: Confronting our most urgent social problem.* New York: Basic Books.

Catlett, B. S., & Artis, J. E. (2004, November). Critiquing the Case for Marriage Promotion. *Violence Against Women, 10,* 1226–1244.

Edleson, J. L. (1999a). Children's witnessing of adult domestic violence. *Journal of Interpersonal Violence, 14*(8), 839–870.

Edleson, J. L. (1999b). The overlap between child maltreatment and woman battering. *Violence Against Women, 5*(2), 134–154.

Edleson, J. L., Mbilinyi, L.F., & Shetty, S. (2003). *Parenting in the Context of Domestic Violence.* San Francisco, CA: Judicial Council of California.

Fantuzzo, J. W., DePaola, L. M., Lambert, L., Martino, T., Anderson, G., & Sutton, S. (1991). Effects of interparental violence on the psychological adjustment and competencies of young children. *Journal of Consulting and Clinical Psychology, 59,* 258–265.

Fantuzzo, J. W., & Mohr, W. K. (1999). Prevalence and effects of child exposure to domestic violence. *The Future of Children, 9,* 21–32.

Felix, A. C., III, & McCarthy, K. F. (1994). *An analysis of child fatalities, 1992.* Boston: Commonwealth of Massachusetts Department of Social Services.

Fleury, R. E., Sullivan, C. M., & Bybee, D. I. (2000). When ending the relationship does not end the violence. *Violence Against Women, 6,* 1363–1383.

Gondolf, E. W. (2002). *Batterer intervention systems: Issues, implications and outcomes of a multi-site evaluation.* Thousand Oaks, CA: Sage.

Gondolf, E. W. (2004). Evaluating batterer counseling programs. *Aggression and Violent Behavior, 9,* 605–631.

Hardesty, J. L. (2002). Separation assault in the context of postdivorce parenting. *Violence Against Women, 8,* 597–625.

Holden, G. W., & Ritchie, K. L. (1991). Linking extreme marital discord, child rearing, and child behavior problems: Evidence from battered women. *Child Development, 62*(2), 311–327.

Holden, G. W., Stein, J. D., Ritchie, K. L., Harris, S. D., & Jouriles, E. N. (1998). Parenting behaviors and beliefs of battered women. In G. W. Holden, R. Geffner, & E. N. Jouriles (Eds.), *Children exposed to marital violence: Theory, research, and applied issues* (pp. 185–222). Washington, DC: American Psychological Association.

Holtzworth-Munroe, A., Smutzler, N., & Sandin, B. (1997). A brief review of the research on husband violence. Part II: The psychological effects of husband violence on battered women and their children. *Aggression and Violent Behavior, 2,* 179–213.

Hughes, H. M. (1988). Psychological and behavioral correlates of family violence in child witness and victims. *American Journal of Orthopsychiatry, 58,* 77–90.

Hughes, H. M., Parkinson, D., & Vargo, M. (1989). Witnessing spouse abuse and experiencing physical abuse: A "double whammy"? *Journal of Family Violence, 4,* 197–209.

Jaffe, P. G., & Crooks, C. V. (2007). Assessing the best interests of the child: Visitation and custody in cases of domestic violence. In J. L. Edleson & O. J. Williams (Eds.), *Parenting by men who batter* (pp. 45–64). New York, NY: Oxford University Press.

Jaffe, P. G., Lemon, N. K. D., & Poisson, S. E. (2002). *Child custody and domestic violence: A call for safety and accountability.* Thousand Oaks, CA: Sage.

Leighton, B. (1989). *Spousal abuse in metropolitan Toronto: Research report on the response of the criminal justice system* (Report No. 1989–02). Ottawa, Canada: Solicitor General of Canada.

Levendosky, A. A., & Graham-Bermann, S. A. (1998). The moderating effects of parenting stress on children's adjustment in woman-abusing families. *Journal of Interpersonal Violence, 13*(3), 383–397.

Levendosky, A. A., Lynch, S. M., & Graham-Bermann, S. A. (2000). Mothers' perceptions of the impact of woman abuse on their parenting. *Violence Against Women, 6*(3), 247–271.

Maker, A. H., Kemmelmeier, M., & Peterson, C. (1998). Long-term psychological consequences in women of witnessing parental physical conflict and experiencing abuse in childhood. *Journal of Interpersonal Violence, 13,* 574–589.

Margolin, G. (1998). Effects of witnessing violence on children. In P. K. Trickett & C. J. Schellenbach (Eds.), *Violence against children in the family and the community* (pp. 57–101). Washington, DC: American Psychological Association.

Mathias, J. L., Mertin, P., & Murray, A. (1995). The psychological functioning of children from backgrounds of domestic violence. *Australian Psychologist, 30,* 47–56.

Mbilinyi, L. F., Edleson, J. L., Beeman, S. K. & Hagemeister, A. K. (in press). What happens to children when their mothers are battered? Results from a four city anonymous telephone survey. *Journal of Family Violence.*

McGuigan, W. M., & Pratt, C. C. (2001). The predictive impact of domestic violence on three types of child maltreatment. *Child Abuse and Neglect, 25,* 869–883.

Oregon Child Welfare Partnership. (1996). *Cohort two: A study of families and children entering foster care 1991–93.* Salem, OR: State Office for Services to Children and Families.

Osthoff, S. (2002). But, Gertrude, I beg to differ: A hit is no a hit is not a hit. *Violence Against Women, 8,* 1521–1544.

Pardue, M. G., & Rector, R. E. (2004, March 30). *Reducing domestic violence: How the healthy marriage initative can help* (Backgrounder#1744). Washington, DC: Heritage Foundation. Retrieved June 25, 2004, from http://www.heritage.org/Research/Family/bg/1744.cfm

Parke, M. (2004). *Marriage-related provisions in welfare reauthorzation proposals: A summary* (Publication No. 04–16). Washington DC: Center for Law & Social Policy. Retrieved June 25, 2004, from http://www.clasp.org/DMS/Documents/1056725608/view_html

Peled, E. (1998). The experience of living with violence for preadolescent children of battered women. *Youth and Society, 29,* 395–430.

Peled, E. (2000). Parenting by men who abuse women: Issues and dilemmas. *British Journal of Social Work, 30*(1), 25–36.

Peled, E., & Edleson, J. L. (1995). Process and outcome in small groups for children of battered women. In E. Peled, P. G. Jaffe, & J. L. Edleson (Eds.), *Ending the cycle of violence: Community responses to children of battered women* (pp. 77–96). Thousand Oaks, CA: Sage.

Popenoe, D. (1996). *Life without father.* New York, NY: Martin Kessler Books, the Free Press.

Rossman, B. B. R. (1998). Descartes's error and posttraumatic stress disorder: Cognition and emotion in children who are exposed to parental violence. In G. W. Holden, R. Geffner, & E. N. Jouriles (Eds.), *Children exposed to marital violence* (pp. 223–256). Washington, DC: American Psychological Association.

Rossman, B. B. R., Hughes, H., & Rosenberg, M. S. (2001). *Children and interparental violence.* Philadelphia, PA: Brunner/Mazel.

Sternberg, K. J. (1997). Fathers, the missing parents in research on family violence. In Lamb, M. E. (Ed.), *The role of the father in child development* (pp. 284–308). New York: John Wiley & Sons.

Sternberg, K. J., Lamb, M. E., Dawud-Noursi, S. (1998). Using multiple informants to understand domestic violence and its effects. In G. W. Holden, R. Geffner, & E. N. Jouriles (Eds). *Children exposed to marital violence: Theory, research, and applied issues.* (pp. 121–156). Washington, DC: American Psychological Association.

Sternberg, K. J., Lamb, M. E., Greenbaum, C., Cicchetti, D., Dawud, S., Cortes, R. M., et al. (1993). Effects of domestic violence on children's behavior problems and depression. *Developmental Psychology, 29,* 44–52.

Straus, M. A., & Gelles, R. J. (Eds.) (1990). *Physical violence in American families.* New Brunswick, NJ: Transaction Publishers.

Sullivan, C. M., Juras, J., Bybee, D., Nguyen, H., & Allen, N. (2000). How children's adjustment is affected by their relationships to their mothers' abusers. *Journal of Interpersonal Violence, 15*(6), 587–602.

Vaux, W. G. (1997). Are fathers really necessary? Retrieved May 30, 2006, from http://www.ncfm.org/liter.htm

Whitehead, B. D. (1993, April). Dan Quayle was right. *The Atlantic,* p. 47–84.

Williams, O. J., Boggess, J., & Carter, J. (2001). Fatherhood and domestic violence: Exploring the role of men who batter in the lives of their children. In J. Edleson & S. Graham-Bermann (Eds.), *Future directions for children exposed to domestic violence* (pp. 157–187). Washington, DC: American Psychological Association.

2

Shared Parenting After Abuse

*Battered Mothers' Perspectives on Parenting
After Dissolution of a Relationship*

Carolyn Y. Tubbs
Oliver J. Williams

The story has become increasingly familiar. They were an attractive, suburban couple with an 11-year marriage and a bright future. After years of hard work, they were a year into their dream job. Close family ties supported the couple and their young children. However, recently, the relationship turned sour and they separated. Divorce papers were filled with intimations of emotional, financial, and sexual coercion, physical threats, intimidating gun play, and veiled threats directed toward her. He countered with reports of mental instability, physical violence, and child abuse. After years as a stay-at-home mother, she began learning word processing skills in preparation for her life as a single parent. She was ready for a new life, but he vowed to never let her go.

She did what she could to manage the risks of their volatile relationship. Consultations with a divorce lawyer had been secretive. She moved out of their home prior to filing for divorce. Because of the nature of his work, she tried to limit disclosure of damaging information to a few close friends and her immediate family. Since tension and conflict in the relationship were high, she promised her family that she would never be in his presence alone. Knowing his love for the children, she hoped that an informal agreement to weekend visits would foster goodwill. They agreed to use her parents' home as the pick-up and drop-off site.

On a Saturday afternoon in April 2003, a chance meeting placed them in her car at a local drug store. He was less than 24 hours into his weekend visit with the kids and had taken them on errands. On a whim, she decided to pick up cold medication and parked her car in front of the store only seconds before he arrived. She was on the cell phone with her mother just as she realized the chance encounter. Her mother begged her to leave immediately, but she hung up before the gravity of her mother's concerns could be impressed on her. Seven more calls to her cell phone went unanswered over the next 12 minutes. He had shot her in the head, then shot himself; and the couple lay dying in her car. A short distance away, the children were locked in his car—witnesses to the murder-suicide that unfolded. They were the children of Crystal Judson Brame and David Brame, the police chief of Tacoma, Washington. (Modeen, 2004)

The 2003 murder-suicide of the Brames is the story of shared parenting in the wake of intimate-partner violence and with the imminent prospect of relationship dissolution. Ultimately, their story illustrates the ubiquitous risks inherent to shared parenting after intimate partner violence.

The Parenting Context

Relationship Dissolution

In social science research, relationship formation has been of greater interest than relationship dissolution (Cherlin, 1992; Sweeney, 2002). However, trends in relationship trajectories toward the latter half of the past century broadened the range of relationship research to include the process of dissolution, and it was through this research that the fragile state of American marriages became apparent. From the 1940s to the 1970s, the rate of legal relationship dissolution for first marriages (i.e., divorce) rose 50% (Bramlett & Mosher, 2002). In 2002, the probability of first marriages ending in divorce after 5 years was 20%, and 33% after 10 years. Outcomes for de facto unions, or those involving couples in common-law or cohabiting arrangements, were considerably worse. The probability of premarital cohabitation ending in 5 years was 49%, and 62% after 10 years (Bramlett & Mosher, 2002; Wilson & Daly, 2001).

In examining the causes of these seemingly dismal prospects for relationship longevity, Olson and DeFrain (2000) found that chronic financial problems, lack of communication, and infidelity were primary reasons for relationship conflict. Relationship distress and the probability of relationship dissolution, as well as mismanaged conflict, increased with negative interactions arising from these difficulties (Gottman, 1994). However, it was the manner in which couples handled conflict, rather than the presence of conflict itself, that ultimately predicted dissolution (Markman, Stanley, & Blumberg, 1994; Sprecher, 1999).

Shared Parenting

When relationship dissolution occurs, it transpires on multiple levels with asynchronous timelines (Demo, Find, & Ganong, 2000). Depending on the level of involvement, couples negotiate several types of dissolutions in the process of ending a romantic relationship. Dissolution of emotional, financial, and legal ties typically occurs individually and collectively when committed cohabiting relationships end. Clearly, all couples (whether legally married or in unions) must deal with the dissolution of emotional ties, which includes romantic and sexual attachments. In addition, whether married or not, cohabiting couples also deal with disentangling finances and joint economic investments. However, rarely do all of these dissolutions occur spontaneously and simultaneously. Cherlin (2002) notes that "the unmaking of a marriage [or committed relationship] occurs in many stages over a period of time that often begins well before the couple separates and that extends well after they are granted a divorce [or the relationship ends]" (p. 430).

One of the most difficult areas to fully disengage as a couple is around the common bond of children (Margolin, Gordis, & John, 2001). Children forge an enduring bond between intimates—one that lasts at least 18 years, if not a lifetime. As estranged intimates initiate various forms of dissolution, they must also face the reality that the shared parenting relationship cannot be readily terminated. Shared parenting begins, in earnest, at the birth of the child and morphs developmentally as the child, each parent, and the family collectively transition to new developmental phases (Rodgers & White, 1993). In most cases, shared parenting is an intergenerational endeavor that transcends the bonds of the romantic or sexual relationship, whether the relationship is committed or noncommitted, legal or de facto, involving cohabitation or separate residences. However, its nature changes, at least quantitatively, when the couple relationship ends.

Shared parenting, in general, describes a negotiated, yet often implicit and unspoken, agreement between parents (typically, the child's biological parents) to supervise, educate, and financially support the child. Margolin et al. (2001) suggest that three important relational dimensions inevitably become part of the agreement: conflict (disagreement about child-rearing practices), cooperation (support and respect for the other's parenting skills and burden), and triangulation (forming a coalition with the child for the purpose of undermining the perception or authority of the other).

After a relationship dissolves, shared parenting is almost inevitably complicated by conflictual interactions and lingering negative emotions (Furstenberg & Cherlin, 1991; Maccoby & Mnookin, 1992). It becomes a parallel, rather than a cooperative, endeavor with former partners opting for as little interaction as possible. Maccoby and Mnookin (1992) reported that couples were more likely to adopt a parallel, disengaged style over cooperative or conflicted styles of shared parenting. In this style, estranged parents who prefer as little contact and conversation as possible often communicate through children and choose to parent separately.

For an unknown number of couples, the complications of shared parenting are further challenged by a history of domestic violence. Reports of domestic violence during marriage are the best predictors of interpersonal violence after relationship dissolution, which is a major cause of concern for women contemplating the prospect of shared parenting (Campbell, Sharps, & Glass, 2001). There are only a few studies that have examined the dynamics of shared parenting in couples where domestic violence has occurred (Johnston, Kline, & Tschann, 1989; Pruett & Hoganbruen, 1998). The domestic violence literature strongly suggests that the probability of negative emotions and escalating conflict not only makes interacting uncomfortable in a couple with a history of violence, but it also renders it dangerous because of the often volatile disposition of batterers. The conflict, cooperation, and triangulation dimensions of coparenting could assume unhealthy, and potentially abusive, dimensions when battered women attempt to negotiate child support and father-child contacts with men who have battered them. However, the outcomes from the interaction of domestic violence and shared parenting are unknown.

Conversely, the relationship between domestic violence and child outcomes are better known. Research on outcomes for children living in violent households indicated that between 1993 and 1998, 41% of female victims of domestic violence lived in households with children, and children in these homes were the victims of child mistreatment (Appel & Holden 1998; Bureau of Justice Statistics [BJS], 2000). Children are more likely to be harmed by or be victims of intimate-partner violence in their homes (Parkinson, Adams, & Emerling, 2001; Rumm, Cummings, Krauss, Bell, & Rivara, 2000). In addition, child witnesses to highly conflictual interactions between parents, as well as domestic violence, were more likely to experience behavioral problems (Hetherington & Stanley-Hagan, 1999).

A review of the literature on shared parenting underscores the lack of data on shared parenting among couples with a history of domestic violence, leaving one to wonder what women's and men's expectations are of shared parenting after a history of abuse. The prospect of having to make joint decisions in a relationship that has historically been characterized by domination and coercion (at least from the battered woman's perspective) would seem unfavorable to both partners. For women, concerns exist over revictimization and being able to assert personal rights and control, as well as advocating for the child. For men, concerns arise over capitulating to external controls and conceding perceived rights to have overt control over his former partner and the child. Paradoxically, by ending the abusive relationship with their former partners, the ex-partners must forge a new relationship with the same partners, especially when children are involved—one that ideally requires redefined power dynamics and greater boundary definition and equity.

This chapter describes an initial effort to investigate African American women's perceptions of shared parenting with men who have battered them in the past. The primary research question guiding the study was: "what types of shared parenting expectations do battered women have in reference to men with whom they have a history of violence?" The larger goal of this study was to seek women's perspectives on the decision-making processes involved in shared parenting with men with whom they have a history of domestic violence. However, its findings may help to spark, or even inform, additional research into this realm of shared parenting, which is often fraught with tensions about violence, whose ramifications can often turn catastrophic, and which continues to linger below the research radar. We hope that men, women,

and children from various ethnic backgrounds will ultimately be the benefi-
ciaries of more focused, and systematic, research on this topic.

A Focus-Group Study

In this chapter, we report on focus-group data from African American
women residing in two large urban areas. The focus groups brought together
women who were in the process of shared parenting or had experienced
shared parenting with an ex-batterer. In using a focus-group approach, we
wanted to tap the subjective experiences of a group who have individually
shared a similar situation through focused questioning and group interaction
(Merton, Fiske, & Kendall, 1990). This approach provides an opportunity
to learn what aspects of the topic of interest are important to the participants
(Patton, 2002; Stewart & Shamdasani, 1990). It also results in detailed responses about respondents' cognitive, perceptual, and affective interpretations
of the situation while also stimulating similar or divergent thoughts in the
group. The goal of the focus-group approach is to expand our understanding of the range of respondents' experiences of the situation—for example,
specific feelings, observations of others' reactions and activities, and respondents' attributions.

Informing Perspectives

In engaging the topic of women's perspectives on shared parenting with men
who have battered in the past, we utilized four informing perspectives to
provide structure for the research design. These perspectives not only informed
the design, but they also acted as sensitizing concepts for guiding our data
analyses (Patton, 2002). Symbolic interactionism posits that the symbols,
rituals, and behaviors employed by a particular cultural group are imbued
with unique meanings and provide essential insights into the values and goals
of the group (Blumer, 1969; Kuhn, 1964). We used it here to increase our
sensitivity to taken-for-granted words and implicit concepts familiar to specific locales and experiences by the study's respondents. We also employed a
life-course perspective to provide the frame for examining various trajectories and impacting variables that describe the lives of individuals sharing similar
life experiences (Featherman, 1983; Elder, 1991). In the case of domestic
violence, it was helpful in understanding the impact of time and developmental phases and transitions, as well as how these factors affect psychological processes.

　　In addition, we draw on human-ecological theory and family-systems
theory to understand the family in context and the context of family interactions. Human-ecological theory acknowledges individuals' and families'
embeddedness in social networks, communities, and larger institutional and
cultural systems that exert various levels of overt and covert influence in their

lives (Bronfenbrenner, 1979). Similarly, family-systems theory provides a helpful lens for describing the relational aspects of interactions between various families that are and have been affected by the domestic violence without the onus of ascribing blame (Hill, 1971; Straus, 1973). Family-systems theory has been criticized by feminist scholars for this failure to ascribe culpability, especially in instances of abuse and violence (Whitchurch & Constantine, 1993). Therefore, we are careful to employ it as a descriptive, rather than an explanatory, framework for understanding the collocations of relationships and events identified by respondents.

Participants

In the spring of 2003, a purposeful, convenience sample of African American women was recruited from two women's programs. Both programs were located in large, Midwestern urban cities and were considered "culturally sensitive." Here, "culturally sensitive" describes a specific intent to address the cultural, physical, and emotional needs of a specific group of color (sometimes, several groups of color). In this case, the programs were chosen for their sensitivity to African American women. The majority of the 18 women respondents were informed of the study by program directors and staff.

This population was important for three reasons. Initially, this population was chosen to explore the unique interaction of domestic violence and shared parenting because of our interest in its impact on and manifestation in African American communities. African Americans emphasize the inherent value of children and the importance of family relationships, especially as they relate to kinship networks; therefore, it would seem that shared parenting would be an important kinship interaction (Burton & Sorenson, 1993). Second, proportionately, African American women are more likely than women of other ethnic groups (except Native Americans) to experience domestic violence; hence, we suspect that they are also more likely to be in positions of shared parenting with partners with whom they have conceived a child and at whose hands they have experienced domestic violence (Tjaden & Thoennes, 2000). Third, this population was also targeted because of the increased likelihood that it would contain women in various stages of relationship dissolution; therefore, perceptions and expectations based on a variety of shared-parenting negotiations and agreements would be present.

Data Collection and Analysis

The primary research question guiding this effort was: "what types of shared parenting expectations do battered women have in reference to men who have battered them in the past?" In order to explore this question, we conducted focus groups using a semistructured interview guide covering topics related to contact and isolation issues, safety concerns, services, and perceptions of fathering. In addition to the interview, respondents were asked to complete closed-ended questions providing demographic information. For the demographic survey, respondents provided data about age and marital status, help-seeking, domestic violence, and children. Several open-ended questions were also posed in reference to shared parenting and counseling experiences.

We relied on the focus-group transcripts and survey questions for insight into the shared-parenting experiences of women who had experienced physical abuse from their child's father. Focus groups were audiotaped for purposes of generating transcripts. The transcripts were reviewed and coded by the primary interviewer (C. Y. T.). Both descriptive and interpretive coding were part of this process (Miles & Huberman, 1994). In addition, research assistants served as scribes and noted important thoughts or ideas. Scribes' notes were employed as a way of facilitating group interaction and as a check of topics covered by the group. In the focus-group interview, participants discussed their needs and their children's needs in reference to facilitating the father-child relationship. Therefore, we examined the interviews to discern perceptions of contact, visitation, safety concerns, and the services needed, as well as to provide descriptive information on women's expectations.

Each participant responded to 22 survey questions about her relationship with the batterer with whom she shared parenting. Questions covered current marital and living status with the batterer; marital and living status during the relationship; the number of years in the relationship; current quality and nature of the relationship; types of violence experienced in the relationship; types of services sought during the relationship and from whom; and the batterer's current contact with the child being coparented.

We employed generalized content analysis, using conceptually ordered matrices (Miles & Huberman, 1994). Conceptually ordered matrices provide the researcher with the opportunity to cluster responses to conceptually related questions in a meaningful way. As noted earlier, a variety of sensitizing concepts guided our analysis and the development of these matrices (Patton, 2002). During coding and analyses, we utilized sensitizing concepts from symbolic-interaction theory, life-course-perspective theory, ecological theory, systems theory, and the literature on shared parenting (Bengston & Allen, 1993; Klein & White, 2002).

In understanding the findings from our interviews, it is important to note that the findings are based on description and interpretation of respondents' comments. Therefore, some findings may be congruent with and others contradictory to prevailing views in the field of domestic violence. As noted earlier, the findings describe the women's perceptions of the phenomenon of interest rather than define causal relationships. In addition, during the data-collection process, pseudonyms were used by all respondents in order to protect confidentiality. Participants were asked to pick a name by which they could be identified in the group and on tape. Therefore, names cited in the inserted quotations are pseudonyms.

Focus-Group Participants

Demographic data and survey data were collected for the 18 participants in the study. Sixteen women (89%) were African American, one was of African heritage (5.5%), and one was European American (5.5%). One half of the women were between 18 and 33 years of age (n = 9), while 78% fell between 18 and 40 years of age. Sixteen participants provided information on relationship status; therefore, two respondents were missing data on relationship status. At the time of our interviews, 25% (n = 4) of the 16 participants were single and never married, but they were cohabiting with a partner, while 31% (n = 5) were single, never married, and not cohabiting with a partner. Two women were legally married; one was cohabiting with her husband (6%), and one was not (6%). Of the 16 participants, 25% (n = 4) were divorced and not cohabiting with a partner; one person (6%) was divorced and cohabiting with a partner (not necessarily her husband).

Fifteen of the 18 participants provided information on their children. Of these, 40% (n = 6) had one child, 20% (n = 3) had two children, 13% (n = 2) had 3 children, 7% (n = 1) had 4 children, 13% (n = 2) had 5 children, and 7% (n = 1) had 6 children. Children were almost evenly split in terms of gender, with 55% female (n = 21) and 45% male (n = 17). In reference to their current relationship with the referent batterer, 72% (n = 13) of the 18 participants reported that they "do not see each other," 11% (n = 2) reported that there was contact with some conflict, 5% (n = 1) had contact with no conflict, 5% (n = 1) reported a friendly relationship, and data were missing for 5% (n = 1). When asked about their current relationship with the referent batterers, 83% (n = 15) of respondents reported that they were estranged, while 17% (n = 3) reported still being involved or married.

Emergent Themes

Three major themes emerged from the analyses of the focus-group data. First, respondents acted from assumptions about shared parenting. The need for safety and the need for fathers' access to their children were the two assumptions that framed the group's discussion and were the background to the other two salient themes. Second, respondents emphasized conditions for shared parenting, including the issues involved with initiating and terminating contacts with the father. Finally, the third salient theme focused on the impact of time on the shared-parenting process. What emerged for us was a metaphorical "picture" with safety and access composing the frame, and conditions for shared parenting being the content of the canvas. Figure 2.1 illustrates these themes.

Assumptive Beliefs: Safety and Access

The two crosscutting, foundational themes that tied together and provided the context for the remaining themes emerging from the analysis were: (1) safety for mothers and children; (2) children's and fathers' inherent need to have access to one another. In examining the relationship of these themes with other salient themes in the study, it became apparent that safety and accessibility were assumed givens or understandings that underlay respondents' perceptions of shared parenting with an estranged, violent partner and framed the values that guided their interactions with their child's coparent. We refer to these themes as *assumptive beliefs*. These assumptive beliefs were the implicit guiding values underlying mothers' decisions to facilitate the parent-to-parent and father-child relationships. The belief about the need for safety was related to fathers' histories of violence toward the mothers, while fathers' access to their children appeared more closely related to the kinship values of this community.

Safety

Unequivocally, safety was the touchstone issue framing the conversations and the ensuing comments about respondents' experiences, expectations, and needs related to shared parenting with a former batterer. It was implicit in most of the responses provided in the focus groups, and it shaped the expectations, contexts, and logistics of shared parenting. If verbalized, this parameter would have been voiced as: "if it were safe, . . ." with safety being understood as the lack of physical or verbal violence or intimidation. It was clear that respondents were most concerned about safety for their children; their own safety was secondary. Therefore, when respondents discussed initiating shared-parenting contacts, determining parameters of contact, and terminating

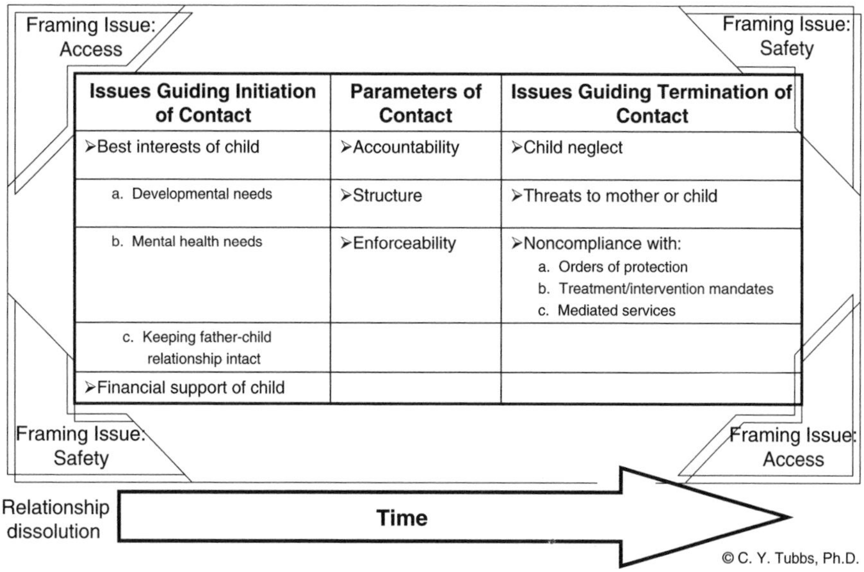

Framing Issue: Access		Framing Issue: Safety
Issues Guiding Initiation of Contact	**Parameters of Contact**	**Issues Guiding Termination of Contact**
➤Best interests of child	➤Accountability	➤Child neglect
a. Developmental needs	➤Structure	➤Threats to mother or child
b. Mental health needs	➤Enforceability	➤Noncompliance with: a. Orders of protection b. Treatment/intervention mandates c. Mediated services
c. Keeping father-child relationship intact		
➤Financial support of child		

Framing Issue: Safety

Framing Issue: Access

Relationship dissolution

Time

© C. Y. Tubbs, Ph.D.

Figure 2.1. Emergent themes among mothers regarding parenting after abuse

father-child contacts, safety was the orienting factor. Julia stated, "I really think that the most important thing is safety. Safety! So that you always feel that it's okay to take the child . . . [to the] father."

Access

Similarly, children's and fathers' access to one another was an assumption that informed respondents' comments. Respondents did not struggle with question of "if" contact should take place but, rather, "how" and "when." Consequentially, since father-child contact was a given, the conditional parameters of "how" and "when" occupied more of the discussions:

> His father wasn't in the picture. So I figured that even though there was abuse going on, I wanted my young son to be around and be with his father. And we set up, as you said, "a structured visitation." I felt like this: he was a no-good s.o.b. for a husband, but maybe he could be a better father, and the two—they're separate—roles, and so what I tried to do was kind of stay out of it and let him find out who his father was.

Conditions for Shared Parenting

Within the context of safety, respondents identified several other conditions for shared parenting with their former partners. We divided these conditions into three categories: initiating shared-parenting contacts; determining parameters of contact; and terminating shared-parenting contacts (see Figure 2.1). Parameters of contact included facilitators and barriers to visitation logistics, with facilitators further broken into three types of components: accountability components; structural components; and enforceability components.

Initiating Shared-Parenting Contacts

Shared parenting is a personal parenting decision. In other words, it is as much about a mother's personal decisions to act in the best interest of the child as it is a joint decision between a child's mother and father to work together (Pruett & Hoganbruen, 1998). It is a personal decision to put the child's needs before one's own relational needs or expectations, especially when the child's father is uncooperative or inadequate in fulfilling his parenting responsibilities. Desiring to act in the best interest of the child was the overarching motive among the mothers we interviewed in initiating shared-parenting contacts with a former batterer. Therefore, respondents reported that children's developmental and mental-health needs, as well as children's material needs, prompted their decisions to initiate conversations about shared parenting.

Respondents' knowledge of children's developmental needs was premised on a mixture of cultural mores and popularized scientific findings. Although this mix did not always agree with the current literature on child development and on the impact of domestic violence on children, it anchored respondents' beliefs about what is best for their children. As the following quotation illustrates, respondents factored in their knowledge of children's developmental needs when pondering decisions to initiate contact:

> I think the child should be able to see [his or her] biological father, that's all. Because basically, it's been shown through research that children [who] have that father figure fare better throughout their life or something like that. I think it's a void for them [that] a mother can't fill, but I also think it depends on other circumstances, like if there were drugs, drug use, or the father was abusive to the children. Also, the children's ages. . . . I guess if they determine that they don't want to see him that should be considered.

Conversely, one mother noted that the stress of single parenting and parenting children during developmental transitions was the precipitating factor in her decision to contact her children's father:

> It was like very extreme stress to handle, to try to handle all of the individual needs and responsibilities and behaviors and attitudes of the kids as they grow up. So that was one of the reasons that I would initiate the visitation with their dad for a while, I mean, just visitation once a week [was] like to deserve it, just to give me something for me, okay?

Child mental health and a sense of emotional security were also primary motivators cited for initial contacts or negotiations with former batterers. Although these two reasons seem to be the very reasons that mothers would choose to leave abusive relationships (i.e., because of the very real possibility that children were negatively impacted by exposure to violence), one participant referenced her own experience of growing up without an invested father as a much worse prospect than the possibility of recovering from violence. In addition to growing up without a father, respondents expressed personal beliefs about child development and mental health, considering it inappropriate for mothers to ignore the manifestations of children's anguish over the absent parent. In addition, they felt no right to disrupt growing father-child bonds by withholding contact rights from either the child or their ex-partners. Just as importantly, participants did not want to increase the probability that fathers would abandon their children because of parental hostilities precluding contact.

In articulating their motives for initiating contact with former batterers, several respondents also stated that they hoped fathers would separate the couple relationship from the father-child relationship. These respondents firmly believed that the father-child relationship would not be tainted by abusive behavior and would continue to grow. This group of respondents believed that the intimate-partner violence directed at them was not transferable to children. Karen explained, "I say 'yes' also because I feel like the situation is totally different as far as, you know, father and child and me and the father, it is just totally different." Similarly, Jan stated, "I wouldn't personally want to have anything to do with him, but I still would want [him] to have something to do with his child, though." However, others held the belief, evidenced by their comments on safety, that the batterer's abuse was more global and not affected by the best interests of children. Sarah captured this sentiment:

> do they really love their kids and want to be [with them]? . . . I don't believe they have the child's best interest in mind. And I think [that] when they say they want to see the kids that they really want to get to the mother. . . . Is [it] possible for them to make that switch and really feel like they want to be responsible for having to raise their child when all these years they've not been, and not responsible and abusive? And so, I'd really question the validity of their decision.

A more muted emergent theme important to initiating contact centered on child support. Mothers acted to share parenting with ex-batterers when they feared that compliance with formal or informal child-support arrangements might be contingent on fathers' access to their children. Respondents appeared willing to entertain the risk of having contact with a former batterer in order to enhance the probability that they and their children would receive needed monetary support. This theme was entangled with, but clearly secondary to, the theme of the developmental impact of child abandonment. That is, mothers were not hesitant to contact fathers about some form of child support. Sarah's comment evinces a mixture of assertiveness about boundaries and concerns about child support:

> I don't believe I would ever go back. PPO [personal protection order] or no PPO, but I don't want to, these are just my feelings. [I do not want to] jeopardize anything that has to do with his importance because I want it to be guaranteed that [he] give[s] me my child support.

Parameters of Contact

Respondents reported that their primary shared-parenting goal was being able to facilitate a father-child relationship while decreasing the probability that their ex-partners might be abusive. Personal safety during times when children were transferred from their care to the care of their fathers was the most salient personal-safety concern. Julie commented, "he should not come to the home for the children. As a matter of fact, I feel that [for] a woman that's been battered, the child should be brought to the courthouse."

Respondents reported being afraid that being in the batterer's presence again would be too much of a temptation for unresolved negative feelings and abusive relationship dynamics to emerge. In other words, even if respondents felt comfortable with children visiting their fathers, they were not confident that their direct involvement in transferring the child would not lead to some form of violence. Suggestions for dealing with transfer-of-care situations ranged from formal arrangements involving transfers monitored by law-enforcement officials (e.g., police precincts) or at visitation centers to informal arrangements using relatives' homes. Visitation centers are neutral locations where children can safely interact with at-risk, noncustodial parents in a monitored environment. They are also venues where battered parents can "drop off" children for mandated visits with the noncustodial parent. Jane related her experience with both formal and informal arrangements:

> what I did was supervised visitation, and it was downtown, in the [name of facility], and eventually, for a few months, it was like that. Then it was supervised by my sister in that she went everywhere, she met up with them, she took our son to meet his dad, or she got in a cab, or whatever. I think that it went pretty well because my sister at that point was out of the loop, and he trusted her to not to tell anything and so on and gave my son a chance to have some contact with his father.

Similarly, respondents expressed concerns about making contact before they could coach children on the appropriate types of information that they should divulge about their current living arrangements. They reported being afraid that children would be placed in situations where they disclosed guarded information about the mother's residence, place of employment, or the location of beloved family members. This concern was expressed for all children but especially for younger, approval-seeking, or cognitively unsophisticated children:

> I have to agree with you because in some instances, depending upon the age of the children and how sophisticated they are, there can be some manipulation techniques—just as you were saying—trying to find out from the child "what's going on in the house, who's coming and going?"; and sometimes children, because they want to be acceptable [sic] by both mom and dad, especially when they are separated, will tell dad what they think dad wants to hear, only because they want to stay on dad's good side.

Therefore, they suggested that certain precautions needed to be in place prior to considering shared parenting contact options with their former batterers.

Contact Logistics

Facilitators of Contact

When asked about the logistics of visitation and custody, respondents reported that *who* would make the decisions about the specifics of visitation was just as important as the when, how, what, and where of visitation. The majority of respondents felt that judges, in collaboration with mediators or child advocates, were most qualified to make these decisions. A few respondents supported the involvement of respected family members (e.g., grandparents) or respected members of both the respondents' and ex-batterers' social networks. Mothers felt that physical safety was enhanced by a mediated, enforceable structure (i.e., including mediation and involvement by the courts) with immediate and tangible consequences. By *mediated,* participants indicated that they invited the prospect of input from an impartial referee whose primary directive was the best interest of the child. Enforceable components would require that the stipulations of the agreements be operationalized to

Fathers' Voices on Parenting and Violence

Tricia Bent-Goodley and Oliver J. Williams

Following is a brief summary of fathers' comments on their parenting and violence. We interviewed 17 men who batter, 15 of whom were African American and 2 Caucasian, about their perspectives on coparenting with their victims after violence. The men were interviewed in two focus groups, one in Michigan and one in Minnesota, and asked a set of 27 questions in a semistructured interview format. The men were asked questions about (1) coparenting, (2) custody issues, (3) safety issues, and (4) fatherhood. The focus-group interviews lasted about two and one half hours at each site and were audiotaped, transcribed and then analyzed by an independent researcher (Bent-Goodley) not involved in the interviewing.

Fathers' Views on Their Role in the Family

Most of the fathers in the focus groups did not view the battered woman or any woman as their equals; in fact, they viewed women and children as having a lower but similar status. As one man put it "Men should be in charge . . . and I should be the man of the house and the disciplinarian." This refers both to the children and their female partner, as one man said, "We need to be there to discipline the children. . . . Like children, she needs to be disciplined too." Generally, these men held rigid sex-role stereotypes and tended to fit the traditional stereotype of men who batter as being controlling.

Another impression was that most of these men did not want to separate the child from their mother, unless there was evidence that she was not a fit parent and the child was unsafe. Yet they were very clear that fathers were important in their child's life, too. They described how important it was for fathers to be valued beyond a provider role or in terms of economics alone. Comments included the following:

"Children need to know their daddy and to know where they come from on the daddy's side of the family. . . . The mother can't give them that. . . . I can teach my son how to be a man. . . . He can't get that from his momma." Another man stated, "I don't have a job, but I should be able to spend time with my child and for them [sic] to get to know me."

Another reported regarding the narrow perspectives of fathering,

"It seems that all my wife and kids want from me is money. . . . I should be viewed as more than just a paycheck."

Fathers' Rights in Light of the Violence

When listening to the comments of the fathers, it was sometimes difficult to determine whether men were minimizing the effect that their violence had on the battered woman and exposed children or were just stressing the significance of fatherhood and the importance of their having continuous contact with their children. For instance, most of the fathers acknowledged that exposing the children to violence was harmful and could impact the children's feelings toward them, but as one respondent noted,

"Time and distance from the father would only make the ability to reunite with the father more difficult in the future. . . . Regardless of what happens between the parents, a child should always be allowed to be around their father."

What was absent from the respondents' comments was an awareness that a child's exposure to their mother's victimization could traumatize the child. There was neither acknowledgment that such events could affect children's fears and reluctance about interacting with him, nor that the children may require additional time away from him because of those fears.

A final impression is that the fathers believed that they have a right to contact with their children, that they have a desire to be with them, and that they have something to offer them. What tends to be absent is a recognition that children and battered women may not always be able to rebound from the impact of their behavior as quickly as fathers would want. Rather, the fathers seemed to suggest that their violence and abuse should be overlooked without evidence of real change or a guarantee of safety from his violence and abuse.

Fathers' Recommendations on Coparenting

Fathers recommended the following ideas regarding what they wanted from their battered partners concerning their children and what could strengthen their capacity to engage her in positive coparenting interactions. These recommendations must be taken with seriousness but also with caution. The issue is not whether the recommendations are unfounded and without merit; rather, it is how to interpret and balance their suggestions with evidence of how batterers behave, the stories and voices of the battered women and children, and the specific behaviors and actions of the man.

Strengthen the Coparents' Capacity to Communicate About the Children

Most of the fathers felt that one impediment for them was communication about the children's needs with the mother. When they did communicate, they reported, "it often would disintegrate into an argument and she would become oppositional with me." Other times they had to communicate through someone else and not directly with her. The respondents reported, "this was difficult because the person you speak with, does not like you." They felt it was important to speak with her directly, or with someone else that they could relate to, and then "find a way to stay positive." They felt they needed help "to keep it positive" in this area.

Another issue that arose and seemed to cause conflict was the role of the mothers' new partner. Fathers suggested that "arguments happen because her new man would put himself into issues that had nothing to do with him. . . . It was between the father, mother, and children." They recommended that the father and mother set boundaries about the new partner's involvement in their issues.

Most men also felt that their battered partners tended to be unclear when they communicated with them. For example, one stated, "They would say one thing about what they were willing to let me do with the children and then renege on their promises." The men also discussed how she might be sexually suggestive or want to re-establish a romantic or sexual relationship. In this regard, some men reported "that if I did not cooperate then she would withdraw and become more difficult about what I wanted to do with the children." Other fathers stated "that it was important that the mothers were clear and consistent. . . . that when the relationship is over they treat it like it is over and not send mixed messages and mixed signals."

Set Clear Expectations

A source of irritation for these fathers was the unpredictability of their interactions with the mother and children. They felt that everything was up in the air and under her control. They wanted things to be more predictable, consistent, and routine. One father felt "that both parents should say what they were trying to achieve from all this and how they were going to accomplish it." Visitation was another issue they wanted resolved. Another father felt that "the mothers would sometimes agree to a time and date and then change it. . . . I feel like this is unfair but there is no consequences [sic]to the woman or reason for her to change what she is doing."

Use an Objective Third Party

The fathers reported that there were times when the conflict and ability to communicate on issues were beyond the parents' capacity to agree. This was often when trouble and problems would escalate. As one man noted, "We may be locked in and unwilling to move from our position, or she may be unwilling to give. . . . This is the time to bring in a neutral and objective third party to resolve the dispute."

Inform the Children

Most fathers felt that their children were very confused about what was going on when parents separated. They cited the child's confusion in their interactions with the father, the mother and between parents. One man reported, "Many of the children did not understand why things were so different regarding their visit and family interactions." Another recommended, "Children should be told about what happened, why things have changed, and what the rules are, and how it's going to be, and what things are going to stay the same."

Encourage Positive Parenting

Finally, the men stated that in order to assist them to become healthy and positive fathers, they needed help. Especially if they were poor and they had few resources, they wanted helping systems to direct them to resources that would help them help their children. It seemed that the resources highlighted by these men primarily focused on financial resources.

allow for accountability and evaluation. Structural components would also provide guidance for visitation, custody, and support. Although the following discussion artificially separates these components, the reader will quickly recognize that accountability, structure, and enforceability are inextricably intertwined.

Accountability Components

In the discussion of enforceable structure, participants referred to components or mechanisms that would provide consequences to batterers for failing to act responsibly toward their children; that is, they would hold him accountable. Most respondents advocated formal arrangements. Some suggested that informal arrangements would also work; however, they provided no concrete details on how enforcement would take place. Either way, respondents wanted assurances that men's issues with reference to controlling their violence and/or alcohol and substance abuse were being addressed. Violence control was essential because of the inappropriate and dangerous behaviors directed toward children out of anger toward or in attempts to manipulate mothers. In addition, if their children's fathers were still drinking or using drugs, mothers saw no reason to enter into conversations, no matter how promising, about allowing them to care for their children. One respondent succinctly surmised, "there should be some help before he sees his child." Another respondent stated:

> I don't think that person would be the appropriate parent if they're under the influence, if they're only keeping the child [on the] night that they're drunk. I don't think they're thinking the right thing. They shouldn't even have the child.

Respondents felt that children would be abused, neglected, or abandoned if allowed to visit with or if left in the custody of a substance-abusing father. Exposure to individuals under the influence of alcohol or drugs, individuals too impaired or disinterested to consider child welfare, and the dangers inherent in substance-abusing cultures (such as unsavory persons, unknown persons, and illicit substances) were the types of abusive and neglectful behaviors noted by respondents.

Structural Components

In the discussion about facilitators of visitation, respondents also suggested that agreements provide structure. Participants expressed a desire to have a structure in order to decrease the likelihood of being entangled in the various forms of emotional manipulation that were typical in their abusive relationships. Veronica recalled: "he did a lot of manipulating with our son, you know. He would put him on the phone and let him call, but [say,] 'Don't tell her where I am or anything, don't say where you are,' and so on."

The types of emotional manipulation of greatest concern involved passive-aggressive behavior and using ambiguous threats and threatening behavior toward children for leverage. Passive-aggressive behavior was manifested in disrespectful behavior toward respondents (such as being constantly late or acting outside of agreements), failing to provide child support, making indirect or veiled threats, or seeking information about the respondent's private life. Threats of harm to the children were another form of emotional manipulation from which respondents sought to be freed. Children had been taken without mothers' consent (i.e., kidnapped) during scheduled visitation for periods of several hours to several days. In one case, two children were picked up after school without the mother's consent; they were released to the father because the school was not informed of the custodial arrangements. In another family, the child had been driven across state lines during a couple of short-term visits with his father:

> it had to be supervised because he had kidnapped him twice and taken him over the state line, and so enough was enough. I tried, and it didn't work! I went to, I kind of pumped up the volume a little bit, you know, until eventually he was sitting downtown on the fifth floor watching his kid through a window because that's where he had put himself, but yeah, his past abuse of me, my son's father, my ex-husband, was so abusive, and he didn't see that taking the child over state lines [was abusive]. [He] figured that was his son, he could do whatever he wanted to do with him.

For these mothers, the emotional burden of weighing their children's desires to see their fathers against the threats of the fathers' spurious decisions to take them without prior arrangements was difficult.

Finally, respondents felt that fathers who fostered negative attitudes in children during visits emotionally manipulated their children. These negative attitudes manifested as externalizing behaviors by children toward the respondents, behavior that typically occurred after visits with the father.

Two additional services were mentioned during the discussion about structural components. Although mothers did not use the formal term, those advocating for mediated and structured arrangements preferred that some form of guardian *ad litem* be appointed. None indicated prior experience with such an individual (at least not in the legal use of the term); however, they were cognizant enough of their own biases to understand the need of an impartial advocate—someone who could understand and represent the needs of their children. As mentioned earlier, for some, it was important that the impartial mediator be affiliated with institutionalized structures, such as the courts, while others expressed comfort with a respected, impartial member of the family or social network:

> I would just like to say I think every woman that enters into a shelter or expressing the fact that she's been through a domestic-violence case should be appointed, free of charge, a counselor or something for the children. Forget the parents—obviously, they have their own issues —but if the child is appointed a counselor or something, it can make the appropriate decisions for the child. I think it'll be much better, because either person is pulling in their direction and is being selfish, you know.

The second service relevant to structural arrangements was the potential for access to various court services and officials during stays in women's shelters so that formal and enforceable arrangements are in place while services are available, memories are fresh, and protection is offered. One respondent noted:

> why couldn't we go through, if you're willing to participate through a family court, to set all of the procedures, like that the mother and father [are] willing to go through family court. . . . That way, it will all be taken care of before you go out into the world unprotected from the shelter.

Enforcement Components

The secondary intent of advocating for arrangements that provided account-ability and structure was their enforceability. This issue was salient when respondents referenced ex-batterers' alcohol and substance abuse, as well as needing some assurances that the fathers were receiving treatment or supervision for other mental-health issues, such as anger management. Respondents also reported that they felt more comfortable with shared parenting with former batterers if they had some assurance that violations of personal protection orders (PPOs), visitation, or custodial arrangements would be sanctioned. Many hinted that court mandates had not been enforced. In part, several admitted that mandates had not been enforced because they were unwilling to engage the difficulties and consequences of seeing the mandates enforced.

Barriers to Contact

The mothers we interviewed identified two primary barriers to visitation and shared parenting. First, the lack of safety was an important impediment. As indicated earlier, respondents were unwilling to expose themselves or their children to fathers (and individuals in his environment) who might harm or neglect the child. Understandably, those mothers who felt that their situation with the children's fathers was too volatile had made little or very limited contact. For those who had more extended contact, referencing past experiences with the fathers helped to determine the levels of risk to children. If children were not perceived as targets of abuse or revenge, then respondents were more willing to further shared-parenting negotiations, regardless of perceived danger to themselves.

Second, the mothers reported that limited financial resources, as well as safety concerns, would prohibit them from seeking, enlisting, or abiding by structured and enforceable arrangements. In one group in particular, the nu-anced differences in class status shaped respondents' expectations for and per-ceived use of court and mediation services. Those who reported limited resources stated that they were not certain if they would use or expect their children's fathers to use supervised transfer locations; therefore, they advocated for infor-mal structures. The following respondent indicated that finances would be a barrier to her use of formal structures once she left a shelter and its supports:

it's like [a group member's name] said: everybody don't have the financial [resources], and legal aid—it's a waiting list to even get in there. As far as the lawyers and all the rest of that stuff, I mean, a lot of people can't afford all that. Me, myself, I can't really afford all that.

On the contrary, those with more resources appeared more rigid about the need for mediated forms of contact and less concerned about the legal or financial impacts of noncompliance on the father.

Terminating Shared-Parenting Contacts

Similar to the barriers impeding contact logistics, respondents stated that they had terminated or would terminate shared-parenting contacts if fathers' behaviors or lifestyles placed them or their children in danger. Threats or threatening behavior directed toward the children or the respondent, refusals to comply with formal or informal contact and visitations agreements, and attempting to manipulate children were unacceptable behaviors. Violations of court mandates (e.g., personal protection orders), noncompliance with treatment recommendations (i.e., substance- or alcohol-abuse counseling, anger management), or mediated services would also prompt termination, at least temporarily. Interestingly, respondents did not make direct reference to failure to participate in batterers' intervention programs as a precondition for termination. Sonja noted that she would terminate contact if the ex-batterer made "threats towards me or [if] any of my children told me that he threatened them. And if he had [given] any punishments that I felt was inappropriate for them."

The noteworthy aspect of mothers' conditions for terminating contact was that they balanced mothers' clear preference for children having contact with their fathers with concerns about safety. Respondents seemed to assume a position of fathering within parameters (especially if they assumed physical custody) versus either extreme of "no fathering at all" or "fathering at all costs." The data suggested that respondents were reasonable in their expectations of fathers in terms of providing for children's physical and emotional safety and well-being while under their care. Providing for children's emotional well-being included cessation of imminent threats against the mother, especially if she was involved in the transfer of children during visits.

Impact of Time

Time was another muted theme in respondents' comments. Time was especially important in terms of life-course issues, as developmental transitions often signaled transitions in the decision-making processes around shared parenting. Mothers' concerns with safety decreased when children transitioned from preverbal to verbal, to school age, then adolescence, and beyond. Participants reported that they felt less protective when children's cognitive, verbal, and physical maturity increased the probability that they could report problems and care for themselves in the event of adult neglect or abuse:

> I feel that it depends upon the age of the child, it has a lot to do with it. I also feel that [it's about] how the abuse was done. If it was done in front of this minor, it could have a dramatic effect on the child, okay? Yet, I still think that the child should be able to be involved with the father; but then it depends upon the age of the child. Because if you have a teenager or son, as I do, you know, he has a lot of resentment, you know, so within time, he will have to heal. He is at the age where he can make his own decisions. If I had young children, they don't quite understand what's going on . . . [,] then I probably would still be involved with their father. But with teenagers, I would let them make up their own mind.

The nature of the shared-parenting relationship also undergoes a parallel developmental progression. Understandably, parents must modulate more intense anger and conflict during the time immediately after the dissolution of their relationship. The passage of time provides distance and perspective on the partner relationship and what forged it, as well as the needs of the child and the immediacy of attempting to make the family work:

> my child is now an adult with his own children, but as time went on, he—the batterer, the shared parent, ex-father—he ending up paying for the relationship that he had made with his son by using him to get to me and find out what I was doing. . . . [S]o he asked him questions and put him in the place where I never could, 'cause I can't ask you why you don't want to be a good father, but your child sure in the hell can.

Discussion

This chapter examined the responses of women who have shared or who share parenting with men who battered them in the past. Focus-group data were analyzed to understand women's expectations for and experiences with shared parenting. The findings indicated that shared parenting was perceived as a necessary obligation of parenting, even with heightened concerns about one's own and one's children's safety. In order to decrease the likelihood that the abusive dynamics that drove them from their relationships would not seep into the shared-parenting and father-child relationships, respondents identified ground rules that would increase the probability of contact. Participants' expectations of shared parenting supported the existent literature in terms of shared-parenting dynamics, safety, and structured arrangements (Pruett & Hoganbruen, 1998).

Shared parenting in an intact union is difficult in itself since it involves merging the two disparate family cultures from which the couple emerged (Margolin, et al., 2001). Creating consensus about parenting children is part of this complex process, especially since parenting is an emergent, individually- and relationally-oriented, life-course process occurring parallel to child development. The dynamics of abuse greatly diminish the aspects of trust and cooperation needed to share parenting, and estrangement strains even further the desire to cooperate (Pruett & Hoganbruen, 1998). Tension in the couple relationship negatively charges the affective context for joint decision making in reference to children.

Based on the data, two beliefs were important in reference to shared parenting in the context of African American couples with histories of domestic violence: the importance of father-child accessibility, and the need for safety. In many instances, these two beliefs conflicted, and this conflict created ambiguity and tension in respondents' decision-making processes. With reference to accessibility, despite the turbulent and traumatic relationships that they experienced with their children's fathers, respondents assumed that children's developmental and mental-health needs dictated some form of contact with their fathers. Even though these beliefs were predicated on popularized or outdated notions of child-development theory, or cultural mores, they nonetheless fueled mothers' sense of guilt about prohibiting father-child contact. As indicated in Carlson's (2000) research review, children benefit less, rather than more, from contact with abusive or neglectful parents (also see Giles-Sims, 1985). In addition, mothers' fears of violence deferred to concerns that lack of contact with the fathers would trigger the withholding of financial support and an increase in hostilities, and encourage divestment of the children.

Second, respondents' focus on safety underscored their realism about the need to keep themselves and their children physically and emotionally protected in the context of contacts with men who had a penchant for control. Respondents used safety to frame and contextualize their responses. When the prospect of initiating contact was on the table, respondents first considered current risks that the batterer posed either in perpetrating physical violence or being too impaired to be safe or provide safety. Once issues of initial contact had been addressed, then respondents outlined parameters that would increase the likelihood of an ongoing and less conflicted shared-parenting relationship that was safe for them, the children, and the fathers. This group of respondents believed that the intimate-partner violence directed at them was not transferable to children. However, many also enacted measures to increase children's safety and well-being when in contact with or when visiting their fathers.

Pruett and Hoganbruen (1998) suggest that parenting plans for estranged couples previously involved in intimate-partner violence should include safety plans for the mother and the child; mechanisms for facilitating equity in decision making between the shared parents; mechanisms for detriangulating the child; and interventions focused on communication skills and accruing information pertinent to shared parenting. Respondents' comments were congruent with this research. The unique aspects of this study emerge in the source of data, the explicit focus on African Americans, and respondents' emphasis on mechanisms for enhancing informal, as well as formal, contact and visitation arrangements.

Our intent in writing this chapter is not to suggest that shared parenting after domestic violence should occur at all costs. We neither suggest nor condone this notion. However, in sharing this research, we assert that women's voices need to be heard—without judgment or censorship—so that researchers and practitioners know what they are thinking and thus can act appropriately to address their needs. In asking respondents to share their stories, we wanted to respect their words. We sought to amplify their voices without assuming the editorial authority of turning down the volume on the comments with which we did not agree or knew to be out of sync with the broader community of voices weighing in on the topic. The chapter provides no directive on what women should be doing—instead, it shares what *this* group of mothers are doing (and will keep doing), why they think they are doing it, and the process. Conversations encouraging behavioral and policy-related change cannot honestly occur unless there is acknowledgment of *where* those affected are and *why* they are there. We hope that this work is an initial step in the process of building a bridge from *what is* to *what can be* for shared parenting in African-American and other communities.

Acknowledgments

We gratefully acknowledge the financial support of the Family Violence Prevention Fund. We would also like to extend our gratitude and thanks to the women who participated in this research for sharing their stories, suggestions, and experiences. We also thank the staffs at Black, Indian, Hispanic, and Asian Women in Action (BIHA) in Minneapolis, MN, and the Interim House in Detroit, MI. In addition, we extend our appreciation to the executive directors of the facilities that allowed us to recruit respondents. Finally, we acknowledge the funding received from and the research and logistical support of the Institute on Domestic Violence in the African American Community and its staff: Lorraine Haley, Shelia Hankins, Patience Togo, and Dawn York.

References

Appel, A. E., & Holden, G. W. (1998). The co-occurrence of spouse and physical child abuse: A review and appraisal. *Journal of Family Psychology*,12, 578–599.

Bengston, V. L., & Allen, K. R. (1993). The life course perspective applied to families over time. In P. G. Boss, W. J. Doherty, R. LaRossa, W. R. Schumm, & S. K. Steinmetz (Eds.), *Sourcebook of family theories and methods: A contextual approach* (pp. 469–498). New York: Plenum Press.

Blumer, H. (1969). *Symbolic interactionism.* Englewood Cliffs, NJ: Prentice Hall.

Bramlett, M. D., & Mosher, W. D. (2002). Cohabitation, marriage, divorce, and remarriage in the United States (National Center for Health Statistics, *Vital Health Stat 23*(22).Washington, DC: U.S. Government Printing Office.)

Retrieved 2004, February 15, 2004, from http://www.cdc.gov/nchs/data/series/sr_23/sr23_022.pdf

Bronfenbrenner, U. (1979). *The ecology of human development.* Cambridge, MA: Harvard University Press.

Bureau of Justice Statistics (2000). Special report: Intimate partner violence (BJS report No. NCJ 178247). Retrieved May 30, 2004, from http://www.oip.usdoj.gov/bjs/pub/pdf/ipv.pdf

Burton, L. M., & Sorensen, S. (1993). Temporal dimensions of intergenerational caregiving in African-American multigeneration families. In S. H. Zarit, L. I. Pearlin, & K. W. Schaie (Eds.), *Caregiving systems: Informal and formal helpers* (pp. 47–66). New York: Erlbaum Associates.

Campbell, J. C., Sharps, P., & Glass, N. (2001). Risk assessment for intimate partner homicide. In G. F. Pinard & L. Pagani (Eds.), *Clinical assessment of dangerousness: Empirical contributions* (pp. 136–157). New York: Cambridge University Press.

Carlson, B. E. (2000). Children exposed to intimate partner violence: Research findings and implications for intervention. *Trauma, Violence and Abuse, 1,* 321–342.

Cherlin, A. (1992). *Marriage, divorce, remarriage* (Rev. ed.). Cambridge, MA: Harvard University Press.

Cherlin, A. J. (2002). *Public and private families: An introduction.* (3rd ed.). New York: McGraw-Hill.

Demo, D. H., Find, M. A., & Ganong, L. H. (2000). Divorce as a family stressor. In P. C. McKenry & S. J. Price (Eds.), *Families and Change,* (pp. 279–302). Thousand Oaks, CA: Sage.

Elder, G. H. (1991). Family transitions, cycles, and social changes. In P. A. Cowan & M. Hetherington (Eds.), *Family Transitions,* (pp. 31–57). Mahwah, NJ: Lawrence Erlbaum Associates.

Featherman, D. L., (1983). The life-span perspective in social science research. In P. B. Baltes & O. G. Brim, Jr. (Eds.), *Life-span development and behavior* (Vol. 5, pp. 1–57). New York: Academic Press.

Furstenberg, F. F., & Cherlin, A. J. (1991). *Divided families: What happens to children when parents part?* Cambridge, MA: Harvard University Press.

Giles-Sims, J. (1985). A longitudinal study of battered children of battered wives. *Family Relations, 34,* 205–210.

Gottman, J. (1994). *Why marriages succeed or fail.* New York: Simon & Schuster.

Hetherington, E. M., & Stanley-Hagan, M. (1999). The adjustment of children with divorced parents: A risk and resiliency perspective. *Journal of Child Psychology and Psychiatry, 40,* 129–140.

Hill, R. (1971, August). *Payoffs and limitations of contemporary strategies for family theory systematization.* Paper presented at the meeting of National Council on Family Relations, Estes Park, CO.

Johnston, J. R., Kline, M., and Tschann, J. M. (1989). Ongoing postdivorce conflict: Effects on children of joint custody and frequent access. *American Journal of Orthopsychiatry, 59,* 576–592.

Klein, D., & White, J. (2002). *Family theories: An introduction.* Thousand Oaks, CA: Sage.

Kuhn, M. (1964). Major trends in symbolic interaction theory in the past twenty-five years. *Sociological Quarterly, 5,* 61–84.

Maccoby, E. E., & Mnookin, R. H. (1992). *Dividing the child: Social and legal dilemmas of custody.* Cambridge, MA: Harvard University Press.

Margolin, G., Gordis, E. B., & John, R. S. (2001). Shared parenting: A link between marital conflict and parenting in two-parent families. *Journal of Family Psychology, 15,* 3–21.

Markman, H. J., Stanley, S. M., & Blumberg, S. L. (1994). *Fighting for your marriage: Positive steps for a loving and lasting relationship.* San Francisco: Jossey Bass.

Merton, R. K., Fiske, M., & Kendall, P. L. (1990). *The focused interview: A manual of problems and procedures* (2nd ed.). New York: Free Press.

Miles, M. B., & Huberman, A. M. (1994). *Qualitative data analysis: An expanded sourcebook* (2nd ed.). Thousand Oaks, CA: Sage.

Modeen, M. (September 16, 2004). Brame ends wife's hopes for new life. *The Tacoma News Tribune,* p. A01.

Olson, D. H., & DeFrain, J. (2000) *Marriage and family: Diversity and strengths.* Mountain View, CA: Mayfield Publishing.

Parkinson, G. W., Adams, R. C., & Emerling, F. G. (2001). Maternal domestic violence screening in an office-based pediatric practice. *Pediatrics,108,* E43.

Patton, M. Q. (2002). *Qualitative research and evaluation methods* (3rd ed.). Thousand Oaks, CA: Sage.

Pruett, M. K., & Hoganbruen, K. (1998). Joint custody and shared parenting. *Child and Adolescent Psychiatric Clinics of North America, 7,* 273–294.

Rodgers, R. H., & White, J. M. (1993). Family development theory. In P. G. Boss, W. J. Doherty, R. LaRossa, W. R. Schumm, & S. K. Steinmetz (Eds.), *Sourcebook of family theories and methods: A contextual approach* (pp. 225–257). New York: Plenum Press.

Rumm, P. D., Cummings, P., Krauss, M. R., Bell, M. A., & Rivara, F. P. (2000). Identified spouse abuse as a risk factor for child abuse. *Child Abuse and Neglect, 24,* 1375–1381.

Sprecher, S. (1999). "I love you more today than yesterday": Romantic partners' perceptions of changes in love and related affect over time. *Journal of Personality and Social Psychology, 76,* 46–53.

Stewart, D. W., & Shamdasani, P. N (1990). *Focus groups theory and practice.* Newbury Park, CA: Sage.

Straus, M. A. (1973). A General Systems Theory approach to a theory of violence between family members. *Social Science Information, 12,* 105–125.

Sweeney, M. M. (2002). Two decades of family change: The shifting economic foundations of marriage. *American Sociological Review, 67,* 132–147.

Tjaden, P., & Thoennes, N. (2000). Extent, nature, and consequences of intimate partner violence: Findings from the National Violence Against Women Survey (Report for Grant No. 93-IJ-CX-0012). Washington, DC: National Institute of Justice and the Centers for Disease Control.

Whitchurch, G. C., & Constantine, L. L. (1993). Systems theory. In P. G. Boss, W. J. Doherty, R. LaRossa, W. R. Schumm, & S. K. Steinmetz (Eds.), *Sourcebook of family theories and methods: A contextual approach* (pp. 325–352). New York: Plenum Press.

Wilson, M., & Daly, M. (2001). The evolutionary psychology of couple conflict in registered versus de facto marital unions. In A. Booth, A. C. Crouter, & M. Clements (Eds.), *Couples in conflict* (pp. 1–26). Mahwah, NJ: Erlbaum.

3

Assessing the Best Interests of the Child

Visitation and Custody in Cases of Domestic Violence

Peter G. Jaffe
Claire V. Crooks

Domestic violence has been on the public agenda for 30 years, since the inception of the first shelters for abused women. The first wave of public policy, legislative change, and service delivery has emphasized an effective criminal-justice response. The overriding principles have been victim safety and perpetrator accountability. The issue of appropriate legal and clinical interventions for perpetrators remains one of many controversies. In particular, perpetrators' amenability to treatment, the effectiveness of various interventions, and the most effective model(s) for coordination between the court's and community systems' responses are major debates (Gondolf, 2002). This issue is further complicated when men's roles as fathers are added to the discussion. An emerging focus has become the role of the family court and its court-related services in determining a man's role as parent following allegations of domestic violence.

This chapter outlines some of the controversies that arise in postseparation parenting plans for couples with a history of domestic violence. The need for comprehensive assessment and differentiated intervention strategies for these families is emphasized. Implications for training, community collaboration, and promising future directions are also discussed.

The ultimate challenge for the court is assessing individual fathers in the context of children's best interests. These best interests have to be viewed through the lens of the emerging knowledge in both the divorce and domestic-violence fields. It is important to recognize that fathers are an extremely heterogeneous group with respect to the interactions and level of involvement that they have with their partners and children at the point of separation. Many men have close and nurturing relationships with their children and are able to maintain shared-parenting plans in an amicable fashion with their ex-partners. These men are not involved in the court system. The critical concerns in the field are the level of conflict between some parents and, at the extreme, the level of violence that children may experience. For some children, this conflict and/or violence is limited to the period of separation;

for others, the violence is part of a longstanding pattern that continues post-separation. There is consensus that children's adjustment may be adversely affected by exposure to both parental conflict and violence (Kitzmann, Gaylord, Holt, & Kenny, 2003; Wolfe, Crooks, Lee, McIntyre-Smith, & Jaffe, 2003). Indeed, courts and community services have an emerging mandate to limit and redress this potential harm by limiting the opportunities for children's exposure to this toxicity (Jaffe, Crooks, & Wolfe, 2003). Strategies to achieve this goal include minimized contact between parents or possibly limiting the role of one parent. The appropriateness of applying any of these individual strategies is predicated on a systematic approach and consensus about definitions of conflict and violence.

Conflict and Domestic Violence

The terms *conflict* and *domestic violence* each represent a continuum of behavior. In the divorce field, conflict refers to disagreements between parents on how to live their lives and raise their children. Both parents are seen to contribute to the conflict, either by arguing with each other or remaining unhappily silent. Underlying dynamics of relationship conflict have been identified to include poor communication and conflict-resolution skills; lack of motivation to negotiate; poor role models in the family of origin; and incompatibility of personality styles (Dalton, Carbon, & Olesen, 2003). In our custody and visitation assessments, we also often recognize these families by their rigid focus on the past and their difficulty in shifting their energy and focus to future parenting plans (Jaffe & Cameron, 1984). In contrast, domestic violence refers to a range of abusive behaviors that occur in the context of an intimate relationship. This abuse may include criminal conduct, such as physical and sexual assaults, as well as emotional and financial control. Perpetrators and victims represent a heterogeneous mix of individuals and relationships that differ with respect to intent, impact, frequency, and severity (Frederick & Tilley, 2001). Although perpetrators of domestic violence are often indiscriminately labeled as *batterers* or *men who batter,* we would argue that these terms should be reserved for individuals who demonstrate a pattern of abusive behaviors that continue over time and that are designed to control, dominate, humiliate, or terrorize their victims. Conversely, individuals who perpetrate minor, isolated incidents of violence that are not part of a pattern of behavior over time are perpetrators or individuals involved in *an incident* of abusive behavior. The terms *batterer* or *men who batter* would not be accurate in these circumstances.

Some conflict is a normal byproduct of most parental separations and can be remedied by brief parent-education programs that help focus on the needs of children (Kurkowski, Gordon, & Arbuthnot, 1993) or, simply, the passage of time. One source of confusion has come from the term *high conflict,* which has been used to describe more intense and protracted disputes that require considerable court and community resources and include domestic-violence cases (Johnston, 1994). To compound this confusion, the original and most popular measure of intimate-partner violence is called the *Conflict Tactics Scale,* which involves a range of behavior from "insulted" to "used a knife or gun" (Straus, Gelles, & Steinmetz, 1980; Straus, Hamby, Boney McCoy, & Sugarman, 1996). In the average courtroom, the terms *domestic violence, conflict,* and *abuse* may be used interchangeably, without any clear definition or understanding of these terms.

More recently, it has been argued that a clearer distinction needs to be made between high-conflict and domestic-violence cases in terms of assessment and intervention strategies (Jaffe, Lemon, & Poisson, 2003). In any event, the use of terms underscores a major controversy in the family court, whereby domestic-violence advocates are concerned that domestic violence will be euphemized as conflict, and others argue that any conflict may be interpreted as domestic violence. Even when domestic violence is identified, is the term *batterer* accurate in describing the perpetrator, or is the incident minor, historical, or isolated? This chapter will focus on the role of courts and court-related services in deciding the appropriate visitation and custody plan in cases of alleged domestic violence. Critical issues of assessment and intervention are discussed, followed by research challenges and future directions for this field.

Why Is Domestic Violence Relevant to Child Custody?

It has only been within the last decade that legal and mental-health professionals have acknowledged that domestic violence is even relevant to the determination of child custody. Prior to this time, domestic violence was seen as an adult issue not relevant to the adjustment of children, and it was accepted that a man could be a violent spouse but still a good father. Many groups have challenged this notion and encouraged major legislative reform to recognize domestic violence as a critical factor to consider in these cases, based on the following rationale.

- *Abuse does not end with separation.* Research has shown that physical abuse, stalking, and harassment continue at significant rates post-separation, and they may even become more severe (Statistics Canada, 2001; Liss & Stahly, 1993). In fact, promoting contact between children and a violent ex-spouse may create an opportunity for renewed domestic violence through visitation and exchanges of children (Leighton, 1989; Sheeran & Hampton, 1999).
- *High overlap between domestic violence and child maltreatment.* The presence of domestic violence is a red flag for the coexistence of child maltreatment. In a review of studies investigating this overlap, results suggested that between 30% and 60% of children whose mothers had experienced abuse were themselves likely to be abused (Edleson, 1999).

- *Batterers are poor role models.* As discussed throughout this book, children's socialization with respect to relationships and conflict resolution is negatively affected by exposure to a perpetrator of domestic violence. For example, when children witness one parent inflicting abuse on the other or using threats of violence to maintain control within a relationship, their own expectations about relationships may come to parallel these observations (Bancroft & Silverman, 2002). The potential of violence in a batterer's subsequent intimate relationships represents a threat that children's exposure to poor modeling will continue.
- *Victims of domestic violence may be undermined in their parenting role.* Perpetrators of domestic violence may undermine their (ex-)partners' parenting in a range of obvious and more insidious ways. For example, batterers may blame the children's mother for the dissolution of the family or even explicitly instruct the children not to listen to her directions (Bancroft & Silverman, 2002). Intervention with these fathers requires that this facet of their parenting be addressed; fathers need to both recognize the ways in which they undermine their children's mother and to commit to stopping these behaviors (Scott & Crooks, 2004).
- *Perpetrators may use perpetual litigation as a form of ongoing control and harassment.* The family court can inadvertently become a tool for batterers to continue their abusive behavior in a new forum. Litigation exacts a high emotional and financial price for abused women already overwhelmed with the aftermath of a violent relationship. Some authors have suggested that many batterers have exceptional skills in presenting themselves positively in court and convincing judges to award them custody (Bowermaster & Johnson, 1998; Zorza, 1995).
- *In extreme cases, domestic violence following separation is lethal.* Domestic violence and homicides are inextricably linked. National figures from the United States and Canada suggest that women are most at risk of homicide from estranged partners with a prior history of domestic violence (Fox & Zawitz, 1999; Statistics Canada, 2001; Websdale, 2003). Thus, risk of homicide in domestic-violence cases requires diligent investigation because of this growing literature linking domestic violence, separation, and homicide. To assist with this work, risk-assessment tools have been developed (Campbell, 1995; Campbell, Sharps, & Glass, 2001). In these extreme cases, children may become involved as witnesses to homicides or become homicide victims themselves (Websdale, Town, & Johnson, 1999). Child abduction represents another traumatic outcome in these cases, representing a batterer's ultimate desire for control after separation through punishment of his ex-partner.

In summary, domestic violence is an important area of inquiry in addressing child-custody and visitation disputes. A history of domestic violence demands a unique analysis. Legal and mental-health professionals need a paradigm shift to view the information and competing allegations in the determination of a child's best interest. A mother who lives in fear of her ex-partner is not paranoid, nor may she be able to promote a paternal relationship in the face of danger. Although the vast majority of divorcing parents need minimal legal resources to resolve their postseparation parenting plan, parents who have experienced domestic violence require the highest standard of care. When parents express concerns about their safety and their children's safety, the issue must be closely examined.

One size does not fit all parents in custody and visitation disputes. Lawyers, judges, and mental-health professionals need to ensure that the right interventions are matched to the right clients. The best innovations of the late 1900s, such as mediation and joint custody, are not appropriate solutions to child-custody disputes involving domestic violence because these remedies require two parents who have some basic respect and trust in each other, as opposed to fear and hesitancy to even be in the same room (Hirst, 2002). Furthermore, the power differential between parties in domestic-violence cases makes it difficult for the more vulnerable party to raise concerns about the process. Legal and mental-health professionals who ignore warning signs of domestic violence can endanger children and parents by minimizing, denying, or excusing the reality of domestic violence.

Clinical Issues: Assessment and Intervention

Trying to understand what dynamics led to a marital breakdown and sorting through allegations of mistreatment and fault are highly complex undertakings. When children are involved, and their future care is at stake, intense emotions may cloud parents' accurate portrayals of the marriage to an independent third party. Conflicts about parents' postseparation arrangements for children may take a number of different pathways. Many parents are able to develop amicable shared-parenting arrangements without court intervention; others require an assessment of the nature of the conflict and the potential existence of domestic violence.

Even in domestic-violence cases, there is a range of outcomes that may not include the formal court system. For some abuse victims, their abuser leaves the jurisdiction and may move on to other relationships, showing no interest in maintaining an ongoing relationship with their former partner or children. In other cases, the abuse victim may flee for her safety, and the perpetrator takes no action to find her. In our survey of abuse victims, some avoided any engagement with their perpetrator over financial or child-related issues by ignoring their legal rights and entitlement (e.g., living in poverty was seen as favorable to living with ongoing violence and harassment) (Jaffe, Crooks, & Poisson, 2003). For cases that do enter the formal court system, the assessment and intervention issues are complex. The cases that pose the most significant challenge to legal and mental-health professionals are ones where the parents present diametrically opposed versions of reality with respect to preseparation events and parental involvement.

Assessment

Domestic-violence allegations represent one of these thorny issues that require thorough assessments and investigation. At the outset, it is important to recognize that domestic violence is not a homogenous phenomenon but rather an umbrella term for a range of patterns and behaviors that differ in frequency, severity, intention, and impact (Frederick & Tilley, 2001). Different patterns have been identified, including Ongoing/Episodic Male Battering, Female Initiated Violence, Male Controlling Interactive Violence, Separation/Divorce trauma, and Psychotic/Paranoid (Johnston & Campbell, 1993). These categories are not without controversy, particularly with respect to the concept of mutual violence. Many domestic-violence advocates suggest that mutual violence is often misinterpreted without a power-and-control analysis of the primary aggressor (Frederick & Tilley, 2001).

To understand the context for these assessments, it is important to be cognizant of the zeitgeist in family courts in North America and elsewhere (Jaffe & Crooks, 2004). Courts want cases settled in a cost-efficient and timely manner by precourt interventions, such as mediation and settlement conferences. Cooperation is highly reinforced and seen to be synonymous with children's best interests. Common wisdom in the divorce field suggests that the parent who is best able to promote a relationship between the child(ren) and the other parent is most appropriate for a custodial role.

Domestic-violence allegations raised in this context are often met with skepticism and concern that the allegation is being utilized to limit the involvement of the other parent. In this vein, the allegations represent a double-edged sword for abuse victims. If the allegations are proven on the preponderance of evidence, the victim and her children may find safety, provided by recent legal reforms and appropriate community resources. However, if the allegations appear unfounded and are deemed to be malicious, the abuse victim may lose custody. In some of these cases, mothers are accused of willful alienation of the children against their father.

In the absence of investigation and clear documentation of family violence by the police or child-protection services, the family-justice system may be faced with conflicting allegations and denials by the two parents. One California-based study of high-conflict separation cases in the family courts found that more than one half involved an allegation of spousal or child abuse (Johnston, Lee, Oleson, & Walters, 2005). About one half of the abuse allegations were substantiated, and in about one quarter of the cases in the study, some form of child or spousal abuse was perpetrated by both parents. The rate of substantiation of spousal abuse was much higher than the rate of substantiation of allegations of child abuse. This finding may reflect the fact that spouses in a high-conflict separation are likely to be accurate in reporting their own victimization by a partner. However, in high-conflict separation cases, parents may have considerable difficulty in accurately understanding and reporting on how their partner may have treated their children.

Even in cases where the violence has been substantiated and documented by police and/or court records, that information may not find its way into family court. In a study of all families undergoing dissolution of marriage in Seattle over a two-year period, results indicated very poor transmission of information across formal systems (Kernic, Monary-Ernsdorff, Koespell, & Holt, 2005). For example, almost one half of those cases with a history of police- and/or court-reported spousal violence had no mention of this abuse in the marriage-dissolution file, and more than one half of the remaining case files documented allegations without corroborating evidence, despite its existence. Overall, the court was made aware of fewer than one fourth of those cases with a substantiated history of spousal violence. The authors point to a number of potential contributors for this lack of information sharing, including lack of coordination of domestic-violence services across different courts and the absence or inadequacy of screening for domestic violence.

In cases where there are spousal-abuse allegations but no conclusive police- or child-protection service investigation, the family-court system is left to try to determine what occurred (Bala, 2004). Even in a family-law case, there is an onus on the party making an allegation to prove it, though the standard of proof is the civil standard of "proof on the balance of probabilities," making it less difficult to establish in family court that abuse occurred than in a criminal-court proceeding, where there must be "proof beyond a reasonable doubt."

In some family-court cases, a genuine victim may be unable to establish the fact or significance of spousal abuse because of the lack of effective legal representation. Even a good family lawyer may have considerable difficulty in establishing that abuse occurred if there is a lack of corroborative evidence of the victim's allegations, for example, from a doctor, neighbor, or babysitter. In these cases, a victim who is unable to prove abuse may find herself accused of alienating the children from their father.

This alienation has even been labeled as a "syndrome," although there is no research to support the reliability and validity of this diagnosis (e.g., Ragland & Fields, 2003). At the same time, there is no question that some separating parents actively undermine children's relationships with the other parent. Children may actively reject a parent postseparation for a host of reasons.

More recently, increasingly sophisticated frameworks have been proposed to understand this rejection process and to develop appropriate interventions (Bala & Bailey, 2004; Drozd & Olesen, 2004; Johnston & Kelly, 2005; Johnston, 2005). In high-conflict cases, it is quite common for both parents to make hostile and derogatory comments about the other to the children and to attempt to enmesh the children in their disputes. While children emotionally suffer in these cases, it would seem that most children struggle to maintain a relationship with both parents, despite the parental conduct. When children do reject one parent, it is necessary to consider the role that both parents are playing in the lives of their children and the specific circumstances of the child. In some cases, a child will become aligned with the warmer and more effective parent and reject the other as a way of resolving conflicting feelings of loyalty.

An alienation analysis is especially inappropriate in cases of family violence, where children's reticence about contact with a parent is better understood as hypervigilance or fear (Drozd & Olesen, 2004). A decision-tree framework has been proposed by Drozd and Olesen to assist judges, lawyers, and assessors in dealing with the difficult issues surrounding perceived alienation. Other advances in the area include a framework that looks at multiple contributors to parental rejection, including the stage of children's development, events surrounding separation, primary caregiver's behavior, and the rejected parent's behavior (Johnston & Kelly, 2004).

In contrast to the empirically unsupported notion of Parental Alienation Syndrome, these more complex, multidimensional models have received preliminary research support. A comprehensive assessment identifying reasons for rejection is critical, because it provides the basis for appropriate intervention. If a parent is being rejected primarily for reasons such as moralistic thinking by the children (e.g., tied to developmental stage), lack of resources (e.g., not as many toys as the other parent's house), and negative comments by the custodial parent, then therapeutic intervention to rebuild the relationship between the rejected parent and the children would be indicated. In contrast, if a careful assessment found that rejection was more closely tied to the non-custodial parent's history of violence and continued attempts to monitor and harass the children and primary caregiver, then interventions to create safety for the children and caregiver would be more important that treating the alienation. In any case, a thorough assessment of abuse allegations is warranted as part of a custody decision-making process, given the high stakes of a finding of domestic violence.

Assessments or evaluations may be completed by mental-health professionals with expertise about divorcing families or by brief reports completed by a range of professionals and volunteers appointed by the court. Assessment resources vary widely by jurisdiction, and in general, parents with more resources have access to more qualified professionals and more thorough evaluations. Assessing domestic violence requires a number of procedures to identify patterns of behavior over time, as opposed to an isolated incident. Furthermore, less severe or subthreshold behaviors should be interpreted within the context of this larger pattern. A multimethod, multisource approach is required. Figure 3.1 identifies the additional assessment requirements for cases where either party has made allegations of violence. The first layer of the pyramid identifies the essential ingredients of a custody-and-visitation assessment, including understanding the children's individual needs, the parents' skills, the ability of the parents to cooperate, and the developmental considerations of any parenting plan. In a high-conflict case, these initial assessment domains are still pertinent; however, the second layer of the pyramid identifies additional concerns, such as the history of the parental conflict and children's coping strategies. In high-conflict cases without violence, it may be important to identify the less toxic parent. By *toxic,* we refer to the more hostile and angry parent who is difficult for children to be around without being drawn into adult conflict. With domestic violence, the above challenges are compounded by additional assessment consideration (denoted at the top of the pyramid), including homicide-risk assessment and an understanding of the impact of violence on the children.

In conducting an assessment where domestic violence has been alleged, collecting all of the information shown in the pyramid involves a complex process. A starting point is individual interviews with both parents on more than one occasion. While perpetrators may present as very reasonable individuals on one or two occasions, by interviewing them over time and beginning to challenge their perspective on the basis of other information that has been gathered may provide the assessor with the opportunity to see past the veneer. Another important ingredient is a structured inventory of abusive behavior that includes frequency and severity of physically, sexually, verbally,

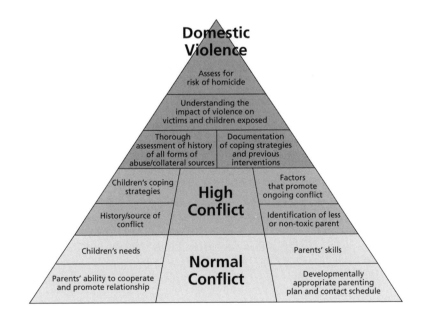

Figure 3.1. Child custody: Specialized assessment needs in domestic violence cases

and psychologically abusive behavior experienced by each partner, as well as injuries suffered (e.g., the Abusive Behavior Observation Checklist; see Dutton, 1992). A follow-up interview to the abuse inventory is helpful for ascertaining the context of the abuse. For example, assessors should gain a better understanding of the impact of the abuse; coping styles; disclosures to friends, family, and professionals; and effects of the violence on the children.

Given that the credibility of claims is an important determinant of custody decisions, collateral information is an important source of documentation. Therefore, interviews with informal and formal support systems, including review of records (police, child protection, emergency-room physicians, and so forth) should be included. Emphasis on this documentation is not meant to imply that allegations of domestic violence are credible only if there is third-party evidence; indeed, the majority of domestic-violence victims may not have disclosed to other people or involved the police. Rather, it is important to review this documentation in cases where it does exist while remaining mindful that lack of such evidence does not imply fabrication.

It is also important to keep the needs of the children first and foremost while assessing these relationship dynamics. In assessing families where domestic violence has been alleged, it is essential to include interviews with the children so as to assess their understanding of events and the impact of their exposure to violence. Collateral sources for children should also be reviewed (e.g., teachers, doctors, counselors) to gain understanding of their reactions to the events that they have witnessed or experienced. Analyzing the information gathered requires an understanding of abuse victims and perpetrators. For example, although the prevailing belief may be that women may lie or exaggerate claims of abuse to gain custody, our experience is more that abuse victims minimize or are reluctant to disclose the extent of abuse that they endured. In our interviews with 62 abused women, they reported that they rarely volunteered information about sexual abuse by their partner. Their reluctance stemmed from feelings of personal embarrassment, lack of trust or rapport with the professional, and the concern that the professional could not handle the information (Jaffe, Crooks, & Poisson, 2003). Perpetrators of domestic violence may deny or minimize the abuse as part of their skill in avoiding responsibility for their behavior and externalizing blame for any difficulties (Bancroft & Silverman, 2003). Without a domestic-violence analysis, these allegations may be misunderstood as more of the "he said/she said" perspectives on a relationship that are often found in high-conflict divorce. Once domestic violence has been identified, this analysis should provide the context for assessing other information, such as communication patterns between the partners. For example, a mother who avoids phone contact with an abusive former partner may be seen to be neglecting her duties for information sharing about the children's activities; however, within the context of domestic violence, this same behavior can be understood as an attempt to protect herself and her children from further harassment and abuse.

There are conflicting claims about the progress of legal and mental-health professionals in understanding domestic violence. Clearly, there has been an increase in the number of training programs available to assist various professionals in becoming more sensitive to the dynamics of domestic violence and more skilled in intervention strategies. The debate focuses on the rate of change in actual practices among professionals. In the custody-evaluation arena, two recent research papers present drastically different pictures of the extent to which the field has changed. Bow and Boxer (2003) surveyed custody evaluators across the United States and found that the vast majority reported that they recognized domestic violence as a critical factor in their work. These practitioners indicated that they considered utilizing specialized assessment resources and made differential custody and visitation recommendations when domestic violence was identified. In contrast, recent studies in the Louisville, Kentucky, courts found that domestic violence was often overlooked in court assessments. Analysis of custody evaluation reports suggested that domestic violence was not a factor in recommendations, even when it was mentioned in the same report (Horvath, Logan, & Walker, 2002). Furthermore, an analysis of court records found that court settlement methods (e.g., mediation, adjudication) did not vary for families with and without domestic-violence histories. Parents with a history of domestic violence were as likely to be steered into mediation as those without, despite the inappropriateness of mediation (for the reasons stated earlier) in these cases. In addition, custody outcomes did not differ between families with and without this history (Logan, Walker, Horvath, & Leukefeld, 2003).

The extent to which these findings from one jurisdiction can be generalized is not clear; nonetheless, recent research emerging from other jurisdictions has replicated these themes. Consistent with this posited gap between theory and practice, one California study found that mediators held joint sessions in nearly one half of the cases in which an independent screening interview had identified allegations of domestic violence, in direct violation of state regulations for separate sessions in these cases (Hirst, 2002).

In the Seattle study discussed earlier, Kernic and her colleagues (Kernic, et al., 2005) found that while some progress has been made in recognizing the need to identify domestic violence in child-custody determinations, in many cases, appropriate safeguards and restrictions are not being put in place. For example, although fathers who were known to have perpetrated violence against children's mothers were more likely to be denied child visitation than those who had not, this restriction was imposed on only 16.8% of fathers from this group. Furthermore, third-party supervision was no more likely to be required for fathers who had perpetrated violence than for those who had not (Kernic, et al., 2005).

In a San Diego–based study looking at mediation practices, it was found that mediators failed to recognize and report domestic violence in 57% of the domestic-violence cases (Johnson, Saccuzzo, & Koen, 2005). Furthermore, revealing information about domestic violence was found to be detrimental to victims with respect to outcomes. In this study, mediators who reported being aware of the existence of domestic violence in the relationships were *less* likely to recommend supervised exchanges than those who did not.

Finally, a study evaluating the application of the Model Code (rebuttable presumption against awarding custody to perpetrators of domestic violence, as recommended by the National Council of Juvenile and Family Court Judges) across several jurisdictions found that these jurisdictions were more likely to award custody to victims of domestic violence than in jurisdictions without the rebuttal presumption, except when there was a competing "friendly parent" provision (Morrill, Dai, Dunn, Sung, & Smith, 2005). However, while victims were more likely to be awarded custody in these jurisdictions and more likely to have restrictions placed on fathers' visits, these restrictions were still only applied in approximately two thirds of cases with a history of domestic violence. Thus, even in jurisdictions with a rebuttal presumption, there appears to still often be a trade-off between physical custody and visitation, whereby perpetrators of abuse may not be awarded custody but are still granted relatively free access.

Intervention

Intervening in child-custody disputes with parental histories of domestic violence is a complex undertaking. In dealing with abusive fathers, there may be a range of remedies over time that depend on access to appropriate services and documented changes in the abuser's behavior. Within the court system, judges have to consider a range of options in dealing with a violent spouse. These options include no contact, supervised visitation, supervised exchanges, exchanges in a public place, unsupervised visitation, liberal and regular visitation, and shared custody/parenting (many states have dropped the term "custody" in favor of "parenting plan" and "residential parent"). Embedded within these options are a multitude of parameters, such as the length of a visit, advisability of overnight access, determination of suitable supervisors, and safe locations for exchanges.

As noted, all of these options exist within a culture that promotes cooperation and shared parenting. Currently, the de facto arrangement appears to be joint-custody or shared-parenting plans, where parents are considered equal partners in decision making and available contact time. The justice system, in our view, attempts to apply a one-size-fits-all solution to separating couples, and all efforts and resources are directed at having parents settle their differences and become parenting partners for life. Figure 3.2 tries to capture this reality by the analogy of a highway leading to shared parenting in which domestic violence cases need an off-ramp to avoid being carried along with the traffic. With a history of domestic violence, shared parenting and the sometimes legislated shared-parenting plans are contraindicated. Shared-parenting plans require good communication between parents, which is un-

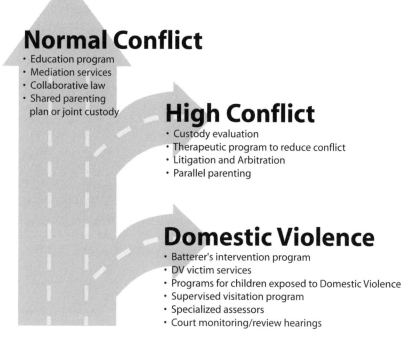

Figure 3.2. Differentiated custody interventions in domestic violence cases

likely in the context of fear and disrespect in a historically abusive relationship. Whereas the majority of families benefit from educational programs and mediation, domestic-violence cases require specialized intervention, including supervised visitation, batterer's intervention, and support services for children. Solutions that require victims and perpetrators to be together in mediation or settlement conferences may endanger victims or intimidate them into accepting remedies without safety.

High-conflict cases involving couples that fully engage lawyers and judges but have no history of violence also require more specialized intervention. Although the physical-safety concerns are mitigated, exposure to ongoing conflict for children is clearly harmful, and the parents require external direction to develop and implement parallel-parenting arrangements. Parallel parenting recognizes that each parent is capable of meeting children's needs by themselves and is a beneficial influence for the child but that any hope of collaboration between the parents is futile and harmful for children. Contained within this arrangement are specific guidelines to minimize contact and communication between the parents.

Further complicating the issue, these decisions may be made at one point in time but require continuous review. These reviews have to consider the abuser's response to previous interventions (legal and clinical), compliance with current undertakings, and readiness of children and ex-partners to accommodate the proposed changes. That is, men's change occurs in a system involving other individuals and their needs; therefore, perpetrator change alone does not necessarily translate to increased access to children. For example, an abusive man may have been involved in extreme forms of violence that traumatized his partner and children to such an extent that they are not prepared to consider contact after his release from jail, regardless of documented changes and a commitment to be nonviolent.

There are systemic problems in providing services for families having experienced domestic violence. First of all, timely access to services may be impeded by poverty, waiting lists, and culturally appropriate service providers. Multiple services need to be accessed, including services for batterers, victims, and children exposed to domestic violence. If these services are in place, there is a critical need to coordinate service delivery and communication of information. Aside from confidentiality concerns, the nature of information required by custody evaluators, lawyers, and judges may be beyond the mandate, policy, and record-keeping practices of individual agencies involved. To compound these problems, it is not clear that anybody is in charge. Practices vary from having a court officer (e.g., master or commissioner) hold regular review hearings to court orders that leave families in limbo with no clear accountability for implementation or mechanism for review. In our experience, the latter is more common.

A further complication in this field is the increasing number of self-represented litigants, who may not even have an awareness of the available legal remedies and community services, let alone know how to navigate these systems. In our experience with judiciary-training seminars, judges report finding these pro se litigants to produce hearings that are more emotionally charged and less informative and productive in decision making in the absence of the organizing and buffering effects of a competent family lawyer. At the extreme, judges may be faced by a perpetrator cross-examining a victim of abuse.

The shortcomings within the court system that relate to gathering important information, making decisions, and monitoring parents' and children's progress with court remedies inadvertently create a benefit for perpetrators. Since many perpetrators of domestic violence minimize their abuse and avoid accountability, the family-court system may reinforce these tendencies through these systemic inadequacies. Similar to the conclusions outlined with regard to the effectiveness of batterer-intervention programs being dependent on their integration into a coordinated justice and community-service system (Gondolf, 2002), family-court interventions for batterers face the same challenge. This challenge is magnified by the number of parties, their relationships to each other, and the multitude of agencies involved. Different aspects of the justice system may also be involved with the same family (criminal, civil, child protection) with inconsistent or even competing decisions.

Future Directions

The preceding discussion illustrates the complexity of assessing and intervening with parents and children with histories of domestic violence within the child-custody arena. The issues raised require major systems change and collaboration among researchers, policymakers, and practitioners. This collaboration has been hampered in the past by the compartmentalization of the domestic-violence and divorce-research fields. The needs of children and families dealing with separation in the context of conflict and/or violence must be understood and addressed in a more holistic manner (Jaffe, Poisson, & Cunningham, 2001).

Research

There is clearly a need for well-designed, longitudinal research to inform practice and policy; however, research faces a tremendous challenge in capturing this same complexity. Some flexibility is required in applying best-practice research methodologies. Obviously, random assignment to different conditions or interventions is not ethical. As a result, research will need to focus on naturally occurring events and trajectories.

Furthermore, we need to expand the possible range of research outcomes which we may consider in a particular study. The impact of a particular visitation arrangement following a history of domestic violence may not be completely positive or negative. For example, a recent study looking at behavioral and emotional outcomes with preschool-aged children following separation in the context of domestic violence identified a potential catch-22 (Smith Stover, Van Horn, Turner, Cooper, & Lieberman, 2003). On the one hand, children who did not see their fathers at all were more likely to have internalizing problems independent of the extent of the violence they had witnessed. On the other hand, children who did see their fathers exhibited externalizing behavior problems, predicted in part by the extent of the violence experienced by their mothers. Overall, the effect size of children's problems if they had been exposed to severe violence was larger than the negative effects of being deprived of contact with their father. Although this small study was innovative in its attempt to look at different aspects of violence (e.g., amount witnessed, severity), it overlooked a major element by excluding children who had suffered from other forms of child maltreatment. The next generation of research needs to follow this direction of including a range of behavioral outcomes and also a more heterogeneous conceptualization of exposure to violence rather than reducing this experience to a dichotomous construct.

Similarly, the impact of a particular outcome may vary across time and developmental stages, underscoring the need for longitudinal research. For example, there may be cases where a child's sense of emotional security and outright physical safety would be greatly facilitated by the cessation of any contact between the father and child. However, this child's needs may change as he or she grows older. It may be that the absence of any contact with the father as a young child may exacerbate difficulties that the child is having in making sense of his or her identity as an adolescent. Unresolved issues with a parent can create a sense of ambiguous loss for the child (Scott & Crooks, 2004). Clinically, we have certainly seen cases where an adolescent who has not had contact with his father (who was abusive to his mother) begins to both idealize and overidentify with the absent parent and may even seek to live with him. The challenge for practitioners in domestic-violence cases is to balance the need for safety in the short-term and healing relationships (when possible) in the long-term. Healing may refer to individuals who are able to come to terms with a traumatic past and develop more effective coping strategies and healthy relationships. It can also refer to reconciliation in previously estranged parent-child relationships, if this can be done in a manner that clearly defines the responsibility for past abuse with the perpetrator, respects the child's wishes and developmental needs, and maintains a sense of safety for the child (Crooks, Scott, Francis, Kelly, & Reid, 2006). This issue of reconciliation must be approached with caution in that there is limited research to inform decision making about whether it should be attempted in a particular family. In order for research to inform this debate, it has to be designed in a manner that captures the complexity of relationships in children's development over time.

Legislation and Community Development

The law has changed to recognize domestic violence in child-custody disputes in many jurisdictions by creating a rebuttable presumption against a batterer receiving custody or making domestic violence a mandatory factor for court consideration (e.g., National Council of Juvenile and Family Court Judges, 2001; Jaffe & Crooks, 2004). As we have argued elsewhere, legislative change without training and resource development may have minimal impact, and in fact, it may trigger unintended negative side effects (Jaffe, Crooks, & Wolfe, 2003). To increase the likelihood of new laws being effective, there is a need for a foundation of comprehensive training programs and specialized resources that extend the mainstream services for separating parents.

Training programs have to do a better job of defining domestic violence in all its forms and providing differential service responses to meet the level of need for a family. Our progress in the domestic-violence arena stands to lose credibility if there is not clear delineation of where conflict ends and domestic violence begins. When domestic violence is recognized, there still needs to be a distinction between minor or isolated acts versus acts that occur as part of a pattern of abuse that engenders fear and harm for victims and children exposed to this behavior. When the most intensive domestic-violence interventions are misapplied to families who may be better characterized as experiencing transitory high conflict, there is the potential to harm parents' reputations, impede their problem-solving, and undermine parent-child relationships. Furthermore, it is an inefficient utilization of scarce resources. Conversely, an abusive husband who engages community members and the court system in a dialogue about his wife making false allegations and being an unfit parent has to be identified early in the process. Failure to identify these cases allows the batterer to manipulate the justice system as a tool to revictimize his ex-partner.

A differential assessment has to lead to differential interventions. Comprehensive assessment without corresponding intervention options is analogous to having a maître d' in a gourmet restaurant giving out menus with a vast array of delicacies while the kitchen staff can only make hamburgers. A finding of domestic violence should give rise to a menu of the following services: a supervised visitation center that can provide safe visits or exchanges; a batterer's intervention program; specialized parenting programs for batterers; specialized counseling programs for children traumatized by violence who have ambivalent and conflicted relationships with their parents; court monitoring of child and parent progress; access to competent legal service; and victim-support services (including parenting and safety planning). The overwhelming problem in this field is the lack of accessible and affordable services outlined above. Ultimately, as these services develop, there needs to be enhanced co-ordination of assessment and intervention strategy. In order for the court to fine-tune agreements and recognize progress (or lack thereof), there needs to be a community plan and a central forum for this information. There is a lingering question about the most effective model that creates accountability for the system as a whole in dealing with these complex cases. At the extreme, domestic-violence death-review committees that have developed across the United States raise some of these questions after homicides by examining what could have been done differently in similar circumstances (Websdale, et al., 1999). The less extreme cases do not receive the same media attention; nonetheless, an effective system response remains illusory.

The first generation of services and policies responding to domestic violence emphasized raising awareness and providing emergency services through police, advocacy, and shelter intervention. Changes similar to those made in the criminal-justice system are now being demanded of the civil courts in their determination of appropriate parenting plans after domestic violence. As researchers and practitioners have come to recognize the heterogeneous nature of domestic violence, the complexity of relationships, and the impact of exposure to violence on children, the need for a flexible and comprehensive set of responses has become apparent. This challenge is compounded by the demands for an integrated court- and community-response strategy. Rather than widening the net to inappropriately label all high-conflict parents as necessarily engaging in cases of domestic violence, it is critical that families receive differential assessment following allegations of domestic violence. The results of these assessments must be matched to services that promote accountability, safety, and healing. The mainstream move toward cooperative settlement strategies and shared-parenting plans is an excellent direction for most families. However, domestic-violence victims and their children require an exit ramp from these presumed solutions. This off-ramp is only as meaningful as the comprehensive assessment and intervention strategies at the end of the road.

References

Bala, N. (2004, July). *Spousal abuse and children: Family law issues*. Retrieved January 7, 2004, from National Family Law Program of the Federation of Law Societies of Canada, La Malbaie, Quebec, Canada, Web site: http://law.queensu.ca/faculty/bala/papers/spouseabuse&familylaw2004.htm

Bala, N., & Bailey, N. (2004). Enforcement of access and alienation of children: Conflict reduction strategies and legal responses. *Canadian Family Law Quarterly, 23,* 1–61.

Bancroft, L., & Silverman, J. (2002). *The batterer as a parent: Addressing the impact of domestic violence on family dynamics*. Thousand Oaks, CA: Sage.

Bow, J. N., & Boxer, P. (2003). Assessing allegations of domestic violence in child custody evaluations. *Journal of Interpersonal Violence, 18,* 1394–1410.

Bowermaster, J., & Johnson, D. (1998, October). *The role of domestic violence in family court child custody determinations: An interdisciplinary investigation*. Paper presented at the Fourth International Conference on Children Exposed to Domestic Violence, San Diego, CA.

Campbell, J. C. (1995). *Assessing dangerousness: Violence by sexual offenders, batterers, and child abusers*. Thousand Oaks, CA: Sage.

Campbell, J. C., Sharps, P., & Glass, N. (2001). Risk assessment for intimate partner homicide. In G.-F. Pinard & L. Pagani (Eds.), *Clinical assessment of dangerousness: Empirical contributions* (pp. 136–157). New York: Cambridge University Press.

Crooks, C. V., Scott, K. L., Francis, K. J., Kelly, T., & Reid, M. (2006). Eliciting change in maltreating fathers: Goals, processes, and desired outcomes. *Cognitive and Behavioral Practice, 13,* 71–81.

Dalton, C., Carbon, S., & Olesen, N. (2003). High conflict divorce, violence, and abuse: Implications for custody and visitation decisions. *Juvenile and Family Court Journal, 54,* 11–33.

Drozd, L. M., & Olesen, N. (2004). Is it abuse, alienation, and/or estrangement? *Journal of Child Custody, 1,* 65–106.

Dutton, M. A., (1992). *Empowering and healing the battered woman: A model for assessment and intervention*. New York: Springer.

Edleson, J. L. (1999). The overlap between child maltreatment and woman battering. *Violence Against Women, 5,* 134–154.

Fox, A. J., & Zawitz, M. W. (1999). *Homicide trends in the United States*. Retrieved February 2, 2004, from the U.S. Department of Justice, Bureau of Justice Statistics, Web site: http://www.ojp.usdoj.gov/bjs/homicide/homtrnd.htm

Frederick, L., & Tilley, J. (2001). *Effective interventions in domestic violence cases: Context is everything*. Duluth, MN: Battered Women's Justice Project.

Gondolf, E. W. (2002). *Batterer intervention systems*. Thousand Oaks, CA: Sage.

Hirst, A. M. (2002). *Domestic violence in court-based child custody mediation cases in California.* Research Update, Judicial Council of California, Administrative Office of the Courts, November 1–12.

Horvath, L. S., Logan, T. K., & Walker, R. (2002). Child custody cases: A content analysis of evaluations in practice. *Professional Psychology: Research and Practice, 33,* 557–565.

Jaffe, P. G., & Cameron, S. (1984). The prediction of successful interventions in the resolution of custody and access disputes. *Canadian Journal of Behavioural Science, 16,* 167–172.

Jaffe, P. G., & Crooks, C. V. (2004). The relevance of domestic violence in child custody determinations: A cross-national comparison. *Violence Against Women, 10,* 917–934.

Jaffe, P. G., Crooks, C. V., & Poisson, S. E. (2003). Common misconceptions and addressing domestic violence in child custody disputes. *Juvenile and Family Court Journal, 54,* 57–67.

Jaffe, P. G., Crooks, C. V., & Wolfe, D. A. (2003). Legal and policy responses to children exposed to domestic violence: The need to evaluate intended and unintended consequences. *Clinical Child and Family Psychology Review, 6,* 205–213.

Jaffe, P. G., Lemon, N. K. D., & Poisson, S. E. (2003). *Child custody and domestic violence: A call for safety and accountability.* Thousand Oaks, CA: Sage.

Jaffe, P. G., Poisson, S. E., Cunningham, A. (2001). Domestic violence and high-conflict divorce: Developing a new generation of research for children. In S. A. Graham-Bermann & J. L. Edleson (Eds), *Domestic violence in the lives of children: The future of research, intervention, and social policy* (pp. 189–202). Washington, DC: American Psychological Association.

Johnson, N. E., Saccuzzo, D. P., & Koen, W. J. (2005). Child custody mediation in cases of domestic violence: Empirical evidence of a failure to protect. *Violence Against Women, 11,* 1022–1053.

Johnston, J. R. (1994). High-conflict divorce. *Future of Children, 4,* 165–182.

Johnston, J. R. (2005). Children of divorce who reject a parent and refuse visitation: Recent research and social policy for the alienated child. *Family Law Quarterly, 38,* 757–775.

Johnston, J. R., & Campbell, L. E. (1993). A clinical typology of interparental violence in disputed-custody divorces. *American Journal of Orthopsychiatry, 63,* 190–199.

Johnston, J. R., & Kelly, J. B. (2004). Commentary on Walker, Brantley, and Rigsbee's (2004) "A critical analysis of Parental Alienation Syndrome and its admissibility in family court." *Journal of Child Custody, 1,* 77–89.

Johnston J. R., Lee, S., Olesen, N. W., & Walters, M. G. (2005). Allegations and substantiations of abuse in custody-disputing families. *Family Court Review, 43,* 283–294.

Kernic, M. A., Monary-Ernsdorff, D. J., Koespell, J. K., & Holt, V. L. (2005). Children in the crossfire: Child custody determinations among couples with a history of intimate partner violence. *Violence Against Women, 11,* 991–1021.

Kitzmann, K. M., Gaylord, N. K., Holt, A., & Kenny, E. D. (2003). Child witnesses to domestic violence: A meta-analytic review. *Journal of Consulting and Clinical Psychology, 71,* 339–352.

Kurkowski, K., Gordon, D. A., & Arbuthnot, J. (1993). Children caught in the middle: A brief educational intervention for parents. *Journal of Divorce and Remarriage, 20,* 139–151.

Leighton, B. (1989). *Spousal abuse in metropolitan Toronto: Research report on the response of the criminal justice system.* Ottawa, Ontario, Canada: Solicitor General Canada.

Liss, M. B., & Stahly, G. B. (1993). Domestic violence and child custody. In M. Hansen & M. Haraway (Eds.), *Battering and family therapy: A feminist perspective* (pp. 175–187). Newbury Park, CA: Sage.

Logan, T. K., Walker, R., Horvath, L. S., & Leukefeld, C. (2003). A random sample of docket records in a circuit court. *Journal of Family Violence, 18,* 269–279.

Morrill, A. C., Dai, J., Dunn, S., Sung, I., & Smith, K. (2005). Child custody and visitation decisions when the father has perpetrated violence against the mother. *Violence Against Women, 11,* 1076–1107.

National Council of Juvenile and Family Court Judges (2001). *Family violence legislative update.* Reno, NV: author.

Ragland, E. R., & Fields, H. (2003). *Parental Alienation Syndrome: What professionals need to know*, Vol. 16(6), Update 14. Alexandria, VA: National Center for Prosecution of Child Abuse.

Scott, K. L., & Crooks, C. V. (2004). Effecting change in maltreating fathers: Critical principles in intervention. *Clinical Psychology: Science and Practice, 11,* 95–111.

Sheeran, M., & Hampton, S. (1999). Supervised visitation in cases of domestic violence. *Juvenile and Family Court Journal, 50,* 13–25.

Smith Stover, C., Van Horn, P., Turner, R., Cooper, B., & Lieberman, A. F. (2003). The effects of father visitation on preschool-aged witnesses of domestic violence. *Journal of Interpersonal Violence, 18,* 1149–1167.

Statistics Canada (2001). *Family violence in Canada: A statistical profile 2001.* Ottawa, Ontario, Canada: Minister of Industry.

Straus, M. A., Gelles, R. J., & Steinmetz, S. K. (1980). *Behind closed doors: Violence in the American family.* Garden City, NY: Anchor Books.

Straus, M. A., Hamby, S. L., Boney McCoy, S., & Sugarman, D. B. (1996). *The revised Conflict Tactics Scales (CTS2): Development and preliminary psychometric data.* Journal of Family Issues, *17,* 283–316.

Websdale, N. (2003). Reviewing domestic violence deaths. *National Institute of Justice Journal, 250,* 26–31.

Websdale, N., Town, M., & Johnson, B. (1999). Domestic violence fatality reviews: From a culture of blame to a culture of safety. *Juvenile and Family Court Journal, 50,* 61–74.

Wolfe, D. A., Crooks, C. V., Lee, V., McIntyre-Smith, A., & Jaffe, P. G. (2003). The effects of children's exposure to domestic violence: A meta-analysis and critique. *Clinical Child and Family Psychology Review, 6,* 171–187.

Zorza, J. (1995). How abused women can use the law to help protect their children. In E. Peled, P. G. Jaffe, & J. L. Edleson (Eds.), *Ending the cycle of violence: Community responses to children of battered women* (pp. 147–169). Thousand Oaks, CA: Sage.

4

Deciding on Fathers' Involvement in Their Children's Treatment After Domestic Violence

Betsy McAlister Groves
Patricia Van Horn
Alicia F. Lieberman

This chapter grows out of the experience of two programs that offer psycho-therapeutic interventions to children exposed to domestic violence: the Child Witness to Violence Project (CWVP) at Boston Medical Center and the Child Trauma Research Project (CTRP) at San Francisco General Hospital. In this chapter, we will review our experience of considering whether and how to include violent fathers in the healing of their children, and we discuss issues that inclusion raises for practitioners and policymakers.

Although violent fathers have not traditionally been directly involved in the treatment of children affected by domestic violence, they are present sym-bolically, emotionally, and frequently physically in the lives of their children. Given this reality, we will consider the following questions.

- How do mothers feel about children's relationships with their abusive fathers and with having fathers involved in their children's healing?
- What do children say and think about their fathers?
- What barriers to engaging fathers might exist in counseling programs that work with children affected by domestic violence?
- Should counseling programs that work with children affected by domestic violence also work with fathers? If so, under what circumstances?

We will begin this chapter with brief descriptions of our two clinical programs for children. We will review what we know about the desires of mothers, children, and fathers for involvement of fathers. We will then use clinical case material from our programs to illustrate some of our dilemmas and successes as we worked to create standards and protocols that would allow for the safe inclusion of violent fathers in their children's healing.

The Programmatic Context of Our Work

We are the founders of two clinical programs for children: the Child Wit-ness to Violence Project in Boston and the Child Trauma Research Project in San Francisco. These are the practice contexts in which we work and struggle with the degree to which fathers are to be involved in children's treatment. Each of our programs and then the overall goals of our work are discussed below.

The Child Witness to Violence Project (CWVP)

The Child Witness to Violence Project has provided mental-health services to children and families affected by domestic violence for over 10 years.[1] Established as an outpatient counseling service in the Pediatrics Department of Boston Medical Center, the project takes referrals of children ages eight and younger who have witnessed significant violence. Nearly 90% of the referrals are for children who have witnessed domestic violence. Referrals come from the health system, the courts and law-enforcement systems, shelters, schools, early child-care settings, and from parents themselves. Licensed mental-health clinicians provide child assessment and intervention. Typically, the child and nonoffending parent are seen, in combinations of individual and child-parent meetings. The decision about seeing the child alone or with the nonoffending parent depends on the age of the child, the functioning of the parent, the severity of symptoms, and other variables. The offender is not seen as part of the evaluation and is rarely involved in treatment. Staff of the CWVP are not trained to provide batterers' intervention, and in many instances, we have assumed that it is neither physically nor psychologically safe to invite the perpetrator to be a part of the evaluation. (In addition, there are often protective orders that limit an abuser's ability to have contact with the child or partner.)

The Child Trauma Research Project (CTRP)

The Child Trauma Research Project has conducted research and provided clinical service to children under the age of six who have been exposed to domestic violence or other interpersonal traumas since 1996. Children are referred by family court, child welfare, advocacy programs for battered women, pediatricians, day-care providers and preschool teachers. Children are seen with their primary caregiver (most typically, their mothers). Both mothers and children are offered intensive assessments before treatment begins. Mothers and children are seen together in child-parent psychotherapy. Our treatment model focuses on restoring children to a positive developmental trajectory by intervening to improve their relationships with caregivers. Perhaps because of this focus, we were asked from the very earliest days of the project to find ways to include fathers in the treatment. The agencies from which we received referrals, and often the mothers of the children we treated, recognized that violent fathers continue to be involved in their children's lives. They hoped that we would be able to intervene to improve the quality of these father-child relationships, which had often been frightening and dangerous. We were willing to consider ways in which to intervene with fathers, but we were mindful that safety for both mother and child had to be the first consideration and that no treatment that compromised protective or stay-away orders could be effective in promoting safety or healing for anyone involved.

Goals of Therapeutic Interventions
With Children Exposed to Violence

For the past three years, both programs, along with two other sites, have established a formal collaboration, focusing on young children and trauma. This collaborative, the Early Trauma Treatment Network, receives funding through the National Child Traumatic Stress Network and has allowed each site to use the child-parent psychotherapy model of intervention, which has been shown to be efficacious for preschool children who witnessed violence between their parents (Lieberman, Van Horn, & Ghosh Ippen, 2005) and for young children who experienced a variety of interpersonal traumas.[2] Although most of our work is with mothers and children, each site provides services to some father-child dyads.

In both programs, the broad goal of therapy with the child is to offer a relationship that provides a safe opportunity to talk about what has happened, to release strong feelings, to recover a sense of stability and mastery, and to ameliorate the symptoms of trauma. Intervention first addresses issues of safety and stability. It also includes helping the parent understand the meaning of the trauma from the perspective of the child, helping the parent understand how emotional and behavioral problems that interfere with the child's functioning are related to the trauma, helping the parent find ways to respond to and manage the child's problems, facilitating the ability of parent and child to talk about what has happened, and assisting the parent in accessing other services, such as legal assistance, medical care, housing, and entitlements.[3] The CWVP has adopted an open-ended treatment model. The number of sessions in which a child and parent may be seen ranges from a few to two or more years of involvement with the program. At the CTRP, clinical services are offered as part of a research trial to test the effectiveness of child-parent psychotherapy, and families are offered one year of treatment, which most commonly takes place in the home.

Hearing the Voices of Mothers and Children

Our clinical work and several qualitative studies give voice to battered women's ideas and wishes about their children's relationships with their fathers. In a study involving focus groups with mothers of color who had survived domestic violence, the majority of participants wanted fathers to be involved in their children's lives, and not only as financial supporters (Atchison, Autry, Davis, & Mitchell-Clark, 2002; Tubbs & Williams, 2007). It did not matter whether the mother wanted to continue to have an intimate relationship with the coparent or not. Her wish was that her children would have relationships with their father. In another study, DeVoe and Smith (2002) reported on focus groups conducted with 43 battered women who had separated from their partners. These women also expressed regret that their children were separated from their fathers, and many of them reported feeling guilty about the decision to separate because it meant that their children would not have these male figures in their lives.

These qualitative findings are supported by anecdotal evidence from our own projects. Women who come to the CTRP with their children frequently report that they want their children to have contact with their fathers. Some recall their experiences of growing up without a father and articulate a strong wish for their children to have a father. These women tell us that they were tortured with indecision about leaving their violent partners because to leave meant depriving their children of their fathers. One mother said,

> I couldn't leave, because I wanted my kids to have a dad. Finally, I had to leave to protect my kids. I couldn't leave and had to leave because of my kids. It's like being torn in two.

We believe that it is essential to listen to the voices of these mothers, whom we consider gatekeepers in their children's process of healing. Practitioners must take mothers' commitment to having children know their fathers into account in thinking about how to involve violent men in the healing of their children.

Many children who have witnessed domestic violence also seem to have a strong, if ambivalent, desire to have a significant relationship with the offending fathers. Some of the children we see have no relationship with their fathers. They do not know their fathers, or their relationships are so distant and sporadic that it is difficult to determine any meaningful connection. While these children may fantasize about an ideal father, their concrete ties to the abuser are minimal. Other children see their fathers very frequently. The CWVP conducted a snapshot survey of its 38 active cases during a one-week period in November 2002. Fifty-two percent of the children included in the survey had no contact with their fathers, and 48% had some contact with their fathers. Of those who had contact, 87.5% of the children had "regular" contact (more than once a month). At the CTRP, we collect systematic data on the amount of contact that the children we treat have with their fathers. The data from 170 children who were referred to the CTRP for assessment and treatment show that 62% had at least weekly contact with their fathers, 2% lived with their fathers, and only 15% had no contact with their fathers.

Our clinical experience with children in our programs leads us to believe that, regardless of the amount of physical contact they have with their fathers, many are emotionally attached to their fathers, sometimes without apparent regard for the quality or quantity of violence to which the child may have been exposed. The attachment is ambivalent and troubling for the child, and the departure of the father does not resolve the child's ambivalence. In fact, the disruption in attachment that comes with the father's departure may lead to periods of intense grief, anger, and guilt in the child (Stover, Van Horn, Turner, Cooper, & Lieberman, 2003).

The children's intense emotional reactions may be difficult for a mother to tolerate if she is also struggling with her own feelings of ambivalence and guilt about having left the relationship and disrupted the bonds between father and children. The following three case examples illustrate the complexities of children's reactions to their abusive fathers.

Benjamin, a nine-year-old boy, was referred for treatment after he witnessed his father attempt to stab his mother. This event had happened about four months prior to the referral, and he had not had contact with his father since the incident. Benjamin was quite willing to talk with the therapist about what had happened. He told the story in some detail, elaborating on how he had felt so terrified that he could not do anything to help his mother. He commented that he had heard his parents argue "every night" and that he was always scared that something would happen to one of them. He expressed great relief to have his father out of the house but then stated that he would miss him at the annual school breakfast for fathers. The therapist wondered if Benjamin might want to see his father at some point. Benjamin thought for a long time and replied, "Yes, if I could be sure that I was big and strong enough to be able to get away from him if I had to."

Elena, age eight, witnessed the arrest of her father after an assault in which he attempted to strangle her mother. As he resisted the arrest, he picked up a kitchen knife and brandished it toward the officers who responded. They called for backup help, and eventually, there were six officers at the scene to effect the arrest. Elena was the terrified bystander to this mayhem. When asked by her therapist if she wanted to talk about what had happened, she decided to draw a picture. She drew a picture of four police officers with their guns drawn, pointing toward her father. He was seated in a chair, a small figure with tears coming down his cheeks. She told her therapist that she was scared the policemen would kill her father.

Betina, age four, had twice witnessed her father choking her mother. After the last incident, Betina's mother called the police and obtained a restraining order. Betina had not seen her father for three months. In one session with her therapist, she sat rocking a baby doll. She said, "Baby, you miss your daddy." Betina looked off into space and said, "Daddy, you called me your princess. Why did you leave and go to the moon?" Later in the same session, Betina drew a picture of a figure behind bars. She said that her daddy was in jail. She told the therapist to put a big lock on the door so that her daddy couldn't get out and hurt her mommy.

These case examples illustrate the complexities of children's appraisals of violence and conflict within the home and of their emotional reactions to their parents' experiences. Each child expresses confusion and ambivalent feelings about the fathers. The children's ability to process the traumatic events that they witnessed, and the impact those events will have on their personalities, varies with their developmental stage (Pynoos, Steinberg, & Piacentini, 1999). Betina, only four, misses her father; and after three months without contact, she seems unable to picture him inhabiting the same world in which she lives. Her idealized yearning for him is not integrated with her view of him as dangerous and needing to be locked behind bars. Benjamin, at age nine, struggles with guilt over the fact that he could not protect his mother. He also expresses the fantasy that things will turn out differently when he sees his father again because he will be "big and strong." Elena, at age eight, can only think about the terror of her father's arrest. Her terror, however, seems to be on her father's behalf, as she draws him small and weeping, surrounded by armed policemen who are larger than life.

The brief examples cited above can give us only a glimpse into children's complex feelings about their fathers. In our experience, a child's reactions are shaped by the quality of the relationship with the father and the specific characteristics of the violence, including the child's belief about the purpose of the violence. The mother's beliefs, experiences, and emotional feelings about the father and the length of separation from the father also affect the child's thoughts and feelings about the violent father.

Because children's feelings are so multifaceted and often conflicting with their mother's feelings, we believe that it is essential for the therapeutic relationship to allow for children's open and complete explorations of their relationships with their father. In child-parent psychotherapy, because the mother is present, this exploration will include an examination of the different feelings that mothers and children may have about the father. It is sometimes difficult for the therapist to maintain neutrality and to tolerate a child's longing for a father, especially if the abuse has been significant, resulting in injury or death. However, for most of these children, the therapeutic space is the only place that will permit the expression of this sadness or ambivalence. In addition, it is our experience that children's feelings, no matter how poignant, are sometimes marked by distortions that can be worked through in the therapeutic space. Elena's case is a clear example. Her view of her father as an endangered victim completely omits the brutality of his attack on her mother.

We believe that it is important to ask whether fathers who are motivated to make amends to their children might be involved in children's treatment to correct some of these distortions and help the child see clearly where the responsibility for the violence and disruption in the family lies. A father's readiness to be involved in this clinical process must be carefully assessed, lest his presence do more harm than good.

Men Who Batter as Parents

Both clinical and empirical reports have begun to emerge about the parenting behavior of violent men. Bancroft and Silverman (2002) have stated that batterers have a consistent group of characteristics that describe them as parents, including the assertion of power and control through authoritarian behavior, neglecting or being underinvolved with their children, undermining their children's mothers, and being self-centered and manipulative. Men who are aggressive against their partners have been observed to be more authoritarian in their interactions with their children than nonaggressive men; they also display more negative affect toward their children, particularly toward their sons (Margolin, John, Ghosh, & Gordis, 1997). Margolin and John (1999) reported that in observed interactions, abusive fathers use more power assertion and display less warmth, nurturance, and support than do nonabusive fathers. Gonzalez and colleagues (2000) found that children's perceptions of conflict and aggression between their parents were linked to the children's statements that their parents were not accepting of them and to the children's perceptions of inconsistent discipline and hostile control by their parents. Most important, in all of these studies, the researchers have found a link between negative parenting practices and negative outcomes for children.

The literature also illustrates that the impact of father violence on children does not stop when parents separate. Violent fathers may use the court system to continue their patterns of control over their former partners. There is empirical evidence that violent fathers seek custody of their children more often than do fathers against whom there is no allegation of domestic violence (Liss & Stahley, 1993) and that they may harass their former partners by refusing to pick up or return children at the agreed-upon time and place or by demanding frequent court appearances to alter visitation arrangements (Walker & Edwall, 1987). They may also use exchanges of the children as occasions for further verbal or physical assaults against the children's mother (Shepard, 1992).

In spite of these negative findings, there is also support for the proposition that children may benefit from safe contact with their fathers, even if the fathers have been violent. Stover and colleagues (Stover, et al., 2003) found that in the CTRP's preschool-age sample of children exposed to domestic violence, children who had rare or no contact with their fathers also had, by their mothers' reports, more symptoms of depression and anxiety than did children who saw their fathers regularly, even controlling for frequency and severity of father violence. There is also research demonstrating the positive effects that fathers may have on their children (Lamb, 1997; Pleck & Pleck, 1997; Sanders, 1996; Daly, 1993). Many researchers agree that constructive father involvement is very important for and beneficial to children. The majority of these studies, however, have concentrated on fathers who have not been abusive.

It also appears that children may motivate some men to change. Litton Fox, Sayers, and Bruce (2001) observed a batterers' intervention program and conducted interviews with eight participants who were fathers. They discovered that many of the men used their relationships with their children and their father role as "a source of re-entry into the moral community" (p. 137).

This qualitative finding that violent men may use the father role as a way to reconnect with their values is consistent with the findings of recent quantitative surveys conducted among batterers. In one study, Mandel (2003) investigated batterers' perception of their children's exposure to violence and abuse. Based on self-reports from a nonrandom survey of 546 fathers enrolled in batterers' intervention programs, Mandel found that most men expressed awareness of the destructive effects of their physical and verbal abuse on their children. Three quarters of participants worried about the longterm impact of their behavior on their children. In another survey, conducted by San Francisco Safe Start,[4] 177 fathers attending certified batterers' intervention programs responded to a questionnaire about their contact and relationships with their children. Thirty-four percent of the fathers were currently living with their children; and, of those men not living with their children, 59% had at least weekly contact with their children. Ninety-five percent of the fathers said that they wanted to improve their relationships with their children, and 94% said that they wanted more contact with their children.

The fathers surveyed in the batterers' intervention groups express concern for their children and want continued contact with them. Our experience, as we stated earlier, is that many mothers also want continued father involvement and that the young children we treat have strong attachments to their fathers and yearn for them if they are absent from the children's lives. These wishes are not enough, however, to assure children's safety. This was certainly true of the mothers and fathers interviewed by Tubbs and Williams (2007) and described earlier in this book.

Peled (2000) argues that men who batter need direct parenting intervention if they are to assume a positive role in their children's healing. She cited a qualitative evaluation of the children's program of the Domestic Abuse Project in Minneapolis, Minnesota (Peled & Edleson, 1999), which found that children who participated in the program were placed in a potentially hurtful bind. If their fathers knew of their participation and disapproved, the children were required to side with one parent against the other: aligning with their mothers against their fathers if they participated in the program or siding with their fathers against their mothers if they did not. On the one hand, if the fathers were not told about the program, however, and the children had contact with them, then the children were required to keep their participation secret, increasing the tension in the father-child relationship. On the other hand, if fathers knew and approved of their children's participation, then the children were free to participate more fully in the groups. This finding suggests that fathers' participation may play a positive role in supporting the healing of children. Because the involvement of abusive men in children's work can pose a danger to children and their mothers, Peled recommends that their involvement be encouraged only if the father has demonstrated his rehabilitation and if his involvement does not put children and mothers at risk. How rehabilitation and safety can be assured is complex and must be the subject of careful assessment.

It is clear from the literature that there are risks if violent men are involved in their children's healing. The potential benefits, however, taken together with our knowledge that many violent men continue to have contact with their children after separation, make us hesitant to take a rigid stance against incorporating fathers in the work. Our willingness to consider involving fathers is reinforced by what women and children tell us about their wishes for children's relationships with their fathers. The scant empirical findings cited here indicate that these fathers need support and intervention in order to form positive and safe relationships with their children.

Key Questions When Deciding on Fathers' Involvement in Child Treatment

Over the past several years, both the CWVP and the CTRP have engaged in discussions regarding cases in which fathers might be involved. In some cases, we have hesitated; in others, we have offered to include fathers, with varying results. Based on our experience with these cases, we believe that the question of whether a father who has been violent should be involved in his children's treatment must be answered on a case-by-case basis and only after careful assessment. The assessment must be continuing as treatment proceeds. The clinician is responsible for making ongoing judgments about whether father involvement is beneficial to the child and safe for all family members. Based on the literature and on our clinical experience, we propose the following guidelines for considering whether and how a particular father should be involved in the clinical treatment of his children. These guidelines are not linear and should not be thought of as a decision tree but instead consist of a set of questions that should be considered by the clinician.

The starting point for our assessment is our belief that if the mother is the physical custodian of the child, her comfort with and support of the father's involvement is a nonnegotiable prerequisite for involving the father in treatment. In some cases, mothers request that fathers be involved. In other instances, the father may request involvement, or the child may initiate the request. Women are generally good judges of the dangerousness of their partners (Weisz, Tolman, & Saunders, 2000), and their concerns in this regard must be carefully considered. Beyond this basic issue of safety, we believe that to involve fathers without the full support of the mother would undermine the child's relationship with the mother and put the child in the awkward bind of being forced to choose between father and mother. If we believe that it is important from the perspective of the child's treatment to involve a father, we would discuss our reasons with the mother, explain our perspective to her, and listen carefully to her doubts and concerns. In the end, however, the mother's sense of comfort and support for father involvement remains essential. In addition to establishing the mother's support for including the child's father in the treatment, we will ask the following questions. Schematically, these questions are shown as primary domains to be assessed in the following diagram. Each of these key questions is discussed in greater detail below.

Is the Violent Parent in Compliance With Court Orders?

This is the most basic level of inquiry. We believe that fathers who are not in compliance with orders, including restraining orders, visitation orders, and terms of probation, are demonstrating a lack of awareness of the impact of their behavior on others and a lack of a genuine commitment to change. The risks of involving such uncommitted men in their children's healing are profound. As clinicians, we would anticipate that men who are not willing to demonstrate this minimal level of compliance would be likely to deny their violent behavior.

From our point of view, a father who is not in compliance with court orders is not emotionally ready to participate in his child's healing and may, in fact, jeopardize it. It is not always, however, a simple matter to exclude

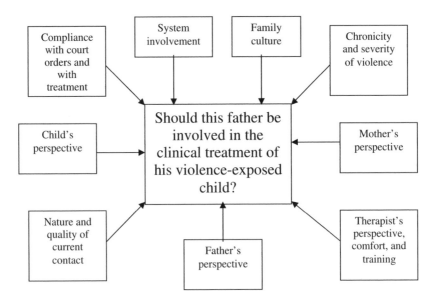

Figure 4.1. Decision-making paradigm for involving fathers in their child's clinical treatment

the father, even if the clinician's assessment reveals that he is not in compliance with orders. Especially if the mother is wishing to salvage the relationship, or if she is fearful, she may side with the father and resist treatment or even leave with the child if the father cannot be included. To minimize this risk, it is essential that the clinician explain the risks of father involvement clearly and involve the mother in assessing and evaluating the father's readiness. The following case example demonstrates this point.

> Jaime is a three-year-old boy who has seen his father, Milton, abuse his mother, Flora, since he was born. When Jaime started coming to the program, his father was incarcerated because of multiple charges, including domestic assault and battery and kidnapping. He lost custody of Jaime.
>
> Three months after Jaime began treatment, Milton finished his six-month jail sentence. As part of his parole, he was mandated to attend a fathering group and was granted unsupervised visitation three times per week. He was not allowed to move back in with Flora.
>
> In the last session before Milton was paroled, Flora told the clinician that she wanted the father to be involved in Jaime's treatment. The therapist told her that she needed to think about it and consult with the clinical team. Thereafter, every time that the clinician attempted to reach Flora, it was Milton who answered the cell phone. When asked about Flora, he always said that she was working and asked to take a message for her.

In this case, the therapist assumed that Milton was back in Flora's life, possibly living in her home, and that Flora felt uncomfortable or scared about coming back and telling the truth. Milton seemed to have regained control and was limiting the therapist's access to Flora. He was apparently out of compliance with the court order that he not live with Flora. The clinician in this case tried unsuccessfully to contact Flora by other means, including leaving messages at her last known work number and with her mother. She could not convey any information to Milton because he had no legal custody of Jaime, and he might not even have known that Jaime was in treatment at CWVP. Giving Milton this information could have been illegal and could have initiated more violence against Flora. In the end, the clinician was unable to reestablish contact with Flora and decided instead to leave a message with her mother so that she could call the clinician any time she desired.

Although the mother requested the father's involvement, the clinician was concerned that it might not be safe, and she was unsure of the legality of the father's involvement. However, her hesitancy to agree may have been interpreted by the mother as criticism or disrespect. In addition, the clinician felt uncomfortable with the prospect of working with a man with his history of violence. The therapist's worries about Milton interfered with her ability to work collaboratively with Flora in assessing the wisdom of bringing Milton into the treatment. She avoided the conversation with Flora and turned instead to the clinical team. If we had been able to continue to see

Jaime and his mother, we would have repaired this breach by meeting with the mother alone to find out more about her wishes to involve the father, to assess if she was being coerced, and to assess his compliance with the court's orders.

Is the Father Attending and Working in the Treatment Programs That Have Been Mandated for Him?

Even when fathers are in compliance with court orders, if they are attending treatment programs without really being engaged, we believe that they still have not taken responsibility for their violent behavior. Until they do, their participation in their children's counseling may put the children at increased risk. These fathers may be more likely to pressure their children to blame their mothers for the family conflict, or they may deny the child's reality. In either event, the child's thoughts and feelings about the father are likely to become even more distorted.

What Is the Level of Violence in the Family?

A cluster of questions must be addressed to assess the severity, frequency, and chronicity of violence in the household. These questions will inform the clinician about how well established the violent pattern is and about whether the father appears to use violence to get what he wants in all of his relationships. How chronic was the violence? How recent? How severe was it? Were there physical injuries? Were children hurt, either intentionally or when they intervened? Were weapons involved? Is the father violent in other relationships outside the family?

Where violence is severe and repeated, where weapons are involved, and where there is a pattern of violence in multiple relationships, the risk that violence may turn lethal under stress increases (Campbell, 2001). In cases where violence has been severe, long lasting, and generalized to a number of relationships, we believe that the risk to the mother's and child's safety may be too great if the father is included in their sessions or in the child's sessions. If the father were having continued contact with the child, we would consider offering him collateral sessions to discuss his relationship with his child, his concerns for his child, his style of discipline, his ways of managing anger when the child arouses anger in him, and his understanding of the impact of his violence on his child's development. We would generally offer these sessions in a different place from the place where we meet with the mother and child in order to minimize the risk of stalking.

If, on the other hand, there were few violent incidents, if they were less severe, and if the father is attending and working with the services that have been mandated for him, he may be able to take part in the child's sessions without undue risk, and he may bring real benefit to the child's healing, as the following case illustrates.

José called to refer his family for services. He said that he had slapped his wife in front of their children, and he wanted to help his children understand that he was wrong to do that. He said he had apologized, but they were still afraid of him. He was worried that his four-year-old son, Ruben, would not talk to him.

With José's permission, the clinician contacted his wife. She said that José had only slapped her one time. She believed that he was really sorry and wanted to change. She said that he had not missed any sessions of his batterers' intervention program. She told the clinician that she intended to stay with José and said that she wanted to help him with the children.

The whole family was involved in the treatment. José answered his children's questions about his behavior, assured them that he had been wrong, apologized for hurting their mother and scaring them, and promised that he would not hit anyone again. In his individual therapy outside the CTRP, José worked on the issues of depression that he believed had led to his violence. In a follow-up session after the treatment ended, José's wife confirmed that there had been no further violence and that things were much better in their family.

This case is an example of how father involvement is potentially healing for children. José's children benefited greatly from hearing him say that he had been wrong to hit their mother and that he would not do it again. Even more than his words, his actions in seeking out help for the family demonstrated to both his wife and his children a genuine desire to make amends. Excluding him from the process of the children's healing would have deprived the children of this benefit.

What Is the Cultural Context Within Which the Family Exists?

In making decisions about the involvement of a father, it is essential that the clinician take into consideration the family's cultural background and beliefs. What is the meaning of marital violence in the family's culture? What does it mean to the family that the courts or other public institutions have stepped in to make decisions that affect the family? If the father is an undocumented resident, he may be reluctant to have any involvement with the system. His reluctance or fear can be misinterpreted as a lack of interest or cooperation. What are the culture's beliefs about male and female adult roles in the family? In some cultures, it is difficult for a woman to challenge her husband's decisions. When a father states that he wishes to see his child, it may be very difficult for the mother to refuse. What does the culture believe about child rearing? In some cultures, the mother is largely responsible for child rearing. How much room is there for emotional expression in the culture? When children's aims or wishes conflict with adult priorities, what takes precedence?

What Do the Family Members Think About Father Involvement, and What Do They Want?

It is important to assess the views of both mother and father. While we would not directly ask the opinions of the very young children with whom we work, we would explore the child's fantasies or fears about having the father involved. Does the child fantasize that a father's presence might lead to reunification of the family? Is the child afraid to see the father? We would also want to know whether one parent or both parents wish to use the treatment as a way to repair the parental relationship. We would want to know whether the mother fears the father. We would want to know about the quality of the father-child relationship and how involved the father was in care for the child.

Cases where both parents are violent or in a high-conflict relationship present a challenge for the therapist, who must form a firm therapeutic alliance with each parent. Without that, neither parent will likely change. At the same time, the clinician must avoid being drawn into either parent's agenda, instead siding with the child and what the child needs. This work is challenging and difficult, and we believe that is essential that the therapist have close supervision or consultation. These difficulties are illustrated by the case of Susan and her parents.

> Susan, age five, was referred for treatment by the family court when her mother, Claire, had been granted a restraining order against Susan's father, Ruben. Susan had witnessed one incident in which Ruben pushed Claire down the stairs, another in which he choked her, and numerous incidents in which he slapped and insulted her. He had never hit Susan, but Susan said that she was afraid that her father would hurt her. After Claire and Ruben separated, he continued to telephone her home and leave long, obscene, threatening messages on her answering machine. He also followed her to work twice. Claire reported these incidents to the police as violations of her restraining order, but Ruben was not arrested.
>
> Susan initially came to treatment with her mother only. Shortly after treatment began, Ruben was granted joint legal custody of Susan and unsupervised overnight visits with her three nights a week. Almost immediately, Ruben contacted the therapist and left a message demanding a report on the progress of Susan's treatment and his inclusion in the treatment. The therapist discussed Ruben's telephone message with Claire, who encouraged the therapist to see Ruben and Susan together. Claire said that since Susan began her overnights, she was more defiant and insulting, and Claire hoped that the therapist could intervene in what Claire believed was Ruben's encouragement that Susan undermine her. For her part, Susan seemed genuinely delighted to spend time with her father. She denied that she had said that she was afraid of him and talked with enthusiasm about how much fun she had at her father's apartment.

The therapist was quite willing to meet with Ruben (as indeed she was required to do, given his status as Susan's joint legal custodian) but was hesitant to hold joint father-child sessions because of the level of violence and because of Ruben's open defiance of court orders. She met twice with Ruben alone and then, because of the major role he played in Susan's life, agreed to offer three joint father-child sessions to explore whether they would be helpful. In view of Ruben's stalking, all sessions with him were held at a different site from the office where Claire and Susan came for their treatment. The joint father-child sessions were discouraging. Ruben was seductive in his behavior toward Susan, although he did nothing that rose to the level of reportable sexual abuse. He told her that she was his little princess and that she was much smarter and more special than her mother had ever been to him. He was obsequiously charming toward the therapist and tried to recruit her to his agenda of obtaining full custody of Susan. He claimed that Claire was "hysterical and overwrought" and that he was better able to provide a stable home for Susan.

The therapist firmly confronted Ruben's seductive treatment of Susan, his demeaning comments in front of Susan about her mother, and his attempts to persuade the therapist to take his side in the custody dispute. After the second father-child session, Ruben contacted the therapist and said that his schedule with Susan had changed and that the two of them would no longer have time to meet with the therapist. He was willing, however, to continue to meet for individual collateral sessions.

In this case, we tried and failed to establish a relationship with Ruben that would let us work with him on his relationship with Susan. He contended that there were no problems in that relationship. He was, however, willing to continue to meet with the therapist individually and, in those meetings, spoke at length about Claire's inadequacies. The therapist continued to work with Claire and Susan together and used the vehicle of that relationship to help Susan, who initially saw her father as "Prince Charming" and her mother as someone to be bullied, move to a more balanced view of her parents. She continued to enjoy time with her father but became able to resist his pressure to demean Claire.

What Is the Involvement of Other Systems?

Families experiencing domestic violence are often involved in a myriad of systems, including civil and criminal courts, domestic-violence advocacy, substance-abuse treatment, and batterers' interventions. If the father becomes involved in his children's treatment and healing, many of these systems may want the child clinician to report to them on his progress. This requires extra time from the clinician, and it can be viewed as a potential breach of confidentiality. In addition, the father may be trying to use clinician reports to gain greater access to the mother through less-supervised visits with their children. Clinicians are often uncomfortable with reporting to such systems, viewing the report as giving sensitive information to a coercive system. Some clinicians are also hesitant to get involved in cases where they may be required to testify in court.

We have found that reporting and communication among the systems serving the family do not have to be unduly burdensome. Most often, these systems are interested not in the content of the sessions but in the clinician's impression of whether the father is making use of the service and making genuine progress toward his goals. If he is, then he will generally welcome the clinician's report. If he is not, then it may be that he is not ready to take part in his child's healing process.

The involvement of other systems has a potential benefit for the clinician as well. Safety concerns are paramount in these families. Open communication among providers can offer a good indication of how well the father is doing generally and can help in the continuing assessment of whether the family's safety is compromised by his involvement in the children's care.

What Is the Clinician's Perspective on the Father's Behavior?

This is an essential area of assessment. Clinicians who include fathers in children's treatment must be trained and able to work with perpetrators of violence. They must understand the men's dynamics and be comfortable confronting them when necessary. They must be able to empathize with the distress and pain of people who have expressed themselves in violent ways. Clinicians must be able to assess the man's attempts to manipulate them and control the information that they are providing others. They must also be able to tolerate the strong feelings that working with violent adults, adult victims, and vulnerable young children will arouse. Clinicians will need support from their agencies and supervision and consultation from their colleagues to handle the burdens of this work.

Conclusion

Each case must be considered on its own merits. It is difficult to generalize a protocol or set a procedure for making decisions about involving fathers. We continue to believe that the willingness of the mother to have the father involved is an essential prerequisite if the mother is the custodian of the child. We also believe that it must be made clear to all involved that the father's participation in his child's treatment is in no way a substitute for other intervention that he may need if he is to stop his violence. Involvement in children's mental-health services should never, for example, take the place of participation in a batterers' intervention program. Yet we cannot be paralyzed by fear or lack of experience. Fathers are in children's lives, both symbolically and in reality. The therapeutic relationship must allow for an open exploration of this aspect of the children's experience.

We are not sure how many of the experiences of the two programs described in this chapter can be generalized to other settings. Both programs see a limited sample of children and families affected by domestic violence. It is likely that our populations have experienced more extreme trauma and are more acutely symptomatic. We know that children show a range of responses to domestic violence and that not all children are equally affected. Our services are also limited to young children, and thus we have less experience with the developmental needs of older children and adolescents.

It is also possible that a child mental-health center might not be the right setting in which to engage fathers in treatment. Perhaps these programs should concentrate on the healing of the child and mother and leave the rest of the process to other settings, such as batterers' intervention programs, after-care programs for abusive men, supervised visitation centers, and adult mental-health centers. We believe, however, that child mental-health programs are uniquely sensitized to the developmental and emotional needs of children. And if intervention in the father-child relationship is the goal, there is no substitute for a setting in which the two can be together in the company of a trained clinician who can facilitate the best possible experience for them both. For these reasons, we believe that children's mental-health programs should be at the forefront in thinking about how to safely engage men who batter in their children's treatment.

We suggest several areas for future exploration. Further research should be carried out to test the criteria for appropriate involvement of fathers in their children's treatment. This includes careful data collection about fathers of children who are exposed to violence and about the nature of their relationships with their children. In addition, we need further research on the definition of "father" as it pertains to children. What are the differences for children between their biological fathers and other men who play a fathering role?

To move forward with the efforts to identify and create strategies for effectively engaging fathers in their children's treatment, we must develop policies and procedures that address institutional barriers to engaging and involving fathers in their children's treatment. We have become aware of institutional barriers to fathers' involvement, even when their presence is clinically advisable. Programs geared toward children may not be welcoming to fathers (Peled & Edleson, 1999). There are both obvious and subtle ways by which programs indicate that they are not particularly father-friendly. In many agencies, the intake and assessment forms are designed for interviewing mothers and are not easily adapted to use with fathers. Some assessment forms do not collect adequate information about fathers, an indication that he is somehow less important. Waiting rooms may not have information or reading material that would be interesting to fathers. A more significant obstacle to fathers' involvement might be the program staff's inexperience and lack of comfort in dealing with men who batter, as well as an organizational infrastructure that has minimized its focus on fathers. If a clinical program that focuses on children is to include fathers in a meaningful way, it must carefully self-assess for these barriers and address them. These institutional barriers communicate subtly (or not so subtly) that fathers are less acceptable and less important than mothers. If violent fathers, many of whom are exquisitely attuned to signals of rejection and abandonment (Dutton & Holtzworth-Munroe, 1997), sense that the program denigrates their importance, they may be unwilling to participate themselves and may even undermine or forbid their children's participation in the program (Peled & Edleson, 1999).

Finally, it will be important to establish closer connections between mental-health services for children exposed to domestic violence, batterers' intervention programs, and supervised visitation programs. In addition to ensuring safety for all family members, increased communication among these care providers can further the goals for treatment for each person.

Acknowledgment

The authors gratefully acknowledge the contributions of Juan Carlos Areán. The Family Violence Prevention Fund supported the development of an earlier version of this chapter, which was coauthored by Mr. Areán.

Notes

1. For more information about the Child Witness to Violence Project, go to the project website at http://www.childwitnesstoviolence.org

2. The Early Trauma Treatment Network is a consortium of four agencies funded through the National Child Traumatic Stress Network (NCTSN) to develop interventions for traumatized children ages five and under and to meet the training needs of caregivers in early childhood settings who work with children affected by trauma. The broader mission of the NCTSN, funded by the Substance Abuse and Mental Health Services Administration (SAMHSA), is to raise the standard of care and to improve access to services for traumatized children and their families. For more information, see their website, www.nctsnet.org

3. For a more in-depth discussion of the impact of domestic violence on children and treatment issues, see Groves (2000).

4. The authors acknowledge the work of the San Francisco Safe Start Initiative and its local evaluator, ETR Associates, in collecting and analyzing these data.

References

Atchison, G., Autry, A., Davis, L., & Mitchell-Clark, K. (2002). *Conversations with women of color who have experienced domestic violence regarding working with men to end violence.* San Francisco, CA: Family Violence Prevention Fund.

Bancroft, L., & Silverman, J. (2002). *The batterer as parent.* Thousand Oaks, CA: Sage.

Bent-Goodley, T & Williams, O. J. (2007). Fathers' voices on parenting and violence. In J. L. Edleson & O. J. Williams, *Parenting by men who batter: New directions for assessment and intervention* (pp. 32–35). New York: Oxford University Press.

Campbell, J. C. (2001). Safety planning based on lethality assessment for partners of batterers in intervention programs. *Journal of Aggression, Maltreatment & Trauma, 5,* 129–143.

Daly, K. J. (1993). Reshaping fatherhood. In W. Marsiglio (Ed.), *Fatherhood: Contemporary theory, research, and social policy* (pp. 21–40). Thousand Oaks, CA: Sage.

DeVoe, E & Smith, E. (2002). The impact of domestic violence on urban preschool children: Battered mothers' perspectives. *Journal of Interpersonal Violence,* 17(10), pp. 1075–1101.

Dutton, D. G., & Holtzworth-Munroe, A. (1997). The role of early trauma in males who assault their wives. In D. Cicchetti & S. L. Toth (Eds.), *Rochester Symposium on Developmental Psychopathology: Vol. 8. Developmental perspectives on trauma: Theory, research, and intervention* (pp. 379–402). Rochester, NY: University of Rochester Press.

Edleson, J. L. (1999). Children's witnessing of adult domestic violence. *Journal of Interpersonal Violence, 14*(8), 839–870.

Gonzalez, N.A., Pitts, S. C., Hill, N. E., & Roosa, M. W. (2000). A mediational model of the impact of interparental conflict on child adjustment in a multiethnic, low-income sample. *Journal of Family Psychology, 14,* 365–379.

Groves, B. M. (2002). *Children who see too much.* Boston: Beacon Press.

Lamb, M. E. (2004). Fathers and child development: An introductory overview and guide. In M.E. Lamb (Ed.), *The role of the father in child development* (pp. 19–31). New York: John Wiley and Sons.

Lieberman, A. F., Van Horn, P., & Ghosh-Ippen, C. (2005). Toward evidence-based treatment: Child-parent psychotherapy with preschoolers exposed to marital violence. *Journal of the American Academy of Child and Adolescent Psychiatry, 44,* 1241–1248.

Liss, M. B. & Stahly, G. B. (1993). Domestic violence and child custody. In M. Hansen & M Harway (Eds). *Battering and family therapy* (pp. 175–184). Newbury Park, CA: Sage Publications, Inc.

Litton Fox, G., Sayers, J., & Bruce, C. (2001). Beyond bravado: Redemption and rehabilitation in the fathering accounts of men who batter. *Marriage & Family Review, 32*(3–4), 137–163.

Mandel, D. (2003). Highlights from the national study on batterers' perceptions of their children's exposure to the violence and abuse. *Issues in Family Violence,* 5(1), 26–37.

Margolin, G. & John, R. S. (1999). Children's exposure to marital aggression: Direct and mediated effects. In G. K. Kantor & J. L. Jasinski (Eds.), *Out of the darkness: Perspectives on family violence.* (pp. 57–78). Thousand Oaks, CA: Sage Publications, Inc.

Margolin, G., John, R. S., Gosh, C., & Gordis, E. (1997). Family interaction process: An essential tool for exploring abusive relations. In D. D. Cahn & S. A. Lloyd (Eds.), *Family abuse: A communication perspective* (pp. 37–58). Thousand Oaks, CA: Sage.

Peled, E. (2000). Parenting by men who abuse women: Issues and dilemmas. *British Journal of Social Work, 30*(1), 25–36.

Peled, E., & Edleson, J. (1999). Barriers to children's domestic violence counseling: A qualitative study. *Families in Society, 80,* 578–586.

Pleck, E. H., & Pleck, J. H. (1997). Fatherhood ideals in the United States: Historical dimensions. In M.E. Lamb (Ed.), *The role of the father in child development* (pp. 33–48). New York: John Wiley and Sons.

Pynoos, R. S., Steinberg, A. M., & Piacentini, J. C. (1999). A developmental psychopathology model of childhood traumatic stress and intersection with anxiety disorders. *Biological Psychiatry, 46,* 1542–1554.

Sanders, H. A. (1996). *Daddy, we need you now! A primer on African American male socialization.* Lanham, MD: University Press of America.

Shepard, M. (1992). Child-visiting and domestic abuse. *Child Welfare, LXXI,* 357–367.

Stover, C. S., Van Horn, P., Turner, R., Cooper, B., & Lieberman, A. F. (2003). The effects of father visitation on preschool-aged witnesses of domestic violence. *Journal of Interpersonal Violence, 18,* 1149–1166.

Tubbs, C. Y. & Williams, O. J. (2007). Shared parenting after abuse: Battered mothers' perspectives on parenting after dissolution of a relationship. In J. L. Edleson & O. J. Williams, *Parenting by men who batter: New directions for assessment and intervention* (pp. 19–44). New York: Oxford University Press.

Walker, L. E. A., & Edwall, G. E. (1987). Domestic violence and determination of visitation and custody in divorce. In D. J. Sonkin (Ed.) *Domestic violence on trial: Psychological and legal dimensions of family violence* (pp. 127–152). New York, Springer.

Weisz, A., Tolman, R., & Saunders, D. G. (2000). Assessing the risk of severe domestic violence: The importance of survivors' predictions. *Journal of Interpersonal Violence, 15,* 75–90.

5

A Conceptual Framework for Fathering Intervention With Men Who Batter

Einat Peled
Guy Perel

As a therapist you need to be aware of what you feel. . . . [S]ometimes I feel angry at them, or repulsion, or stuff like this. What now, you and fathering? Where were you, go to hell or to jail or I don't know what they should do to you, burn you in hell.

Before I started the [fathering] group and got to know them, I said that parents are tools for saving these children. Unequivocally, that's what I thought. I want the father to understand what the child is going through when he (the father) beats up the mother. That he will experience this shit, this abomination. . . . I was all mad about this, I want them to understand, to see, to take responsibility. That something will be moved inside them. That's how I came to this. Later, when I started to see the children, . . . I started to regard them as the direct goal.

The reflections above by two experienced practitioners demonstrate the emotional and moral complexity of fathering intervention with men who batter. We experienced this emotional and moral turbulence firsthand when we embarked on our project of designing, implementing, and evaluating a fathering group-intervention program for men who batter their partners (Perel & Peled, in press a). Questions that we confronted revolved mainly around the *why* and the *how*—why dedicate time, money, and effort to supporting the fathering of men who batter, and how to do it without further endangering the women and children or violating our perception of social justice?

Fathering Intervention With Men Who Batter Can Be Problematic and Even Dangerous

Intervention with men who batter, though common and established, raises moral, ideological, and economic questions (Caesar & Hamberger, 1989). A therapeutic approach to men who batter contributes to their construction as victims of individual pathology rather than executioners of a morally twisted social order (Dobash & Dobash, 1992). Providing them with intervention competes with services for their victims for the limited available resources, and it is not clear whether this intervention is actually successful in ameliorating domestic violence as a social problem (Gondolf, 2004). Intervention directed at the parenting of men who batter raises additional concerns regarding its potentially harmful effects on the abused women and children.

The provision of such intervention reflects a supportive stance toward the men's capacity to father. However, several authors have questioned the ability and right of these abusive, negligent fathers to continue their fathering relationships with their children (Haddix, 1996; Harne & Radford, 1994; Hooper, 1994). Some consider the exposure of children to violence against their mother a form of child abuse (Peled, 1998, 2000). The exposure to violence may terrify and terrorize children, create an unstable atmosphere in the home, expose them to narrow, rigid, destructive, violent, and antisocial role models, and lead them to experience both externalized and internalized behavior problems (Haddix, 1996; Peled & Davis, 1995; Margolin, 1998; Saunders, 1994). The violence may also harm the mothering of the abused woman by hampering her daily functioning, undermining her self-esteem and parental authority and inciting the children against her (Bancroft & Silverman, 2002; Holden, Stein, Ritchie, Harris, & Jourliles, 1998; Levendosky & Graham-Bermann, 1998). Additionally, there appears to be a considerable overlap (30%–60%) between woman abuse and child physical and sexual abuse (Edleson, 1999; McCloskey & Figueredo, 1995).

Men who batter have also been found to be uninvolved in their children's lives and negligent of their children's basic needs (including those thwarted by the abuse) (Holden & Ritchie, 1991; Sternberg, Lamb, Greenbaum, Dawud, Cortes, & Lorey, 1994), self-absorbed and possessive of the child (Ayoub, Grace, Paradise, & Newberger, 1991), and manipulative (Bancroft & Silverman, 2002; Vock, Elliot, & Spironello, 1997). A frequently cited aspect of their fathering in the context of divorce proceedings is their view of their children as a means for continuing their attempts to exert control over their partner's life and their abuse of her (Bancroft & Silverman, 2002; Geffner & Pagelow, 1990; Harne & Radford, 1994; Hester, Humphries, Pearson, Qaiser, Radford, & Woodfield, 1994; Hooper, 1994; Saunders, 1994; Vock et al., 1997). The available research on the characteristics of the fathering of men who batter suggests that they may misuse the fathering intervention to continue and even elaborate their controlling and abusive behavior toward their partners and their children. For example, a fathering intervention may be used by the man as a *certificate of good character*—a proof of his competence as a father, which may be waved in the woman's face in times of conflict or during various interactions with social and criminal-justice-system agencies. It may also delay and even block further rehabilitation of fathering skills and relationships by serving as a token effort in that direction.

Fathering Intervention With Men Who Batter
Is Justified and Important

All this notwithstanding, we suggest that fathering intervention with men who batter is called for and important. It is important because we believe that all fathers, abusive fathers included, are responsible for the well-being of their children and that they deserve adequate social support in performing this complex task. It is important for many children of men who batter who either live with their fathers or continue to have ongoing contact with them, many of whom care about their fathers and wish that they could have a gratifying relationship with them (Peled, 1998; McAlister Groves, Van Horn, & Lieberman, 2007). It is important for many women who coparent with their (ex-)abuser and who could benefit greatly from positive changes in the fathering behavior and relationships of their coparent (Jaffe & Crooks, 2007). And we believe that men who have ended their violence or made significant progress in this direction and would like to become better parents to their children deserve an opportunity to rehabilitate their fathering.

Our support of fathering intervention with men who batter was shaped by a critical examination of the literature on fathering in general and the fathering of men who batter in particular and by our research on the experience of fathering for men who batter (Perel & Peled, in press b). A distant and pathological perspective seems to characterize the construction of fathering in the academic discourse (Lupton & Barclay, 1997). Research on fathers tends to identify them as "variables" affecting their children, while the emotional and pleasurable aspects of fathering are mostly absent. This "role-inadequacy perspective," which is a part of a deficit paradigm (Hawkins & Dollahite, 1997, p. 1), is evident in much of contemporary family scholarship on men and fathers. From this perspective, fathering is associated with a multitude of structural flaws. These may correctly describe many fathers but are inappropriate for others. The deficit paradigm is reflected in the literature in the meager writing on the culture of fathering, and in the emphasis on the problematic nature of men and fathers (unaware, emotionally detached, and so forth) and their lack of involvement in the home life.

Set against the deficit paradigm are new efforts to understand fathering within the social context in which it takes place and which are based on a recognition of the uniqueness of the father role. Examples of this trend are the growing number of studies directed at the fathers' experience of fathering, the growing recognition among developmental psychologists of the complexity and the importance of the father-child relationship (Marsiglio, Amato, Day, & Lamb, 2000), and the expansion of the concept of "paternal involvement" to include the father's responsibility to his children even if he does not take care of them directly or does not live near them (Lamb, Pleck, Charnov, & Levine, 1985; Marsiglio, et al., 2000). These changes in the concept of fathering can best be observed in the "generative fathering" approach, which adopts a positive viewpoint toward fathers and fathering and claims that viewing fathering from a deficit perspective fails to provide an understanding of fathers and cannot propel them toward change and growth (Hawkins & Dollahite, 1997; Gerson, 1997; Snary, 1993). "Generative fathering" assumes that fathers intrinsically have the ethical imperative and the desire to commit themselves, to choose, to create, to guide, to show concern, to change, to relate, and to communicate—all on behalf of the next generation (Dollahite, Hawkins, & Brotherson, 1997; Hawkins & Dollahite, 1997; Palm, 1997).

The literature on fathers who abuse their partners focuses entirely on their negative traits and their deficient functioning. This observation, characteristic of the general literature on fathering, is understandable in light of their violent behavior. Despite this, the literature on the fathering of men who batter seems lacking by being one-dimensional, alienated from lived experience, and filled with sweeping generalizations. For example, the attempt to learn about the fathering of men who batter by relying on research findings regarding the general characteristics of violent men is methodologically problematic (Bancroft & Silverman, 2002). As a minimum, the significant variance found among "types" of men who batter (Holtzworth-Munroe & Stuart, 1994; Johnson & Ferraro, 2000, Dixon & Browne, 2003) calls for a more comprehensive and systematic approach to the qualities of their fathering. Caution and even suspicion are imperative in dealing with fathers who are abusive— their parenting is deficient and abusive by virtue of their violence toward the mother of their children. Still, an exclusive reliance on the deficit paradigm for learning about these fathers is restrictive. Our current knowledge about men who batter as fathers enhances our ability to protect their victims but does not help us to understand these men as fathers.

Our own research, which aimed at understanding the experience of fathering for men who abused their partners, exposed a complex picture of contradictory forces and processes shaping the fathering of these men (Perel & Peled, in press b). The study applied a naturalistic qualitative methodology and was shaped by phenomenological, feminist, and interpretative interactionist influences. In-depth interviews were conducted with 14 men who were abusive toward their partners and who had been identified through domestic-violence intervention centers.

The men's basic attitude toward fathering was positive: fathering was perceived as being of the utmost importance, the men devoted considerable efforts to being a "good father" as they perceived it, and they felt that they were indeed good fathers. Their aspirations, however, were undermined by internal and external forces, which included their own childhoods, their personal limitations, the children's exposure to violence, and their coparenting. The men experienced these forces, independently and jointly, as constricting their fathering. They diminished their involvement and presence in their children's lives and focused their fathering on providing for their children and controlling them. Their partners, in their view, were responsible for accelerating the process of constriction. However, despite the constriction, and possibly as a reaction to it, many fathers were left with a strong yearning for a closer and warmer relationship with their children. In an overall review of their fathering experience, the men could be located on a continuum extending from feelings of failure and missed opportunities to a sense of growth and improvement as part of a wider change process bound up with the cessation of violence.

Our findings seem to echo a more complex understanding of violent men voiced by experienced domestic-violence practitioners. They expanded our view of the flawed and abusive parenting of these men to include also their vulnerability, distress, and yearning. Such yearning for connection could be an expression of the need to control the woman and the children, but it could also arise from the gap between a desired close and warm connection with one's children and the reality of a remote and constricted relationship. Support for the latter view can be found in descriptions of men who batter as being characterized by a yearning for intimacy (e.g., Denzin, 1984; Dutton & Browning, 1988; Vaselle-Augenstein & Erlich, 1992; Borochowitz, 2003). It is possible that under certain conditions, and if it is their wish, some of these abusive fathers could repair their damaged parenting. Allowing men who batter an in-depth exploration of this meaningful and sensitive aspect of their lives may also facilitate changes in other domains of intervention with them by providing access into inner worlds otherwise cordoned off from practitioners.

The Challenge: Duality in Practice

The above examination of the pros and cons of fathering intervention with men who batter reflects the multifaceted nature of their experience and highlights both the risks and opportunities involved in such intervention. Fathering intervention with men who batter takes place within a complex web of various dimensions of practice in this domain, relating to the goals, methods, and therapeutic approaches of the intervention. Models of intervention with men who batter as fathers can be distinguished by the extent to which they see the issue of fathering as an end in itself or as an entry point into the men's inner world and into other potential areas of change, such as the violent behavior. They can aim primarily at cognitive behavioral changes or focus on the examination of fathering as an experience and an identity. They can strive for concrete outcomes or emphasize the processes of intervention. They can regard the men or the men's victims as the focus of the intervention. Finally, they can stress the men's responsibility and accountability or emphasize a caring and empathic approach.

In the conceptual framework and intervention model presented in this chapter, we try to find a balanced middle ground, preferring a "both-and" approach to an "either-or" one. We see men who batter as simultaneously harmful and vulnerable. We are aware of the potential dangers involved for the women and children in the offering of a fathering intervention to men who batter and to the possibility of the men misusing the intervention so as to strengthen their control over their family (Peled, 2000). Hence, we have to demand that the men be accountable for their abusive behavior and for the damage that it created. We also believe that a fathering intervention with them, as with any other fathers, will be effective only if it is based on respect and empathy for their experiences and views (Hawkins & Dollahite, 1997). Fathering is seen as an end but is also understood as a powerful component of a man's identity and close relationships. Though the men who batter are our direct clients, we are also responsible for the well-being and safety of their partners and children, as these are involved in the intervention, and we aspire to create an intervention from which all three groups will benefit. We advocate for the creation of an intervention space that is both empathic and critical and for a reflective examination of the fathering experience, leading to some concrete parenting outcomes.

The challenge facing anyone who wishes to intervene with men who batter as fathers is how to do it all—protect and respect, trust and suspect, empathize and criticize. Our answer, in one sentence, is: "maintain this *duality in practice.*" This implies a condemnation of the harm the fathers cause to the children and to the children's mother and striving to put a stop to the abuse, while also being attentive to the fathers' distress and providing them with support. Intervention of this kind with men who batter requires grasping both ends of a long rope. At the one extreme, there is empathy, acceptance, and even sometimes love; while at the other extreme, there is repudiation of the violent behavior, emotions of anger and even rage, and the provision of protection and support for the victims. In the rest of this chapter, we present the theoretical premises and a brief outline for such an intervention, but we first provide a note on the context in which we developed our approach.

Our Context

Over the past three decades, domestic violence has been constructed as a major social problem worldwide. In Israel, where we practice and study, this interest has resulted in, among other things, the establishment of a country-wide public service system dedicated to protecting and supporting victims, intervening with abusers, and prevention efforts.

This chapter is based on knowledge that we cocreated as part of a four-year project aimed to develop, implement, and evaluate a parenting group-intervention model with men who batter in Israeli community centers for domestic-violence prevention and intervention. Currently, there are about 60 such centers in Israel, varying in size and in the range of interventions provided. These centers are responsible for the bulk of interventions with men who batter, offering services to hundreds of men each year. All of the centers offer basic and advanced groups for men who batter, aimed at eliminating their violent behavior, as well as group intervention for abused women and individual and family intervention, when required. In addition, most centers offer intervention to children exposed to domestic violence. The centers are cofunded by the local municipalities, the Welfare Ministry, and women's organizations; they employ experienced social workers trained for intervention in this domain.

The male client population of the centers is heterogeneous in age, education, income, religion, and ethnicity (Jews and Arabs, new immigrants from various countries), religiosity (secular, religious, and orthodox), marital status, and severity of violence committed. Most of the men are referred to the centers by the police or the courts but are never court-mandated to treatment. Others are self-referred, with or without the ultimatum of a partner. Most of the male clients are fathers, and most of these fathers either live with their partner and children or have ongoing contact with the children. This distinctive characteristic may be explained by the centrality of the family in Israel, maintained by formal and informal institutions, both religious and secular. For example, divorce is still perceived in terms of "failure" and as an undesirable deviation. Women's wages, the policies of housing, education, and employment, as well as the tax system, all further reflect and preserve this perception (Fogeil-Bijaoui, 1999; Katz & Peres, 1996).

As in other countries, the dominant intervention approach with men who batter in Israeli domestic-violence centers is cognitive-behavioral group treatment with a growing influence of psychodynamic therapy in advanced phases of the intervention. A tendency to prolong the intervention with the men, sometimes up to two years, is also evident in the centers in the last decade.

Theoretical Premises for Safe and Effective Fathering Intervention

As expected, no single theoretical approach could account for the complexity involved in fathering intervention with men who batter that is aiming to maintain the dualities described above. A multifaceted reality requires a conceptual *mélange*. We found feminist and phenomenological approaches to be particularly useful in providing us with premises and guidelines for an intervention model that could account for both the social context and individual experiences of fathering of men who batter. In addition, we drew on several tenets of dynamic psychotherapy to complement additional aspects of intervention deemed important in light of the literature and our own practice with and research on fathering by men who batter.

Fathering Intervention as a Feminist Issue

Fathering intervention with men who batter is a feminist issue. If done properly, it can greatly improve the lives of the men's partners and children and generally advance a more egalitarian and less violent society (Silverstein, 1996). Intervention with men who batter, and particularly a fathering intervention, must be grounded in a feminist analysis and praxis regarding men's use of violence against women. "Domestic violence" is one aspect of wide-ranging social processes aimed at maintaining male domination over women and children (Kelly, 1988). Though occurring within the complex setting of family relationships and interactions, men's abuse of their partner and children is first and foremost a crime calling for a criminal justice–system response. It is conceptually flawed and practically dangerous to view men's violence toward their partners outside the social context in which it takes place and without consideration of their victims. Thus, violence and fathering are inseparable experiences in the context of intervention with men who batter. This feminist perspective translates to the following intervention safeguards and guidelines.

- Fathering intervention with men who batter must be framed as such, not concealing the violence or minimizing it, though this would likely be the preference of many participating men. Rather, the intervention should focus on abusive parenting and the impact of violence on exposed children as major areas of reflection and change. This framing of the intervention should be openly presented to potential participants and accepted by them before entering the intervention program.
- Fathering intervention with men who batter can never replace the criminal-justice response and punishment. Furthermore, fathering intervention should constitute but one aspect of wider intervention efforts aimed at eradicating the man's violent behavior and should be offered in this context. It should be offered only to men who batter who have acknowledged and taken responsibility for their abusive behavior, as well as made significant progress in stopping it. Offering parenting intervention to men who batter prior to a successful completion of intervention directed at the abusive behavior could strengthen denial of the violence by seeming to reframe their problem as that of deficient parenting.
- Designers of fathering intervention, though directed at the men who batter, must also see abused women and children as their clients. Victims' safety should precede all other intervention agendas.

While a feminist perspective centers on issues of justice, accountability, and victims' safety, phenomenology facilitates an understanding of the men's experiences of fathering.

Phenomenology

A phenomenological approach to fathering intervention with men who batter is centered on the men's experience of fathering and the meaning they attribute to it. Men's experiences of fathering are located within the interpersonal, social, and political environments and shape the meaning of fathering for them. This client-centered, humanistic approach assumes that the meaning of experience precedes interpretation or theory and that all objective understandings are based on subjective perception (Eisikovits & Buchbinder, 1996). We find the phenomenological approach to be particularly suitable to fathering intervention with men who batter. It encourages a reflective stance, multiple perspectives, and competing explanations regarding the phenomenon at hand (Eisikovits & Buchbinder, 1996). It thus corresponds well with the ambiguous nature of fatherhood in our era. The available literature on contemporary fathers suggests that they are faced with a multiplicity of norms, definitions, and images of the father role, some of them contradictory, and they may thus experience confusion, distress, and inner conflicts (Lamb, 2000; Marsiglio, et al., 2000). At the same time, much criticism and little support are offered to fathers by various social institutions and services (Hawkins & Dollahite, 1997). Under these circumstances, the complex, emotionally loaded process of exploring one's experience of fathering seems to be a prerequisite for a further exploration of the meaning of abusive fathering. By legitimizing the subjective perception of one's experiences as a valid and even crucial source of knowledge and by emphasizing the role of emotionality in human existence, phenomenology facilitates the exploration of both violence and fathering as emotional experiences and thus has the potential to go beyond initial defensive and idealized reactions and engage men who batter in a reflective change process.

It is important to remember, however, that a purely phenomenological approach to the fathering experience of men who batter will blur the problematic social context of this experience and may make the victims invisible. Thus, we propose to integrate the phenomenological notions with a feminist social-interpretive viewpoint by focusing on the meanings attributed by the men to their fathering experiences, as lived in the context of reciprocal relationships between them and their social environment. The aim of the interpretation is to expose the processes, history, and interactions that have shaped and located their experience of fathering. Another important layer in the exploration of men's experiences of fathering is their childhood experience, which, from a psychodynamic perspective, is expected to impact their parenting.

Dynamic Psychotherapy

The inclusion of psychodynamic elements in the conceptual model stems from our assumptions regarding the nature of the parenting experience in general and for men who batter in particular. The experience of parenting is rooted in childhood—in being a child, in being parented, and in observing the parenting of one's parents (Fraiberg, Adelson, & Shapiro, 2003; Simons, Beaman, Conger, & Chao, 1993). Therefore, observing the past and understanding its influence on parenting is part of the process of parental change (McInnis-Dittrich, 1996). The men in our study spoke extensively about their childhood during the interviews, presenting a complex and multifaceted picture and stressing their relationships with their fathers. In most cases, their childhoods seemed to have left them with residues and deficiencies that they had to deal with in the process of becoming fathers. Most of them seemed to have engaged in an inner dialogue with their fathers concerning two opposing desires: to emulate the father and follow in his footsteps; or to be different or "the opposite." The general tenor of most of the men was one of confusion and discomfort; they felt that their childhoods and their parents did not prepare them for fathering (Perel & Peled, in press b). Similar attitudes of abusive men toward their fathers were described by Fox, Sayers, and Bruce (2001).

The psychological salience of childhood in the experience of fathering has implications for both the content and structure of intervention. We believe that it is important to allow the men to reflect on and process their relationships with their parents and the ways in which the parenting models and experiences to which they were exposed impact their own parenting. In order to do so, the men need to experience the therapeutic milieu as an empathetic and compassionate space. Such a therapeutic environment will support the men's use of the intervention as a healing experience, provide them with a modeling opportunity for handling intimacy and emotion in interpersonal relationships, and is likely to facilitate the development of empathy to their own children's experiences.

Goals for Intervention With Fathers

Based on the available literature in this domain, our own research and practice experiences, and the conceptual framework presented above, we derived the following set of goals for fathering intervention with men who batter.

- We expect participating men to be capable of greater self-reflection following intervention.
- We expect the men to perceive the fathering intervention as part of their domestic-violence intervention, to increase their understanding of the impact of violence on exposed children, and to increase their empathy to the children's feelings in general and to those related to their exposure to violence in particular. In addition, we hope that participation in this intervention will lead to a decrease in the men's abusive behavior toward their partners and children.
- We expect the intervention to result in an increased and more varied involvement of the men in their children's lives and in more diversified and improved basic parenting skills. An important set of parenting skills concerns fathers' interactions with their (ex-)partners and co- or parallel parents.

The achievement of all these goals for men who batter is a highly ambitious enterprise, and it is even more so within the constraints of the public social service system. Again, the main challenge is how to do it all? In the final section of this chapter, we present a rough outline of the topics we included in our model for a semistructured, cofacilitated group intervention aimed at "strengthening the fathering of men who batter" (Perel & Peled, in press a).

This intervention model was developed as part of a larger project aiming to establish mothering and fathering intervention as routine practice with battered women and men who batter in Israeli domestic-violence centers. The fathering model was implemented and evaluated, both for processes and outcomes, in seven centers for domestic-violence prevention and intervention in Israel in the years 2001–2003. Five additional fathering groups based on this model in its draft stages were conducted in domestic-violence centers and probation services between 2001 and 2004. Overall, about 85 men have so far completed a short-term fathering group based on the model. Throughout these years, we conducted four supervision groups for group facilitators of both the fathering and mothering groups. The ongoing supervision was a major source of learning and feedback on the model and played a central role in its development process. The ongoing feedback from both group members and facilitators over the past three years was very positive regarding both the usefulness of the model as a tool and its ability to effect change in participating fathers.

A preliminary analysis of the evaluation data, however, calls for a cautious approach regarding the extent to which the expected outcomes can be achieved in a short-term intervention. Our findings suggest that, following their participation in the group, there was some improvement in the men's parenting skills, and an increase in the men's understanding of the impact of violence on exposed children and in their empathy to the children's feelings. These findings notwithstanding, until further support of the program's efficacy is available, we suggest that the main contribution of the short-term group will be in its sowing the seeds of change in the expected directions; but without further fertilization, it may not take root. In accordance, our published version of the intervention model includes reference to both short- and long-term programs (Perel & Peled, in press a).

Structure of Intervention With Fathers

The intervention is modular and includes five major topical sections intertwined throughout the group sessions: (1) introduction to the group and being a father; (2) parenting skills and daily events; (3) my parents and my parenting; (4) my children and the impact of the violence on them; (5) closure and farewell. In the group manual, we offer several alternative sessions, each including a number of alternative activities for each of the sections (Perel & Peled, in press a). The number of group sessions determines the depth and breadth with which each of the topics will be processed. A short-term intervention

(16–20 sessions) is focused on improving parenting skills and functioning, emphasizing learning processes while also allowing some space for exploring biographical, emotional, and relational aspects of the fathering experience. A longer group (more than 30 sessions) is focused on similar topics but allows for a more thorough reflective examination of the dynamics underlying and shaping the men's fathering experiences.

Section I: Being a Father

This section opens the group and lays the ground rules to its formation. While our aim is to bring participants to identify and acknowledge both their capabilities and deficiencies as fathers, we believe that focusing on positive and meaningful aspects of their fathering experiences in the beginning of the group helps to establish a nonjudgmental and nonthreatening atmosphere. Issues dealt with in this section are identifying one's fathering style, men's self-perception as fathers, and the gap existing between this perception and ideal images of fathering, both personal and cultural.

Section II: Parenting Skills and Analysis of Daily Events

"Parenting skills" are various blends of knowledge, attitudes, and behaviors deemed by parenting experts to be helpful in raising children "appropriately." While we do not espouse any particular combination of "golden rules" in this domain and appreciate the cultural diversity in parenting practices, we believe that most men who batter could benefit from an examination and refinement of their current parenting skills and an acquisition of additional ones. This section of the intervention is partly shaped based on the needs and requests of the participants; but in our view, it should include applicable information on normative child development and work on issues of discipline. Other relevant issues include communication, positive reinforcement, parental touch, quality time, coparenting, and the like. We found that approaching the topic of parenting skills through the analysis of everyday life events facilitated a more relevant, applicable, and rich treatment of the issues at hand.

Section III: My Parents and My Parenting

We believe in the existence of an ongoing dialogue between a man's fathering and his experiences as a son of both his father and mother. This section aims to facilitate an exploration of one's fathering vis-à-vis his perception of his parents' parenting. The men's reflection on positive and problematic aspects of their parents' parenting sets the stage for an examination of both positive and problematic aspects in their own parenting. A further step would be to examine ways of revising and enriching the men's current fathering practices.

Section IV: My Children and the Impact of Violence on Them

We assume that many if not most men who batter have difficulties in "seeing their children" or in being empathic toward them. Hence, group time is devoted to "reacquaintance" with their children through an empathic, in-depth observation of their children's distinctive characteristics and experiences. The ability to understand the child's world and perspective helps to lay the foundation for an understanding of the child's experience of exposure to violence. Understanding the impact of violence on one's children and responding to it involves cognitive, emotional, and behavioral work. We expect the men to learn about the potential negative effects of exposure to violence, to try and empathize with the hurting child, to acknowledge the ways in which their own children were damaged by the violence, and to develop or strengthen their commitment to help their children to heal. To complete these processes, the men would be expected to plan and carry out concrete steps in this direction.

Section V: Closure and Farewell

A major goal of the closure sessions is to allow the men to reflect on their group experience; to identify areas of learning, growth, and change; and to commend themselves for these hard-earned achievements. At the same time, it is important that the men identify issues and areas in their fathering that require further work and that they develop some initial plans for continuing this work. Lasting positive effects of the group are likely to be strengthened by a well-processed closure of the various group dynamics and relationships.

Conclusion

Intervening with men who batter as fathers is a challenging, delicate, highly skilled, and political task. The constant effort to walk a tightrope without slipping into any of the pits below may prove exhausting. A constant balance needs to be maintained between conflicting perspectives, agendas, and commitments. Previous experience in intervention with violent men and an ongoing reflective mode are highly recommended for those wishing to lead men who batter on this often painful journey

When considering the practical adaptation of this theoretical framework, it is important to remember the cultural-organizational context in which it was constructed, as presented earlier. We advocate the use of an exploratory, tentative approach in transferring this intervention framework to practice with other populations such as involuntary and court-mandated clients or men who are abusive toward their children. Furthermore, the development and implementation of the proposed intervention in a practice setting serving men who batter, battered women, and exposed children shaped it in significant ways.

The presence of victims' voices in the agencies helped to maintain an awareness of the abuse and its implications while at the same time exploring various dimensions of the men's fathering experiences. The implementation of this model in isolation of women's and children's programs may require direct efforts to ensure that the victims are well represented and protected.

Acknowledgments

Our many partners in this project were Tzipi Nachshon and Ayala Mayer from the Israeli Ministry of Welfare, Sarah Tov and Dr. Shoshana Grinwald from the Ashalim Foundation, group facilitators, and group participants. The in-depth discussions we had with all of them throughout these years have contributed enormously to our understanding of the experience of fathering for men who batter and of the multitude of challenges involved in such intervention. We would like to acknowledge their contribution and thank them for sharing with us their doubts, difficulties, questions, and answers.

References

Ayoub, C., Grace, P., Paradise, J., & Newberger, E. (1991). Alleging psychological impairment of the accuser to defend oneself against a child abuse allegation: A manifestation of wife battering and false accusation. In M. Robin (Ed.), *Assessing child maltreatment reports: The problem of false allegations* (pp. 191–207). New York: Haworth Press.

Bancroft, L., & Silverman, J. G. (2002). *The batterer as parent.* Thousand Oaks, CA: Sage.

Caesar, P. L., & Hamberger, L. K. (1989). Introduction: Brief historical overview of interventions for wife abuse in the United States. In P. L. Caesar & L. K. Hamberger (Eds.), *Treating men who batter: Theory, practice and programs* (pp. xxvii–xxxvi). New York: Springer.

Denzin, N. K. (1984). Toward a phenomenology of domestic family violence. *American Journal of Sociology, 90,* 485–511.

Dixon, L., & Browne, K. (2003). The heterogeneity of spouse abuse: A review. *Aggression and Violent Behavior, 8,* 107–130.

Dobash, R. E. & Dobash, R. (1992). *Women, violence and social change.* London: Routledge.

Dollahite, D. C., Hawkins, A. J., & Brotherson, S. E. (1997). Fatherwork: A conceptual ethic of fathering as generative work. In D. C. Dollahite & A. J. Hawkins (Eds.), *Generative fathering: Beyond deficit perspectives* (pp. 17–35). Thousand Oaks, CA: Sage

Dutton, D. G., & Browning, J. J. (1988). Concern for power, fear of intimacy, and aversive stimuli for wife assault. In G. T. Hotaling, D. Finkelhor, J. T. Kirkpatric & M. A. Straus (Eds.), *Family abuse and its consequences* (pp. 163–175). Newbery Park, CA: Sage.

Edleson, J. L. (1999). The overlap between child maltreatment and women battering. *Violence Against Women, 5,* 134–154.

Eisikovits, Z. C., & Buchbinder, E. (1996). Toward a phenomenological intervention with violence in intimate relationships. In J. L. Edleson & Z. C. Eisikovits (Eds.), *Future interventions with battered women and their families* (pp. 186–200). Thousand Oaks, CA: Sage.

Fogeil-Bijaoui, S. (1999). *Sex, gender and politics.* Tel Aviv, Israel: Hakibbutz Ha-Meuhad.

Fox, G. L., Sayers, J., & Bruce, C. (2001). Beyond bravado: Fatherhood as a resource for rehabilitation of men who batter. *Marriage and Family Review, 30,* 137–163.

Fraiberg, S., Adelson, E., & Shapiro, V. (2003). Ghosts in the nursery: A psychoanalytic approach to the problems of impaired infant-mother relationships. In J. Raphael-Leff (Ed.), *Parent-infant psychodynamics: Wild things, mirrors, and ghosts* (pp. 87–117). Philadelphia, PA: Whurr Publishers.

Geffner, R., & Pagelow, M. (1990). Mediation and child custody issues in abusive relationships. *Social Sciences and Law, 8,* 151–159.

Gerson, K. (1997). An institutional perspective on generative fathering: Creating social supports for parenting equality. In A. J. Hawkins & D. C. Dollahite (Eds.), *Generative fathering: Beyond deficit perspectives* (pp. 36–51). Thousand Oaks, CA: Sage.

Gondolf, E. (2004). Evaluating batterer counseling programs: A difficult task showing some effects. *Aggression and Violent Behavior, 9*(6), 605–631.

Haddix, A. (1996). Unseen Victims: Acknowledging the effects of domestic violence on children through statutory termination of parental rights. *California Law Review, 84,* 757–815.

Harne, L., & Radford, J. (1994). Reinstating patriarchy: The politics of the family and the new legislation. In A. Mullender & R. Morley (Eds.), *Children living with domestic violence: Putting men's abuse of women on the child care agenda* (pp. 68–85). London: Whiting & Birch.

Hawkins, A. J., & Dollahite, D.C. (1997). Beyond the role-inadequacy perspective of fathering. In A. J. Hawkins & D. C. Dollahite (Eds.), *Generative fathering: Beyond deficit perspectives* (pp. 3–16). Thousand Oaks, CA: Sage.

Hester, M., Humphries, J., Pearson, C., Qaiser, K., Radford, L., & Woodfield, K. S. (1994). Domestic violence and child contact. In A. Mullender & R. Morley (Eds.), *Children living with domestic violence: Putting men's abuse of women on the child care agenda* (pp. 102–121). London: Whiting & Birch.

Holden, G. W., & Ritchie, K. L. (1991). Linking extreme marital discord, child rearing, and child behavior problems: Evidence from battered women. *Child Development, 62,* 311–327.

Holden, G. W., Stein, D. J., Ritchie, K. L., Harris, S. D., & Jouriles, E. N. (1998). Parenting behaviors and beliefs of battered women. In: G. W. Holden, R. Geffner, & E. N. Jouriles (Eds.). *Children exposed to marital violence: Theory, research and applied issues* (pp. 289–334). Washington, DC: American Psychological Association.

Holtzworth-Munroe, A., & Stuart, G. L. (1994). Typologies of male batterers: Three subtypes and the differences among them. *Psychological Bulletin, 116,* 476–497.

Hooper, C. A. (1994). Do families need fathers? The impact of divorce on children. In A. Mullender & R. Morley (Eds.), *Children living with domestic violence: Putting men's abuse of women on the child care agenda* (pp. 86–101). London: Whiting & Birch.

Jaffe, P.G., & Crooks, C. V. (2007). Assessing the best interests of the child: Visitation and custody cases of domestic violence. In J. L. Edleson & O. J. Williams,

Parenting by men who batter: New directions for assessment and intervention (pp. 45–64). New York: Oxford University Press.

Johnson, M. P., & Ferraro, K. J. (2000). Research on domestic violence in the 1990s: Making distinctions. *Journal of Marriage and Family, 62*(4), 948–963.

Katz, R., & Peres, Y. (1996). Divorce tendencies in Israel and their implications for family counseling. *Hevrah u-Revahah* (Society and Welfare), *15*(4), 483–502.

Kelly, L. (1988). *Surviving sexual violence.* Minneapolis, MN: University of Minnesota Press.

Lamb, M. E. (2000). The history of research on father involvement: An overview. In H. E. Peters, G. W. Peterson, S. K. Steinmetz, & R. D. Day (Eds.), *Fatherhood: Research, interventions and policies* (pp. 23–42). New York. Haworth.

Lamb, M. E., Pleck, J., Charnov, E. L., & Levine, J. A. (1985). Paternal behavior in humans. *American Zoologist, 25,* 883–894.

Levendosky, A. A., & Graham-Bermann, S. A. (1998). The moderating effects of parenting stress on children's adjustment in woman-abusing families. *Journal of Interpersonal Violence, 13,* 383–397.

Lupton, D., & Barclay, L. (1997). *Constructing fatherhood: Discourses and experiences.* Thousand Oaks, CA: Sage.

Margolin, G. (1998). Effects of domestic violence on children. In P. K. Trickett & C. J. Schellenback (Eds.), *Violence against children in the family and in the community* (pp. 57–101). Washington, DC: American Psychological Association.

Marsiglio, W., Amato, P., Day, R. D., & Lamb, M. E. (2000). Scholarship on fatherhood in the 1990s and beyond. *Journal of Marriage and Family, 62,* 1173–1191.

McAlister Groves, B., Van Horn, P., & Lieberman A. F. (2007). Deciding on fathers' involvement in their children's treatment after domestic violence. In J. L. Edleson & O. J. Williams, *Parenting by men who batter: New directions for assessment and intervention* (pp. 65–84). New York: Oxford University Press.

McCloskey, L. A., & Figueredo, A. J. (1995). The effects of systemic family violence on children's mental health. *Child Development, 66*(5), 1239–1261.

McInnis-Dittrich, K. (1996). Violence prevention: An ecological adaptation of systematic training for effective parenting. *Families in Society, 77*(7), 414–422.

Palm, G. F. (1997). Promoting generative fathering through parent and family education. In A. J. Hawkins & D. C. Dollahite (Eds.), *Generative fathering: Beyond deficit perspectives* (pp. 167–182). Thousand Oaks, CA: Sage.

Peled, E. (1998). The experience of living with violence for preadolescent children of battered women. *Youth and Society, 29,* 395–430.

Peled, E. (2000). Supporting the parenting of battering men: Issues and dilemmas. *British Journal of Social Work, 30*(1), 25–36.

Peled, E., & Davis, D. (1995). *Groupwork with children of battered women: A practitioner's manual.* Thousand Oaks, CA: Sage.

Perel, G., & Peled, E. (in press a). *Fathering and violence: A guide for group intervention with men who are violent toward their partner.* Jerusalem, Israel: Ashalim Press.

Perel, G. & Peled, E. (in press b). The fathering of violent men: Constriction and yearning. *Violence Against Women.*

Saunders, D. G. (1994). Child custody decisions in families experiencing women abuse. *Social Work, 39*(1), 51–59.

Silverstein, L. B. (1996). Fathering is a feminist issue. *Psychology of Women Quarterly, 20,* 3–37.

Simons, R. L., Beaman, J., Conger, R. D., & Chao, W. (1993). Childhood experience, conceptions of parenting, and attitudes of spouse as determinants of
parental behavior. *Journal of Marriage and the Family, 55*(1), 91–106.

Snary, J. (1993). *How fathers care for the next generation: A four-decade study.* London:
Howard University Press.

Sternberg, K. J., Lamb, M. E., Greenbaum, Dawud, S., Cortes, R. M., & Lorey, F.
(1994). The effects of domestic violence on children's perceptions of their
perpetrating and nonperpetrating parents. *International Journal of Behavioral
Development, 17*(4), 779–795.

Vaselle-Augenstein, R., & Ehrlich, A. (1992). Male batterers: Evidence for psychopathology. In C. E. Viano (Ed.), *Intimate violence: Interdisciplinary perspectives*
(pp. 139–154). Washington, DC: Hemisphere.

Vock, J., Elliot, P., & Spironello, V. (1997, June). From child witnesses to pawns:
Post-separation tactics of abusive ex-partners. Paper presented at the Conference
on Children Exposed to Family Violence, London, Ontario, Canada.

Yassour Borochowitz, D. (2003). *Intimate violence: The emotional world of batterers.*
Tel Aviv, Israel: Resling.

6

Guidelines for Intervention With Abusive Fathers

Katreena L. Scott
Karen J. Francis
Claire V. Crooks
Michelle Paddon
David A. Wolfe

Although awareness of the overlapping nature of child abuse and domestic violence dates back at least to the mid–1980s (Edleson, 1999; Wolfe, Crooks, Lee, McIntyre-Smith, & Jaffe, 2003; Wolfe, Jaffe, Wilson, & Zak, 1985), this knowledge has not been adequately reflected in intervention practices. Batterer intervention programs have historically focused on men's relationships with women and not on their role as fathers. Similarly, in child protection services, fathers have tended to be either ignored or viewed as inherently dangerous to children (Edleson, 1998; Featherstone, 2001; Scourfield, 2001). Problems with these strategies of excluding fathers from service have become increasingly apparent. First, focusing protective service efforts and interventions on the mother-child relationship has indirectly allowed maltreating fathers to avoid dealing with the consequences of their abusive behavior, subsequently placing a greater burden on children's mothers (Peled, 2000). Second, problems arise because men who have been abusive in one relationship seldom end relationships altogether. They often have children with other partners and/or become caregivers for children of other partners. These multiple relationships are particularly concerning in light of research suggesting that children who live in homes with a nonbiological father are more likely to be abused than those living with biological parents (Radhakrishna, Bou-Saada, Hunter, Catellier, & Kotch, 2001). Finally, by failing to provide intervention to fathers, communities may be missing an important opportunity to promote children's health and well-being and to break an intergenerational cycle of violence.

In response to growing recognition of these issues, there have been recent efforts in justice, child welfare, and batterer intervention to provide more comprehensive and integrated services for families where men have been violent (Family Violence Prevention Fund, 2004; National Council of Juvenile and Family Court Judges (NCJFCJ), 1999). As part of these efforts, we have developed an intervention program for fathers who have been abusive in their families: *Caring Dads: Helping Fathers Value Their*

Children (Scott, Francis, Crooks, & Kelly, in press). In this chapter, we draw on our experiences with the Caring Dads program to describe issues that arise in designing and providing intervention with fathers who have abused their children and/or intimate partners and to outline a series of guidelines for program accountability.

The Caring Dads Program: Beginnings and Philosophy

The Caring Dads initiative began in 2001 at Changing Ways, an agency in London, Ontario, Canada, committed to ending men's violence, with Emerge in Boston, Massachusetts, as an early partner. Since the first Caring Dads groups were offered in London and Boston, a number of other communities have joined in this effort. These communities serve culturally and linguistically diverse client populations, and the program has been modified and adapted accordingly.

The Caring Dads program provides 17 weeks of group intervention to men who have maltreated their children and/or abused their children's mothers. Specifically, the group serves clients who have been officially identified as having been emotionally or physically abusive or neglectful toward their children only, clients who have abused their children's mothers but have not physically abused their children, and clients who have been abusive toward both their children and their children's mothers. Referrals to Caring Dads are most often made by child protection services or probation and parole personnel, though men also attend voluntarily and in response to referrals from mental health agencies, batterer intervention programs, child and family services, and other community organizations.

The content of the Caring Dads program is informed by five major principles derived from an integration of the parenting, child abuse, change promotion, and batterer intervention literatures (Scott & Crooks, 2004). These principles describe our conceptualization of fathers' needs, the overlap of child and women abuse, men's minimization of responsibility, men's adherence to gender-role stereotypes, and the cumulative harmful effects of abuse on children. The principles are realized in the four broad therapeutic goals of the Caring Dads program curriculum: (1) to develop sufficient trust so that men can be engaged in the process of examining their fathering; (2) to increase men's awareness of child-centered fathering; (3) to increase men's awareness of, and responsibility for, abusive and neglectful fathering behaviors and their impact on children; and (4) to consolidate learning, rebuild trust, and plan for the future (Crooks, Scott, Francis, Kelly, & Reid, 2006; Scott, et al., in press). Addressing fathers' attitudes about children's relationships with their mothers (including biological, step-, and/or adoptive mothers) is a key component of these program goals. For example, child-centered fathering includes the need to support the mother-child relationship, and abuse of children's mothers is clearly identified as a form of child maltreatment. Overall, then,

Caring Dads combines aspects of both standard parenting education groups and batterer intervention to form a program that is distinct to the needs of fathers who have been abusive in their families.

Accountability Guidelines

In providing Caring Dads groups, it has become clear that in order to offer the program in a manner that is responsible to the safety and well-being of women and children victims, issues of accountability must be in the forefront. These guidelines are necessary to ensure that the program is embedded in the broader network of domestic violence, child protection, women's advocacy, mental health, and criminal justice services. Embedding the program in a broader response to families facilitates appropriate monitoring of both fathers and program providers to ensure that child, mother, and community safety needs are being met. In the following sections, we outline 12 guidelines for accountability practice in service to fathers who have been abusive in their families. Some of these guidelines are fairly detailed and prescriptive, and others are designed to raise issues for discussion within communities. These guidelines address accountability and responsibility to: (1) children; (2) children's mothers; (3) fathers; and (4) the broader community. Each of these areas is summarized in Table 6.1 and discussed in separate sections below.

Accountability to the Safety and Well-Being of Children

As a starting point for accountability, we suggest that the needs of children must be the primary consideration for programs intervening with abusive fathers. The following guidelines were developed upon this philosophical foundation. We also recognize that children's safety and well-being needs are not independent of those of their mothers. Guidelines around this issue are discussed in the section on accountability to children's mothers.

1. *Programs targeting fathers who have maltreated their children or abused their children's mothers must have firm collaborations with agencies that can identify maltreating fathers and strongly encourage or mandate men into treatment.* Fathers who have been abusive in their families seldom seek intervention voluntarily. These men are often distrustful of intervention services and angry at personnel from child protection, justice, mental health, or battered women's agencies who have identified problems in their behavior. Moreover, they frequently see any involvement with social service agencies as unnecessary and as interfering in their families (Duggan, et al., 2004; Summers, Boller, & Raikes, 2004).

Current approaches to increasing fathers' involvement with their children often emphasize the need to *invite* men to be better fathers and coparents (e.g. Green, 2003). We maintain that a firmer approach is necessary with men who have been abusive, because if services are limited to men *voluntarily*

Table 6.1
Summary of Accountability Guidelines

Accountability to the Safety and Well-Being of Children
1. Programs targeting fathers who have maltreated their children or abused their children's mothers must have firm collaborations with agencies that can identify maltreating fathers and can strongly encourage or mandate men into treatment.
2. Fathers' participation in intervention must have the potential to benefit children independent of men's progress through intervention.
3. Consideration should be given to whether and how children can access clear and developmentally appropriate answers about their fathers' involvement in intervention.

Accountability to the Safety of Children's Mothers
4. Abuse of children's mothers compromises children's needs for safety, well-being, and stability. As such, men's abuse of children's mothers must be recognized and addressed as part of intervention for fathers.
5. Outreach must be offered to provide women with information about the program and referrals to appropriate therapeutic or advocacy services.
6. Rather than focusing on coparenting, intervention should emphasize the need for men to be respectful and nonabusive of children's mothers and of the mother-child relationship.

Accountability to Fathers
7. Programs for abusive fathers need to maintain respectful and transparent relationships with men.
8. Recognizing that any one program is often insufficient to meet all the needs of its clients, program facilitators should be ready to refer men to alternative or additional services.
9. Intervention programs for abusive fathers are responsible for being accessible to men of diverse cultures and individual circumstances.

Accountability to Communities
10. Programs for fathers who abuse or neglect their children or their children's mothers need to be offered with the guidance and support of a community advisory committee that includes representatives from agencies that provide services to children, women, and men.
11. Programs for abusive fathers should offer training and education to the community as necessary for accountable service.
12. Programs for abusive fathers should engage in continued program evaluation.

pursuing intervention, the safety and well-being needs of the many children of fathers who choose to avoid intervention will not be addressed. Referral and service models, which can strongly encourage or mandate men's involvement in intervention and regulate their access to their children, are therefore necessary. Obvious partners are child protective, probation and parole, and court services. Education of service providers in social and medical service agencies about better identification of early warning signs of fathers' abuse of their children or their children's mothers may result in additional appropriate referrals.

2. *Fathers' participation in intervention must have the potential to benefit children independent of men's progress through intervention.* Fathers' participation in intervention programs targeting their abuse of their children must have the potential to improve children's lives—*whether men are successful or unsuccessful in changing their own behavior.* To achieve this aim, programs for abusive fathers must collaborate with other service providers to make decisions around men's acceptance into the program, to monitor fathers while they are in intervention, and to provide critical feedback after men's involvement.

First, decisions regarding whether to offer men service must be made with the needs of children in mind. Although, in most cases, service has the potential to benefit children, there are also cases in which providing intervention may be detrimental. For example, having a father involved in parenting program while a child protection worker is in the midst of arguing for the elimination of father-child contact may be unnecessarily confusing to children. Similarly, choices may need to be made during intervention about competing treatment goals or strategies to address family difficulties. For example, facilitators may offer guidance as to whether a particular father would best help his family by increasing his contributions to parenting decisions or by being more respectful and accepting of the decisions of his children's mother. Collaboration with those working toward children's safety is necessary when making these decisions so that children's needs may be a primary consideration.

Second, throughout fathers' involvement in intervention, group facilitators must be responsible for proactively monitoring men's risk for perpetrating abuse and for responding appropriately to any abusive behavior. In respect to men referred to a program like Caring Dads, there are almost always ongoing concerns about men's behavior and the safety and well-being of their family members. For example, there may be continued concerns that a father is using access transfers in order to verbally and emotionally harass his partner, or that a father is using illicit substances while caring for his children. Alternatively, referral agents may express concerns about especially severe punishments or extreme emotional uninvolvement. To appropriately protect children's safety and well-being, programs for fathers need to inquire about, address, and respond to concerns about ongoing abuse expressed by referral agents, men's partners, and women's and children's advocates. Moreover, group facilitators should be ready to challenge men's abusive behavior and to encourage nonabusive actions. For example, if a referral agent identifies transfers at access visits as problematic, facilitators of the group should be prepared to ask men about these transfers during intake and to address this issue during intervention. On a more general level, because these fathers have a history of engaging in controlling and abusive behavior, facilitators must be vigilant to changes in men's emotional states and behaviors across sessions and to the potential need for assessment and reporting of risk to children, children's mothers, and other members of men's families (Campbell, 1995).

A final way to ensure that men's participation in intervention has the potential to benefit children is to provide appropriate feedback about their progress to the larger system of professionals dealing with men's families. Ideally, men will make progress over intervention, stop their battering behavior, and become more nurturing fathers. However, when men's behavior continues to jeopardize the safety and well-being of their family members, even at the end of intervention, these concerns must be shared with referral agents and others planning for the needs of children. In extreme cases, the best outcome for a child following his or her father's involvement in an intervention may be that facilitators provide information to the referral agent that leads to further restrictions—or even to termination of father-child contact. To facilitate this goal of providing useful and responsible feedback to the larger system, program group leaders must provide clear and well-conceptualized reports to referral agents on men's progress through the program rather than mere certificates of completion. These reports should focus on direct observations of men's accountability, responsibility, attitudes, and reported behavior and should include concerns expressed by children's mothers about men's behaviors. Limitations of the report (i.e., that no direct observation of father-child interaction was done) and the importance of gathering collateral information also need to be emphasized. Although the process of writing detailed and evaluative reports is resource intensive, it is necessary to ensure the communication of adequate information to guide decision making that best meets the safety needs of children and women. Informative final reports also guard against the inappropriate use of program completion to argue for unrestricted access to children and mothers by men who have failed to make changes in their violent and abusive behaviors.

3. *Consideration should be given to whether and how children can access clear and developmentally appropriate answers about their fathers' involvement in intervention.* A final consideration for accountability to children concerns their knowledge and understanding of their fathers' involvement in intervention. Children who have been emotionally or physically abused often blame themselves for this abuse, and they may believe that their fathers are attending intervention "because of them." Fathers may inadvertently or deliberately support their children's self-blame by complaining about the inconvenience of the group or by directly telling children that their "bad behavior" resulted in fathers' mandatory attendance. Thus, programs providing intervention to maltreating fathers should consider whether to provide children with information that will highlight fathers' responsibility for violence and abuse and/

or counter children's self-blame. Providing this information to children is complicated by differences in their vulnerabilities and developmental stages. Issues for consideration include: differences in information appropriate for older versus younger children; provision of opportunities for children to share their experiences with professionals; coordination with service providers already involved with men's children; and avenues to facilitate referral of children to appropriate intervention services. The decision making of a particular community will depend on its resources. In a community with well-integrated child and family services and strong child and women's advocates, children will likely benefit from supportive and therapeutic sharing of information about their fathers' participation in intervention at multiple time points. In communities that can offer less support, involving children in discussions of their fathers' abuse may leave them feeling anxious and confused and possibly at increased risk of additional maltreatment.

Accountability to the Safety of Children's Mothers

Children's safety and well-being must be considered in the context of their families. Children are dependent on their parents, or parent figures, for the love and support necessary for healthy development and growth. Thus, accountable service to children requires intervening so as to hold men accountable for their violence toward both children and children's mothers and to strengthen the safety of the nonabusive adult victims in the family (NCJFCJ, 1999). A critical starting point is the recognition that when mothers are unsafe, children are also negatively affected. The following three guidelines were developed with this recognition at the forefront.

4. *Battering of children's mothers compromises children's needs for safety, well-being, and stability. As such, men's battering of children's mothers must be recognized and addressed as part of intervention for fathers.* Recognition of the interdependence of children's and mothers' safety needs is a critical component of programs for maltreating fathers. From the perspective of program content, battering of children's mothers must be identified as a possible form of child maltreatment by the men, and it must be directly addressed in intervention. Fathers should explicitly be taught how to be more supportive of their children's mothers and other important figures in children's lives (e.g., grandparents, teachers and neighbors). Rather than supporting men's assertions that their children's mother should behave in "more reasonable ways" or "be a better parent," fathers are encouraged to respect their partners' right to have parenting opinions that differ from their own and to focus on recognizing and supporting positive aspects of the mother-child relationship. Facilitators must send the message that men cannot be bad (i.e., battering) husbands and good fathers at the same time—that children's emotional security depends, in part, on a nonabusive relationship between their parents. Facilitators should also actively seek, monitor, and share with

referral agents any information about fathers' risk for battering the children's mothers.

This approach to men's relationships with their intimate partners is perhaps most challenging to maintain when fathers and mothers are both struggling to provide adequate parenting of their children. Although facilitators must remain vigilant to the possibility that men may fabricate or exaggerate difficulties of the mother, mothers too are sometimes poor caregivers for their children. In cases such as these, facilitators may have empathy for the challenges men face in providing adequate care to their children. Regardless, facilitators must remain firm about the need for men to avoid verbal, emotional, and physical abuse of any member of the family. In addition, facilitators can add clarity to these situations by labeling the other parent's difficulties as "adult problems" from which children should be protected as much as possible. For example, in a case where a father is parenting with a mother with a serious mental disorder, facilitators may need to help the father to avoid derogation of the parenting of the children's mother. At the same time, this father would likely need to be encouraged to take on more parenting responsibilities to ensure that the children's needs are being met (much like a mother parenting with a father who is often away or who is alcoholic).

5. *Outreach must be offered to provide women with information about the program and referrals to appropriate therapeutic or advocacy services.* Given the high rate of overlap of woman and child abuse, there is also a need to provide outreach to mothers of men's children. At a minimum, women who are parenting children with abusive fathers must be provided with information about the program, referrals to appropriate services, and, as required, safety planning. Such contact is necessary to address women's right to safety, children's need to be protected from witnessing men's abuse of their mothers, and the duty to ensure that fathers are not using their involvement in intervention as a justification for further abuse of women or children.

The practice of contacting children's mothers has been very controversial in some of the communities that offer the Caring Dads program. On one hand, fathers often respond to this policy with anger about a perceived double standard (given that information is not provided to them about mothers' involvement in intervention), frustration that the program is "checking up on them," and wariness that their partners will be considered more credible than themselves. Facilitators and program staff sometimes express trepidation over getting drawn into potentially hostile and prolonged battles for child custody and access, or they are concerned that men's participation in the program may be used to unfair advantage by a mother or father. On the other hand, women's advocates point out that children's mothers may have serious concerns about men's parenting that are not being heard or addressed by group facilitators. The varied living, custody and visitation, and parenting situations further complicate the situation, making the development of one-size-fits-all guidelines for contact with children's mothers very difficult (e.g., in a case where a father has sole custody and a mother has no regular contact with the child, the benefits of contacting children's mothers is not clear). Guidelines around the frequency and nature of contact with children's mothers that are responsive to these multiple concerns need to be driven by community consultation and collaboration. Whatever practice a particular community adopts, such decisions must be guided by recognition of women's and children's fundamental right to safety.

6. *Rather than focusing on coparenting, intervention should emphasize the need for men to be respectful and nonabusive of children's mothers and of the mother-child relationship.* Programs for fathers who have been abusive in their families need be aware of the fundamental problems of coparenting in the context of past and/or current abuse and violence. Over the past two decades, there has been a gradual increase in the number and range of interventions available for separated and divorced couples with continued difficulties resolving parenting conflicts. Such intervention approaches include mediation, court-appointed parenting coordinators, divorce-orientation and divorce-education programs, individual or conjoint therapy, and directed coparenting intervention (see Garber, 2004). As these new policies and practices have developed, there has also been recognition that, for a number of reasons, such programs are *not* generally appropriate in families where there has been significant domestic violence or child maltreatment (see Hart, 1990; Imbrogno & Imbrogno, 2000; Jaffe & Crooks, 2007; Maxwell, 1999; Newmark, Harrell, & Salem, 1995). First, equitable resolution of parenting difficulties is not possible in the context of fundamental power differences between men and their victimized partners. Second, working toward parenting consistency (which is the goal of most interventions) is not logical when one parent has attitudes and engages in behaviors that are conducive to child maltreatment. Finally, commonly available coparenting interventions do not adequately recognize or address the continued risk of subsequent abuse and violence against women and children.

Following from these arguments, programs for fathers who have been abusive in their families must recognize that coparenting interventions that encourage men to jointly resolve differences with their children's mothers are contraindicated. Instead, intervention needs to focus on the actions that fathers can take independently to establish more respectful and equitable relationships with their children's mother. Appropriate therapeutic strategies include challenging men's use of emotionally abusive and manipulative tactics against children's mothers; highlighting the negative impact of exposing children to continued hostility and abuse against their mothers; encouraging fathers to respect children's relationships with their mothers; and teaching men skills for supporting the mother-child relationship (e.g., listening to, and supporting, children when they talk about enjoyable mother-child activities). Only after fathers can maintain consistently nonabusive and respectful behavior toward their children's mothers should they be referred to more traditional coparenting interventions.

Responsibility to Fathers

It is essential that intervention with individuals who have maltreated their children or abused their children's mothers have victims' safety and well-being as the primary consideration for accountability. As part of this commitment, these programs need to work in coordination with social systems that can monitor men's behavior and provide sanctions for continued abuse. However, within this framework, intervention programs also need to maintain the fundamental commitments of clinical practice, such as respect, honesty, and compassion, to men in the program (Kelly & Wolfe, 2004). Such values reflect the belief that men *can* change their behavior and attitudes—and, thus, their relationships with their families. The following guidelines were developed in consideration of this responsibility.

7. *Programs for abusive fathers need to maintain respectful and transparent relationships with men.* Respect for clients is necessary for effective intervention in any program. Men referred to a program for abusive fathers typically begin intervention with anger and hostility toward "the system," their partners and children, and sometimes toward group facilitators. This presentation has implications for both program design and therapeutic strategy. Programs should anticipate that many fathers are likely to be reluctant participants, even if they have completed a batterer intervention or similar program. Thus, the initial goals should be to develop rapport and motivate men toward change. The use of motivational interviewing skills during the first few sessions facilitates men's commitment to the program and their motivation to change their parenting behavior (Burke, Arkowitz, & Mencholam, 2003; Crooks, et al., 2006; Miller & Rollnick, 2002). Facilitators must also be ready to support men in the small steps that they take toward healthier relationships with their children and adult partners or ex-partners and to have patience as men fluctuate in their readiness to change their behavior.

Respect for fathers also requires that there be open and honest communication between men and group leaders. Facilitators must clearly inform men about policies of interagency communication, limits of confidentiality, and conditions of their involvement. These policies should emphasize facilitators' commitment to provide men with clear and ongoing feedback about behaviors and attitudes that are of concern for child or partner well-being and safety. In addition, policies of interagency communication should commit group leaders to being open with men about their communication with referral agents and other professionals regarding men's progress through the program, except in cases where such communication would compromise child or adult-victim safety. For example, facilitators should discuss with men any information or concerns that they share with referral agents. Similarly, upon completion of group, facilitators should share their reports on men's progress. This level of openness with men, although time-consuming and difficult, provides an important model of respect for others, and it will likely enhance men's openness to change.

8. *Recognizing that any one program is often insufficient to meet all the needs of its clients, program facilitators should be ready to refer men to alternative or additional services.* Men who abuse their family members often have a variety of comorbid conditions such as substance dependence, depression, socioeconomic disadvantage, cognitive delays, and chronic health problems. These difficulties often contribute to ongoing difficulties that men have in negotiating the multiple systems in which they are involved (e.g., child protection, criminal justice) and in making changes during intervention. Men's problems may mean that they require additional, and potentially long-term, parenting support following the completion of an initial group program. Awareness of the many challenges that men may face allows facilitators to more realistically monitor their progress during group work and to determine appropriate referrals for additional service. It will also help facilitators intervene in ways that will promote men's insights into criminal justice or child welfare restrictions and help them to develop better strategies to work within these systems.

In considering issues around men's needs, it is important to recognize those services and supports that *should not* be provided as part of intervention for maltreating fathers—specifically, advocacy for individual fathers within systems concerned with children's best interests. For example, we would avoid writing letters to child protective services or fathers' lawyers arguing for increased father-child access or for changes in custody. Instead, information would be provided to a family or child case manager who can integrate the perspectives of all family members with a consideration of child needs at the forefront.

9. *Intervention programs for abusive fathers are responsible for being accessible to men of diverse cultures and individual circumstances.* Programs are also responsible for providing accessible service to fathers. There have now been a number of reports written on how to better engage fathers in child-protection and social-service interventions (e.g., National Family Preservation Network, 2001). Recommendations from these reports include: recruiting more male staff; providing training for staff on working with men; offering services at times convenient for men; ensuring that materials appeal to fathers; doing outreach; and developing collaborative relationships with men's programs. These recommendations should be implemented to the extent that resources allow.

A second important consideration is the program's accessibility for ethnically, linguistically, and culturally diverse populations. The use of a collaborative community-based model, which has been emphasized repeatedly in these guidelines, lends itself naturally to the needs of larger and more diverse populations. For example, if a program is offered within a particular cultural group, representatives of this group could join with other community agencies to make critical program decisions. This model empowers communities to address and meet their own unique needs. In cases where culturally specific services cannot be developed, intervention programs must be sensitive and responsive to cultural, linguistic, and ethnic differences. For example, education is needed so that facilitators can assess their own cultural competence, challenge their attitudes, and ameliorate knowledge deficits. Program materials need to be accessible, representative, and attractive to members of diverse communities, and efforts should be made to hire program staff who are representative of community diversity.

Third, programs targeting fathers who have maltreated their children or abused their children's mothers need to be understanding and flexible to a wide range of individual differences in men's nonabusive parenting models and in men's parenting circumstances. Men define fatherhood in many different ways, holding differing ideals about the nature of father-child and father-mother connections and appropriate father-child activities. Such ideals are individually and culturally constructed, so that among any one group of men, views may vary greatly. One of the goals of the Caring Dads program is to help men evaluate their model of fatherhood and ensure that it is respectful and nonabusive. To support men in this process, facilitators need to be aware of their own biases and to be willing to set these aside so that they can be as flexible as possible in helping men develop models of fatherhood that best suit the needs of their children and families. Being supportive of different fathering models may also require consideration of the direct and subtle messages sent by the program itself about men's responsibility for, and involvement in, their children's lives. For example, failing to provide childcare may send a subtle message that fathers should not have primary childcare responsibilities or should be easily able to find appropriate supervision for their children during group sessions.

Accountability to Communities

Finally, programs targeting fathers who have abused their children or their children's mothers must be accountable to the community. As identified in the National Council of Juvenile and Family Court Judges' comprehensive guide to community accountability, *Effective Intervention in Domestic Violence and Child Maltreatment Cases: Guidelines for Policy and Practice* (NCJFCJ, 1999), leadership is keenly needed in a number of areas. These include: developing protocols and policies for cross-agency communication and coordination; advocating with government for greater resources for services; partnering with justice services for appropriate follow-through for child safety; engaging diverse communities; developing prevention and early response initiatives; and building the capacity of staff to assess and respond to child maltreatment and woman battering. We support all of these recommendations; however, we also recognize that there are limits to what any one program or service can achieve. This section of the chapter highlights two aspects of community accountability that we found critical in the initial development and implementation of Caring Dads and that may inform other programs developing services for abusive fathers.

10. *Programs for fathers who are abusive or violent to their children or their children's mothers need to be offered with the guidance and support of a commu-*

nity advisory committee that includes representatives from agencies which provide services to children, women, and men. To ensure that programs are transparent and accountable to the community, it is critical that a community advisory committee oversees them. At a minimum, such a committee needs to include representatives of the various agencies that are stakeholders in the program, including child protection workers, battered women's advocates, probation and parole officers, and providers of men's, children's, and families' mental health services. This advisory committee provides guidance to the program, monitors adherence to the overall vision, and contributes to the identification and resolution of community-level and interagency-level issues that may arise in providing intervention. Finally, the committee can act as a catalyst for greater communication among agencies and for the development of interagency protocols that support coordinated intervention efforts with children, mothers, and fathers (NCJFCJ, 1999).

11. *Programs for abusive fathers should offer training and education to the community as necessary for accountable service.* In addition to training community members about appropriate referrals and the need for a collaborative approach to service, programs for abusive fathers are likely to encounter other training and educational needs (Kelly & Wolfe, 2004). These training and knowledge needs may be considered an *accountability* issue to the extent that gaps in knowledge interfere with the ability of the fathering program to offer services in a way that provides for the safety and well-being of children and children's mothers. For example, if referral agents are using reports from group facilitators about men's progress without independent corroboration of program observations, it may be necessary to educate case managers on the importance of determining if changes noted by group facilitators are being reflected in observations of men's behavior with, or attitudes toward, their children and children's mothers. Similarly, referral agents may need to be educated on how to more effectively engage men for the purpose of making referrals to the fathering program. Broader community training on issues around intervention for abusive fathers may also be warranted. For example, medical and social service agencies may benefit from educational seminars regarding early warning signs of fathers' abuse of their children or their children's mothers. Community partners may require education regarding common characteristics of abusive fathers, approaches by which the community may encourage fathers to be held accountable for their behavior, policy development, and important cautions and considerations when providing services to fathers and planning for child safety. This proactive approach to training and education enhances the probability that a program for abusive fathers will operate within current best practices of service.

12. *Programs for abusive fathers should engage in continued program evaluation.* Finally, as we have argued previously (Scott & Crooks, 2004), it is critical to engage in continued evaluation of programs for fathers who have been abusive towards their children or their children's mothers. Such research is particularly important in the context of the mixed empirical support for

batterer intervention programs (Babcock, Green, & Robie, 2004; Gondolf, 2004) and because without adequate levels of program accountability, men's participation in a fathering program could potentially have unintended negative effects on women and children (i.e., men having increased access without having changed their abusive fathering). It is notable that program evaluations typically measure change in program participants alone rather than in the broader system designed to ensure the safety of abused women and children. As discussed earlier, there are at least two pathways to greater safety and well-being of children. One is through men's change, whereby program participation is associated with reduced rates of father-perpetrated child maltreatment and with reductions in violence and hostility toward the children's mothers. The other pathway involves an appropriate system response to men's failure to change. Evaluation of the latter pathway involves consideration about whether feedback from a program for abusive fathers contributes to the system's responses to men in ways that are beneficial for children's safety and well-being. For example, programs might evaluate whether their report that a man dropped out or made little progress in a fathering program influenced decisions made by child-protection or probation professionals with respect to the father's access to his children. Research models thus need to recognize and evaluate the impact of the program on both men's behavior and on systemic responses to men's involvement in the program.

Conclusion

In recent years, there has been increased recognition that fathers need to be included in efforts to address co-occurring woman abuse and child maltreatment. Caring Dads is one program developed to better meet the safety and security needs of children and their mothers by providing intervention for fathers who have perpetrated violence in their families. Due to the importance of child and woman safety and the complexity of multisystem involvement, the delivery of a program like Caring Dads requires a high level of program accountability. In the preceding sections, we outlined a series of accountability policies to guide Caring Dads and other programs servicing fathers who have been abusive in their families. All guidelines were developed with consideration of the safety, security, and well-being of child and adult victims at the forefront, as well as respect for the unique and diverse needs of fathers and the communities in which these services are offered.

The accountability guidelines emphasize the need for enhancement and integration of resources for fathers and for members of their families. Fathering programs for perpetrators will benefit greatly from being provided within the context of a coordinated approach involving batterer interventions, child protection, battered women's advocacy, criminal justice, men's services, and mental health representatives. Development and follow-through on such partnerships are time-consuming, expensive, and sometimes difficult. However, such relationships can enhance men's attendance at programs and promote greater achievement toward the goal of making children's and their mothers' lives safer. It is our belief that without such coordination, consideration of children's and women's safety and well-being is too easily overlooked. Indeed, as highlighted by the National Council of Juvenile and Family Court Judges (1999), a lack of coordination in efforts to cease abusive behavior may *increase* risk to victims. Finally, such services must be accessible to all fathers, regardless of culture, language, or social situation and including those for whom woman-abuse is not a co-occurring concern. It is only with such comprehensive service that the needs of children and their mothers can be meaningfully addressed.

References

Babcock, J. C., Green, C. E., & Robie, C. (2004). Does batterers' treatment work? A meta-analytic review of domestic violence treatment. *Clinical Psychology Review, 23,* 1023–1053.

Burke, B. L., Arkowitz, H., & Mencholam, M. (2003). The efficacy of motivational interviewing: A meta-analysis of controlled trials. *Journal of Consulting and Clinical Psychology, 71,* 843–861.

Campbell, J. C. (1995). *Assessing dangerousness: Violence by sexual offenders, batterers, and child abusers.* Thousand Oaks, CA: Sage.

Crooks, C. V., Scott, K. L., Francis, K. J., Kelly, T., & Reid, M. (2006). Eliciting change in maltreating fathers: Goals, processes and desired outcomes. *Cognitive and Behavioral Practice, 13,* 71–81.

Duggan, A., Fuddy, L., McFarlane, E., Burrell, L., Windham, A., Higman, S., et al. (2004). Evaluating a statewide home visiting program to prevent child abuse in at-risk families of newborns: Fathers' participation and outcomes. *Child Maltreatment, 9,* 3–17.

Edleson, J. L. (1998). Responsible mothers and invisible men: Child protection in the case of adult domestic violence. *Journal of Interpersonal Violence, 13,* 294–298.

Edleson, J. L. (1999). The overlap between child maltreatment and woman battering. *Violence Against Women, 5,* 134–154.

Family Violence Prevention Fund. (2004). *Breaking the cycle: Fathering after violence: Curriculum guidelines and tools for batterer intervention programs.* San Francisco, CA: author.

Featherstone, B. (2001). Putting fathers on the child welfare agenda. *Child and Family Social Work, 6,* 179–186.

Garber, B. D. (2004). Directed co-parenting intervention: Conducting child-centered interventions in parallel with highly conflicted co-parents. *Professional Psychology: Research & Practice, 35,* 55–64.

Gondolf, E. (2004). Evaluating batterer counseling programs: A difficult task showing some effects. *Aggression and Violent Behavior, 9,* 605–631.

Green, S. (2003). Reaching out to fathers: An examination of staff efforts that lead to greater father involvement in early childhood programs. *Early Childhood Research and Practice: An Internet Journal on the Development, Care, and*

Education of Young Children, 5(2). Available at http://ecrp.uiuc.edu/v5n2/green.html. Retrieved May 19, 2006.

Hart, B. J. (1990). Gentle jeopardy: The further endangerment of battered women and children in custody mediation. *Mediation Quarterly, 7*(4), 317–330.

Imbrogno, A. R., & Imbrogno, S. (2000). Mediation in court cases of domestic violence. *Families in Society, 81,* 392–401.

Jaffe, P. G., & Crooks, C. V. (2007). Assessing the best interests of the child: Visitation and custody cases of domestic violence. In J. L. Edleson & O. J. Williams, *Parenting by Men Who Batter: New Directions for Assessment and Intervention* (pp. 45–64). New York: Oxford University Press.

Kelly, T., & Wolfe, D. (2004). Advancing change with maltreating fathers. *Clinical Psychology Science and Practice, 11,* 116–119.

Maxwell, J. P. (1999). Mandatory mediation of custody in the face of domestic violence: Suggestions for courts and mediators. *Family and Conciliation Courts Review, 37,* 335–355.

Miller, W. R., & Rollnick, S. (2002). *Motivational interviewing: Preparing people for change* (2nd ed.). New York: Guilford Press.

National Council of Juvenile and Family Court Judges. (1999). *Effective intervention in domestic violence and child maltreatment cases: Guidelines for policy and practice.* Reno, NV: author.

National Family Preservation Network. (2001). *An assessment of child welfare practices regarding fathers.* National Child Welfare Resource Center for Family-Centered Practice and The Annie E. Casey Foundation. Buhl, ID: author.

Newmark, L., Harrell, A., & Salem, P. (1995). Domestic violence and empowerment in custody and visitation cases. *Family and Conciliation Courts Review, 33*(1), 30–62.

Peled, E. (2000). Parenting by men who abuse women: Issues and dilemmas. *British Journal of Social Work, 30,* 25–36.

Radhakrishna, A., Bou-Saada, I., Hunter, W., Catellier, D., & Kotch, J. (2001). Are father surrogates a risk factor for child maltreatment? *Child Maltreatment, 6,* 281–289.

Scott, K., & Crooks, C. V. (2004). Effecting change in maltreating fathers: Critical principles for intervention planning. *Clinical Psychology Science and Practice, 11,* 95–111.

Scott, K., Francis, K. J., Crooks, C. V., & Kelly, T. (in press). *Caring dads: Helping fathers value their children.*

Scourfield, J. B. (2001). Constructing men in child protection work. *Men and Masculinities, 4,* 70–89.

Summers, J. A., Boller, K., & Raikes, H. (2004). Preferences and perceptions about getting support expressed by low-income fathers. *Fathering, 2,* 61–82.

Wolfe, D. A., Crooks, C. V., Lee, V., McIntyre-Smith, A., & Jaffe, P. G. (2003). The effects of children's exposure to domestic violence: A meta-analysis and critique. *Clinical Child and Family Psychology Review, 6,* 171–187.

Wolfe, D. A., Jaffe, P., Wilson, S., & Zak, L. (1985). Children of battered women: The relation of child behavior to family violence and maternal stress. *Journal of Consulting and Clinical Psychology, 53,* 657–665.

7

Working With Fathers in Batterer Intervention Programs

Lessons From the Fathering After Violence Initiative

Juan Carlos Areán
Lonna Davis

> *"I want him to support his daughter, no matter what."*
> *"[I want him to] spend quality time with my son."*
> *"It takes love to raise a man. You don't necessarily need a father."*

These are actual comments from survivors of domestic violence about their abusive partners or ex-partners. They were made during a series of focus groups conducted by the Family Violence Prevention Fund (FVPF) in November 2002 in Boston and San Francisco (Atchison, Autry, Davis, & Mitchell-Clark, 2003). Among the many valuable and courageous ideas that these women had to share was a strong message about their desire for fathers to be involved with their children, even if the fathers had used violence in the past. Some women, however, clearly articulated that men have to change and take responsibility for their abuse and that a man cannot be a good father if he is abusive or disrespectful to his partner or ex-partner. These findings are consistent with Tubbs and Williams's (2007) findings discussed earlier in this book.

This qualitative research was undertaken as part of the development of the FVPF's national violence-prevention campaign and has been central to informing initiatives such as Fathering After Violence (FAV), a project focused on both improving the parenting abilities of abusive fathers and using fatherhood as an engagement strategy to help men stop their violence. This article will focus on the work with fathers in the context of batterers' intervention; however, the FAV framework can be and has been used in other services, including supervised visitation, child-protection, and responsible fatherhood programs (see http://www.endabuse.org for more information).[1]

Overview of the Fathering After Violence Initiative

The goal of the Fathering After Violence initiative is to enhance the safety and well-being of women and children by motivating men to renounce their violence and become better fathers (or father figures) and more supportive parenting partners. Father figures include adoptive fathers, stepfathers, mothers' boyfriends, and even uncles, older brothers, and mentors. We believe that men who have used violence can be more respectful and supportive as parents and partners regardless of their level of access or type of custody.

FAV is not a program per se or a quick solution to a complex problem. Rather, it is a conceptual framework to help end violence against women by using fatherhood as a leading approach. Using this framework as a starting point, the FVPF, our partners, and other practitioners have developed culturally appropriate practical tools, prevention and intervention strategies, and policy and practice recommendations. FAV has proposed engaging abusive fathers by helping them develop empathy for their children and then using this empathy as a motivator to change their behavior. It is also exploring an assessment framework to help practitioners discern which fathers might be appropriate for repairing the relationships with their children.

Our intention has been to support and complement other innovative work happening around the country and the world in the fatherhood, child-abuse, and domestic violence fields by contributing a domestic violence prevention strategy that can be integrated by multiple disciplines in various settings; by proposing a culturally appropriate model to impress systememic change; and by playing a role in the larger movement to eradicate violence from our society.

In the first stage of the project, the FVPF partnered with a consortium of Boston-based providers to develop strategies and interventions to help fathers understand the impact of their behaviors on their children and on their relationships with their children. Our partners were the Dorchester Community Roundtable, the Child Witness to Violence Project at Boston Medical Center, and three batterer intervention programs: Common Purpose, EMERGE, and Roxbury Comprehensive Community Health Services. We decided to work with batterer intervention programs because their services target men who have used violence and also to work with a child witness to violence program because its primary clients are the children who have been hurt by that violence.

As with any intervention involving abusive men, their partners, and their children, we have been aware all along that there are risks in implementing this project. Since the onset of the initiative, we have repeatedly invited individuals to communicate their concerns. Predictably, the number-one consideration has involved safeguarding the physical and emotional integrity of the mother and the children. Other concerns have included the fear of the courts overestimating the man's ability to parent, the risk of encouraging men to have more contact or seek custody when it is not appropriate, and pushing fathers to make promises they cannot fulfill.

The FVPF's top priority is the safety of victims of family violence, and we believe that nonoffending mothers should be the gatekeepers for abusive men to have any access to their children. These ideas are similar to those discussed by Groves, Van Horn, and Lieberman (2007) earlier in this book. Court officers and domestic violence experts need to responsibly assess if contact is appropriate and under which circumstances it can be accomplished. We also know that many men who use violence continue to live with their families and have uninterrupted legal or illegal contact with their children, and we are also aware that fathers stay present in the lives of many children, even when those children never have formal contact. We are committed to finding new ways to keep men accountable and to invite them to change and repair the damage they have done.

In the beginning, the FAV initiative concentrated on gathering extensive information from focus groups and interviews with mothers who had experienced intimate-partner violence, fathers who had been abusive, and domestic-violence experts and service providers. Based on all of this information, we developed a series of exercises and policy and practice recommendations for batterer intervention programs.

Cultural Context

Introducing the topic of fathering in batterer intervention programs (BIPs) offers an invaluable opportunity to explore issues of culture and oppression among both the program staff and with group members. Traditionally, BIPs have avoided dealing with these issues due to an understandable fear of giving participants one more chance to justify or rationalize their abuse. However, the reluctance of BIPs to deal with these topics has decreased their credibility and effectiveness in communities of color. We cannot isolate one form of oppression (sexism and gender violence) and totally ignore others (racism, poverty, and so forth). A well-trained and knowledgeable facilitator should be able to invite men to talk about their own experience of oppression in the context of stopping their own violence.

It is essential to understand the cultural context in which fathering happens in communities of color. Racism and oppression are systematic ways in which to dehumanize certain populations. This dehumanization can take various forms; one is to deprive men of their ability to protect and provide for their families. This is most obvious in the cases of slavery and genocide, but it has been perpetuated in other forms of oppression, such as colonization, discrimination, marginalization, and poverty. These injustices have had and continue to have profound consequences on the fathering abilities and styles of men of color.

Batterer intervention programs have the responsibility to start understanding the role of culture in the treatment of abusive men. As Fleck-Henderson and Areán (2004) state in the FAV implementation guide:

> [if] culture and oppression are ignored, these elements will work against the intervention. [To] stop violence in a given cultural group, the intervention has to be based on values generated by that community, rather

than the dominant culture. If participants perceive that the intervention is being imposed from outside their cultural framework, they might interpret it as one more way in which the dominant culture is trying to oppress them by telling them what to do. We run the risk that they will see family violence prevention as a "white" issue and that we just want them to be more "white." BIPs have to make a concerted effort to create a context worthy of the participants' trust. This necessarily involves recognition of and respect for their cultures and the structural barriers they face in establishing a constructive family life. (p. 11)

Program Development

Based on the qualitative research conducted at the beginning of the FAV initiative, we developed a theoretical framework to conceptualize the process of healing between children and their fathers who had renounced violence. This model is a work-in-progress based primarily on in-depth interviews with six men who had stopped their violence and had started to heal their relationships with their children. After analyzing the information from the interviews, we discovered a series of similar actions taken by each of the men. These findings helped us conceptualize the steps needed to be taken in BIPs so as to begin supporting the healing process between men and the children in their lives. We named this the "Reparative Framework" and described the following actions in the initiative's implementation guide (Fleck-Henderson and Areán, 2004, pp. 22–23):

1. *Changing abusive behavior.* It is imperative that fathers stop all kinds of abuse immediately. This is one of the fundamental goals of batterer intervention and, of course, a prerequisite to starting any reparation.

2. *Modeling constructive behavior.* Children learn by example. Fathers need to know that as they stop modeling destructive behaviors, they have to make a concerted effort to model positive ones. A key teaching concept in this initiative is that a father cannot be a good model for his children if he is abusive, disrespectful, or hateful to their mother.

3. *Stopping denial, blaming, and justification.* Most batterer intervention works toward having men take full responsibility for their abusive behavior. In the context of this framework, programs need to teach fathers about the negative effects that denial, blaming, and justification can have on children.

4. *Accepting all consequences for one's behavior.* Violence-prevention activists often think of consequences primarily from the perspective of the criminal justice system. Fathers involved in a reparation process need to understand that facing the consequences of their behavior may also include accepting rejection and the loss of trust, love, and even contact with their children.

5. *Acknowledging damage.* It is important that fathers realize the amount of damage they have inflicted and let their children know that they understand specifically how they have hurt them.

6. *Supporting and respecting the mother's parenting.* Men who are abusive often continue to undermine the authority of the other parent. Fathers need to restore the sense of respect for the mother's authority and decision making and to fully support her parenting, especially if the father finds himself in a secondary parenting role.

7. *Listening and validating.* Fathers need to be prepared and willing to receive anger, hurt, sadness, fear, and rejection from their children. It is essential that they understand that this is part of the healing process and not a way for the children to manipulate the situation.

8. *Neither forcing the process nor trying to "turn the page."* Except for the actions that involve personal-change work, every action in this framework has to take place on the children's own terms and timing. Fathers have to learn how to be patient and to not try to push healing or contact with their children, and they should be open to talking about the past as many times as their children need to do it.

This framework was very valuable for the development of exercises to be integrated into batterer intervention programs. However, we were aware of the fact that the six men we interviewed did not necessarily represent typical participants of batterer intervention groups. For example, we knew for a fact (through partner contact) that they all had genuinely renounced all of their violence and that every one of them had voluntarily sought additional intervention beyond the basic batterer intervention group. Furthermore, to the best of our knowledge, none of the fathers had been sexually abusive with the children.

Clearly, men in batterer intervention groups are at different stages of change, and some, in fact, will not stop their abuse after intervention. We were careful about not encouraging contact between fathers and their children when it would not be legal or appropriate. In the implementation guide for using the exercises below, we emphasized that programs and facilitators must be aware at all times of the legal restrictions that each man in the program has and be very clear that it is never acceptable for a father to pursue contact with his children when there are orders of protection in place.

At this particular time, batterer intervention programs do not have the tools to assess and select the men who might be ready to start working on healing their relationships with their children. Moreover, even men who are committed to stopping their violence could at best take the first four or five actions during a standard period of group participation (such as the 40-week model in Massachusetts).

Taking all of this information into account, we designed the exercises below in such a way that they would not involve any direct actions between fathers and their children or encourage father contact when it is not desirable. Therefore, all batterer intervention program participants can benefit from these exercises, regardless of their level of involvement with their children. In fact, the exercises can be beneficial even for fathers who have no contact with their children. Men who are not fathers can participate as well.

Three Exercises for Use in Batterer Intervention Groups

In developing these exercises for batterer intervention programs, our main concern was to communicate that the reparative framework is difficult, painful, and very slow and that it has to happen on the children's own terms and timing. We also designed exercises that would increase the man's empathy for the children's experience, examine positive and negative modeling behaviors, and increase support for the children's mother.[2]

The Fathering After Violence exercises were developed in Spanish and English and piloted in six groups by the three Boston-area batterer-intervention programs. Two of the groups were primarily African American, one was for Spanish-speaking participants, one was predominantly European American, and two were racially mixed.

Our intention was to provide maximum flexibility of implementation. The exercises can be used in any batterer intervention program based on an educational or psychoeducational mode of intervention. They can be utilized as a group or individually, in sequence or interspersed with other lessons. Due to the advanced nature of the materials, we did make a strong recommendation that these exercises should not be implemented in the first few weeks of intervention. In Boston, they were all piloted in "second-stage" groups, after participants have had a minimum of eight sessions.

Empathy Exercise

The first exercise was designed to help participants see their abuse through their children's eyes and develop a better understanding of how children are affected by it. We called it the *Empathy Exercise.* The facilitators started the exercise by showing a series of five overheads with actual drawings made by children about their fathers. The drawings were created by schoolchildren in Mexico in response to the question, "How do I see my father?" They were compiled as part of a project by the staff of the Men's Collective for Equal Relationships (CORIAC) in Mexico City, which generously shared them with the FVPF for this initiative. The drawings eloquently and movingly depicted both positive and negative modeling by fathers. The negative drawings included pictures of fathers as a devil, a sinister figure overshadowing a devastated mother, and Dr. Jekyll and Mr. Hyde–like cartoons. The positive ones included one depicting a father as a superhero and another of a father helping his son climb the "mountain of life."

After having a group discussion about the drawings, the facilitators asked the participants to use paper and crayons and draw their own pictures depicting how they thought their children might see them as fathers, especially after witnessing an incident of violence. The exercise concluded with a discussion of the ways in which participants believed they might have hurt their children.

Modeling Exercise

The second exercise aimed to encourage participants to reflect on some of the positive and negative behaviors they learned from their own fathers or father figures and to examine the kind of model that they have been for their children. We called it the *Modeling Exercise.* On implementation, men were asked to write down both bad and good examples of behaviors they had witnessed from their fathers in modeling respect and disrespect to their fathers' partners or ex-partners.

After sharing their examples with other men, the participants were asked to repeat the exercise, but this time thinking about ways in which they have given bad and good examples to their own children in showing respect for their children's mothers. Then they proceeded to discuss whether they thought there was a connection between their behaviors and that of their fathers. The exercise closed with a homework assignment in which the men were asked to commit to choosing one act of respect toward the children's mothers that they would perform in the following four weeks so as to become a better model for their children. These actions were chosen with guidance from the facilitators to ensure that inappropriate contact was not encouraged under the guise of "respect." Furthermore, actions that did not involve any verbal or physical contact were discussed as options. Facilitators kept track of the actions each subsequent week as the men checked in to report on their progress.

Michael's Story Exercise

The third exercise was created to help men understand some aspects of the reparative framework between children and fathers who had renounced the use of violence. For this exercise, we produced an audio recording relating the story of a real man (whom we called Michael or Miguel) whom we had previously interviewed for the project. In the first part of the recording, Michael told about his growing up with an abusive father and not being able to ever heal the relationship because of the father's denial and continued abusive behavior. In the second part, Michael talks about his own abusive behavior, his struggle to overcome it, and the difficult journey toward repairing his relationship with his own children.

The exercise opened with the playing of the first part of the story, followed by the group brainstorming about what Michael's father had done wrong and about what he could have done better. The facilitators emphasized key points about the reparative framework, including the following:

- In order to start healing a relationship, the offender has to stop the abuse and begin modeling positive behaviors.
- Denial and minimization can be very damaging to children.
- Taking responsibility for one's behavior means more than doing time in jail or being on probation. Men have to accept all the consequences of their violence in front of their families and communities. Accountability includes recognizing that their relationships with the children might be damaged beyond repair.

The exercise ended by playing the second part of Michael's story, in which he talks about his struggles and successes in healing his relationship with his children. A facilitated discussion followed, concentrating on the following ideas:

- Healing the relationship between an abusive parent and his children is a very slow and difficult process.
- The process has to take place on the children's terms and timing. The offender should not and cannot force the pace of the process.
- Victims and witnesses of family violence need to be listened to and validated for a long period of time, often over many years. The offender should not attempt to "turn the page."

Staff Training

A fundamental element for the successful implementation of the exercises was comprehensive training for batterer intervention program staff. The training was an opportunity to invite all staff (not only group facilitators) to discuss the program's intent and limitations. It also allowed staff to express their apprehensions, hopes, and ideas about the subject matter, to understand the theoretical framework and rationale behind each exercise, and to explore the cultural context in which fathering takes place.

Key training activities included an overview of the initiative and brainstorming potential benefits and challenges, an exercise to help staff understand the cultural context of fathering, a detailed presentation of the reparative framework, and a comprehensive review of each exercise. Because of unplanned circumstances, the staff of the three batterer intervention programs received different amounts of training prior to implementing the exercises. After reviewing the evaluation data, it became clear that the sites that received more training were more successful in achieving the exercises' goals.

Examining the Impact

The evaluation component of the FAV initiative was conducted in partnership with the Dorchester Community Roundtable and Dr. Ann Fleck-Henderson and her colleagues from the Simmons College School of Social Work in

Boston, Massachusetts (Fleck-Henderson, 2004). The evaluators employed multiple methods of data collection to explore the impact of the program. The 60 participants of the project completed evaluation forms after each group session. In-depth interviews were conducted with three men and their partners (separately), one pair from each participating program. Short questionnaires were also used to document the reactions of women whose partners went through this curriculum. (The project required that attempts be made to contact each female partner in order to inform her about the new curriculum and learn how she felt about the increased attention to fatherhood.) The questionnaire probed the woman's reactions to the curriculum, made inquiry into the nature of the relationship between the man and her children, and informed her of local resources for herself and/or her children. Lastly, a debriefing session was held with the group facilitators to hear their experiences after the implementation period was completed.

Overall, the evaluation yielded positive results from the standpoint of batterer intervention group facilitators. The staff consistently reported positive experiences with the project and increased engagement with the men. The facilitators' feedback on the exercises was invaluable, allowing us to modify the training and curriculum to be more user-friendly.

Feedback from the men revealed a range of responses. While some men clearly demonstrated a better understanding of the effects of violence on children and an increased sense of realism respective to their relationships with their children, others remained unable to see a problem and/or demonstrated a significant lack of comprehension of what it takes to build or rebuild relationships with their children after violence.

Data collected on the empathy and modeling exercises suggested a continuum of fathers' acceptance of responsibility for hurting their children and their role in correcting the harm. While some men referred to the need to change their own behavior, other men seemed to refer to the negative effects of "fighting" without mention of their own role. For example, in the postimplementation evaluation forms for the empathy exercise, when group members were asked whether the exercise had changed their view of how a child might feel about an abusive father, 38 out of 52 responded affirmatively.

For the *Michael's Story Exercise,* increased knowledge of the reparative framework was evident only in a minority of the responses from men; however, it appears that other important lessons were learned about the effects of violence on children, particularly the intergenerational transmission of family violence, the need to change, and the value of seeking help. In the postevaluation questionnaire, 38 out of 51 men disagreed with the following statement: "If you really try, the other person should be able to regain trust quickly." On the other hand, 31 participants agreed with the erroneous concept that there are always two sides in a violent conflict, so both people should apologize equally.

The participants' feedback on the exercises in the pilot project gave us some important data to understand some of the differences among men who use violence. The majority of the men were most affected by the "feelings" children had and were least influenced by the "acts of violence" the children saw. Many of the men's comments also indicated some resistance to acknowledging the pain illustrated in the children's pictures, even when their comments indicated increased empathy for children.

The evaluation gave program facilitators valuable information about the participants' relationships with their children which they did not have beforehand. In addition, the men's responses to the exercises and questionnaires helped programs assess the participants' level of empathy toward their children and their willingness to take responsibility for their abusive behavior.

Finally, although efforts were made to reach every partner of the men in the groups, only about one half were contacted successfully. Of those contacted, the reaction to including child-focused exercises in men's groups was unanimously positive.

Conclusion: Lessons Learned

From our experiences working with the batterer intervention programs, we offer the following policy and practice recommendations.

Mothers Who Have Experienced Violence Want More Programming About Parenting for Their Children's Fathers

Both in the FAV implementation and in focus groups (Atchison, et al., 2003; Williams & Tubbs, 2005, Tubbs & Williams, 2007), mothers who have experienced abuse consistently stated that batterer intervention programs should give more attention to issues of fathering. Although women want increased programming in this area, the extent to which they want it still remains unclear. Many women reported that their partners' or ex-partners' relationships with the children was adequate or good; so why, we might ask, the unanimous support for more help? More conversations and research need to be conducted with mothers who have survived abuse to understand how they define "good-enough" parenting from their partners or ex-partners. Program development and policy changes must always be informed by women's and children's experiences. When doing new research with survivors, information should be gathered about whether they stayed with the abusers and, if not, about how much time had passed since they left the abusive relationships.

Batterer Intervention Programs Should Pay More Systematic Attention to the Issue of Fatherhood

Programs for abusive men have a unique opportunity to incorporate universal messages about positive fathering into their sessions. Understanding the effects of violence on children seems to motivate some fathers to stop their abuse. Furthermore, children need to be seen not as "collateral" recipients of damage from the abusers but as direct survivors of violence, even if they did not experience it firsthand.

More Tools Need to Be Developed to Help Programs Deal With the Issue of Fatherhood

Programs need to seek additional financial and educational resources to help participants deal with their parenting. Program staff require ongoing training on the issue, and specialized, culturally relevant curricula need to be developed.

Men Need Concrete Help to Understand What They Have Done to Their Children and, if Indicated, How to Reverse the Long-Term Effects on Their Relationships

Teaching violent men about the effects of domestic violence on children is a beginning, but it is not enough. Programs need to go deeper when addressing the topic of fatherhood. Additionally, a cultural context for fatherhood must be included in the discussions.

Men Must Be Monitored to Make Sure That a New Attention to Fathering Does Not Create Unintended Consequences for Women and Children

Programs need to understand the impact of new work in this area and consider it as a learning process and not just as a new curriculum to be added. Programs need to ensure that the courts and other providers who work with other members of the family or the family together (as in the case of a visitation program) understand the work being done and its limitations.

As Men's Programs Increase Attention on Children and Fatherhood, There Must Be Deliberate Attention to the Child's Well-Being

Many children whose fathers are in batterer intervention programs are not receiving any formal services. Although it is not always necessary for all children to receive services, programs should know who is attending to the child's well-being (the mother, another caregiver, or a program) and develop mechanisms for communication, referrals, and coordination.

Service Coordination Is Needed Between All Programs That Work With Members of a Family That Has Experienced Domestic Violence

When multiple services are involved for the same or different family members, providers should be talking to each other to ensure a consistent message about parenting in the context of violence and to follow up with any concerns or progress.

The Reparative Framework Between Men and the Children in Their Lives Is Long, Painful, and Complex

It is clear from our research that the reparative framework is a long-term and involved project, and it varies according to the circumstances of each man and his children. Very few men will be able to take more than the first few steps during their first year of batterer intervention. Programs should consider expanding their services to include aftercare and follow-up groups where men could focus their attention on concretely repairing their relationships with children and on issues of coparenting (when appropriate). Since follow-up interventions are not usually court mandated, programs will need to develop new strategies to engage fathers on a voluntary basis, using as a model the few programs that have been successful at doing so.

The Reparative Framework Is Not Appropriate for All Fathers

A percentage of men do not stop their violence after attending a batterer intervention group (the actual number is the subject of great and ongoing debate). Fathers who are actively violent should not be encouraged to pursue this work. Accurate assessment tools need to be developed that include the mother's knowledge and experience and the court's recommendations so that providers can determine if particular men should embark in reparative work with their children. Obviously, if a father has been physically or sexually abusive with his children, the reparative framework becomes much more complicated.

Further Evaluation and Research Are Greatly Needed in the Area of Fathering After Violence

Research is needed to understand why mothers who have experienced violence desire increased help for their children's fathers. Studies must address which fathers are more likely to benefit from such programming and what curricula and services would most help them achieve positive results with their children. Additionally, research should focus on the impact of new programming on children.

All Parenting and Fathering Programs That Work With Violent Men Need to Ensure That Men Are Working on Stopping Their Violence Through Appropriate Programs for Extended Periods of Time

Men who are not working toward stopping abuse of their children's mothers should not be encouraged to repair any relationship with their children. Men need to understand the full impact of their violence toward their children's mother before they can adequately begin to understand what their children have suffered and what will be required in terms of healing.

Taking the first steps to develop a coordinated response to improve the fathering of men who have been abusive has proved both challenging and rewarding. The reparative framework is more complex than we ever imagined, and yet our conviction that it is possible to heal the relationships between some fathers who have previously used violence and their children has grown as the initiative has developed. If we want to end family violence, it is imperative that we simultaneously attend to intervention, accountability, safety, and healing.

Note

1. FAV was launched in 2002 with the generous support of the Doris Duke Charitable Foundation

2. To download a free copy of the implementation and training guide *Breaking the Cycle: Fathering After Violence. Curriculum Guidelines and Tools for Batterer Intervention Programs,* please visit http://endabuse.org/programs/display.php3?DocID=342

References

Atchison, G., Autry, A., Davis, L., & Mitchell-Clark, K. (2003). *Conversations with women of color who have experienced domestic violence regarding working with men to end violence.* San Francisco, CA: Family Violence Prevention Fund.

Fleck-Henderson, A. (2004). *The fathering after violence evaluation report.* San Francisco, CA: Family Violence Prevention Fund.

Fleck-Henderson, A., & Areán, J. C. (2004). *Breaking the cycle: Fathering after violence. Curriculum guidelines and tools for batterer intervention programs.* San Francisco, CA: Family Violence Prevention Fund.

McAlister Groves, B., Van Horn, P., and Lieberman, A. F. (2007). Deciding on fathers' involvement in their children's treatment aftr domiestic violence. In J. L. Edleson & O. J. Williams, Eds., *Parenting by men who batter: New directions for assessment and invervention* (pp. 65–84). New York: Oxford University Press.

Tubbs, C. Y. , and Williams,O. J. (2007). Shared parenting afer abuse: Battered mothers' perspectives on parenting after dissolution of a relationship. In J. L. Edleson & O. J. Williams (Eds.), *Parenting by men who batter: New directions for assessment and invervention* (pp. 19–44). New York: Oxford University Press.

Williams, O., and Tubbs, C. (2005). Co-parenting concerns of African American women. In Dabby, C. & Autry, A. (Eds.), *Activists dialogues* (pp. 28–29). San Francisco, CA: Family Violence Prevention Fund.

8

Latino Fathers in Recovery

Ricardo Carrillo
Jerry Tello

I came to "The Circle" to find my father. As a child, I remember seeing him, dark skinned, black curly hair, mole on the right upper lip, bedroom eyes, and a lean muscular body. He worked the mines as a boy, learned to drink and romance women. He romanced my mother into marrying him. I don't remember ever having an intimate time with him, an elder's lesson, a *consejo*, or a warm memory. My father was fire that was ignited with firewater. He drank, used drugs, and caused pain and havoc to my mother and our household. I remember being in my bed and listening to my father yell and my mother scream as he broke her bones. The sounds were so pervasive that they literally went through my body.

My father was murdered over a drug deal. I listened as he burned to death in our Mission District flat in San Francisco. When he died my mother said, "You're the man of the house now, *mijo* [my son]." I proceeded to help raise my brother and sisters, with no training or role modeling. There was no one around that could teach me how to be a father. When I started to have children myself, I was terrified of creating the same havoc on them that had been committed to me. I learned to use narcotics to dull the fear, pain, confusion, and terror that I felt inside.

One day, my son, Naldo, and I were listening to the Stylistics sing "Have You Seen Her." Naldo said, "Dad, that's a sad song, huh?" "Yes, it can be," I responded. "Well," Naldo said, "Mary is my girlfriend, and we are going to get married." He was all of six years old. I was shocked and speechless. What moved me was the fact that he and I were having a conversation that I had never had with my own father. Years later, after Naldo's mother and I divorced, he came to live with me. He had changed. He was moody, sullen, depressed, hostile, and withdrawn. We were not speaking. He was failing all of his classes at school, had very few friends that were also failing at that time. I asked him, after repeated attempts to talk to him, "What happened? What happened to the way we used to be? What did you do with the little boy who used to talk to me, who used to share with me?" Naldo replied, "He left when you did."

I came to the *Circulo* to learn how to be a father. In turn, I learned how to be a man, a son, a husband, an *hombre con palabra* [a man of my word]. I brought the *cargas* [baggage] from my trauma-filled past and left it in the fire of the altar, the sacred place of order, to become free of them. In my father's absence, his horrible death, the loneliness of carrying that baggage alone, the fear of never succeeding, the overcompensation by attaining a graduate degree, and never being satisfied. In the Circulo, I learned to have a place, just because I am human. I learned to love and be loved by men who also shared the same cargas and, in that journey, learned that we all have *regalos* [gifts] to share. I learned that I was someone: I had the medicine. All of the pain and suffering had a purpose. That purpose was to help other men heal. I brought Naldo to the Circulo, and we healed together. We cried, laughed, shared, and asked for permission to love each other openly, truly, and without reservation. We learned that these ways have always been here. We are on a path of rediscovery.

Naldo graduated from high school in 2000. He is an accomplished Mexican folklore dancer, an uncle, and my best friend. Most importantly, he is a balanced and loving young man who does not carry his father's cargas. I am grateful for that.

We men gathered together in *El Circulo* (The Circle) to deal with pain, confusion, and our relationships with our children, our spouses, our addictions, our loss of fathers, our loss of country and culture, and to pray for direction. In the tradition of our indigenous culture, we began by praying to the four directions: to honor our ancestors; to honor the women who are the heart, the givers of life, and the first warriors; to honor the children and their laughter and innocence, who are the ones who will carry our baggage if we do not heal; and to honor ourselves. A song is then offered (*El Amor de Este Hijo,* "The Love of This Son") in gratitude. With this, *El Circulo* begins. This ceremony of gathering in circles to heal, strengthen, teach/learn, and refocus is an ancient way of our ancestors which we have reintegrated into our lives to help Latino fathers in recovery.

The *coyote spirit,* or negative influences and behaviors, remains a constant threat to individuals, families, and communities. The coyote spirit is the trickster element in each one of us that can pull us out of balance and thus harm ourselves and our relationships. It can also include addictive behaviors such as dependence on alcohol, jealousy, or infidelity as defenses against not facing one's cargas (baggage issues). This is the curative aspect of naming the coyote spirit for what it is, a reflection of unbalance. It was in this *Circulo Way* that guidance and healing took place and where reprimands were shared, the first priority always being the respect and safety of everyone, but especially the women and children. In the Circulo Way, we passed the *palabra* (the word), recognizing that everyone has a voice and that everyone has a story.

El Amor de Este Hijo ("The Love of This Son")

El Amor de Este Hijo	The Love of this Son
A mis padres les quiero decir	To my parents I want to say
Que muchisimo los quiero,	That I love them tremendously,
Que no se paga con dinero	That I cannot repay with money
Lo que hicieron por mi.	What you have done for me.
Los amo por la enternidad,	I love you for eternity,
Estare simpre agradecido	I will always be grateful
Por lo que han sufrido	For all you have suffered
Por darme la vida.	To give me life.
Simpre tendran	You will always have
El amor de este hijo,	The love of this son,
El amor que hicieron	The love that you made
Fue amor de verdad.	Was true love.

A popular Tex-Mex song recorded by Jimmy Edwards and the Latin Breed. Translation by the author.

The essential lessons or rooted principals of childhood are traditionally called *La Educacion* (the development of the spirit or character of a person). Our ancestors realized the importance of this foundation to the extent that volumes were written on these teachings. These teachings were called the *Hue Hues* (Teachings of the Elders). At their core are the dual teachings of *Itxtl* and *Yollotl,* in Spanish translated as *Cara y Corazon* (Face and Heart). The *Cara* carried the dual values of *Dignidad y Respeto* (Dignity and Respect), and the *Corazon* carried the values of *Cariño y Confianza* (Love and Interconnected Compassion or Trust). What is not understood is that in order to be a good father, you must first be a responsible man. We attempt to reroot men in these principles, thus allowing them to discover the true essence of *Machismo* (Honorable Manhood). With this as a basis, we are then ready to recover the fatherhood skills that we never experienced from our fathers and are now ready to learn to be an honorable father as well.

We employ a four-stage process for healing and development that seeks to reroot the men in these teachings.

- *Conocimiento,* Acknowledgment (*Dignidad,* Dignity)
- *Entendimento,* Understanding (*Respeto,* Respect)
- *Integracion,* Integration (*Confianza,* Trust)
- *Movimento,* Movement (*Cariño,* Love)

In the first phase of recovery, *Conocimiento,* it is important to acknowledge the men by honoring their spirit, respecting their lessons, and embracing both the gifts and baggage that they bring. We begin this process by giving a man his voice to tell his story. He is able to see (or face) himself—maybe for the first time. Telling his story serves as a way to allow other men in *El Circulo* to see their own reflections as well. More importantly, men are given a *lugar* (place) as a man and/or father (Dignity). The men who find their positive purpose and dignity are able to treat their children and relations positively and with dignity.

As we enter the second phase, *Entendimiento,* men's understanding of the role that multigenerational oppression has played in their lives becomes evident. The understanding that the burdens that they carry are generations old brings much insight and a sense of respect for their issues. It also points to the negative result of not finding a positive way to face life's cargas, or baggage/challenges. As a result, many times, the men in these groups have a distorted view of men and authority. In their view, fatherhood is perceived as being the authority over decision making and, many times, as using violence and force to discipline or oppress others. Teaching men to separate authority from effective administration of family affairs is a major task of any fatherhood education for this population. This phase also includes having fathers understand their journey in learning the false values of manhood and fatherhood and relearning relationship-enhancing values of sacred relationships that come from their culture. Pre-Colombian texts document a different understanding of how fathers and mothers should raise their children and are excellent examples of behavioral administration with clarity about the values of a society (see Leon-Portillo, 1988). In this phase, men also learn about child and life development, which gives them insight into what they did and did not receive in their own childhood and includes instruction in the role of the father in the child's development, guidance, direction, discipline, love, and care.

As we move to the third phase of Fathers in Recovery, *Integracion,* fathers are guided through a process of integrating these teachings into their lives with a sense of *Cara y Corazon* (Face and Heart). This concept of Face and Heart was the basis for healthy child development in some traditional societies. Parents were expected to participate in their child's development with an understanding of *Cara Noble* (Noble Face) and *Corazon Firme* (Firm Heart). One was an honorable parent if he or she demonstrated the values of *Cara y Corazon.* Cara reflected respect and dignity for all life and relationships. Corazon was the summary of *Cariño* (Warmth) and *Confianza* (Trustworthiness). If children demonstrated these values, they were acknowledged as *Bien Educados* (Well-mannered), and the parents congratulated them on their achievements.

The teachings of Cara y Corazon change with each developmental phase, and Jerry Tello and his colleagues use four seasons and four directions to delineate a lifespan framework for parents to use in raising their children. The *Destino* (Destiny) of fathers is likely to change with each stage of development. As they explore how to reintegrate themselves into their children's lives, fathers can begin to learn to rebuild the spirit of trust within them. They learn, maybe for the first time, to rely on others for guidance and advice, which points to the importance of listening to other men who have been through this journey successfully. Through this process, they may begin to learn how to develop a healthy relationship based on trust between their children and themselves.

The final phase is *Movimiento* (Movement), and it provides a structure and process for men to establish an ongoing extended kinship network— *Circulo de Hombres*—with other men who have chosen to rededicate their lives to their children. Men with histories of violence require experiences that allow them to demonstrate *Confianza* (Trustworthiness), and they also need a support system that helps them to maintain accountability. Men learn to give their word and follow through. For men who have multigenerational wounds, the challenge of maintaining this commitment in the midst of ongoing challenges and tests is difficult. For this reason, Circulo de Hombres becomes a way for men to maintain this commitment. Finally, through these Circulos, men begin to form friendships with other men who are also devoted to their children.

Conclusion

Recovering fathers need programs and service providers to advocate for them. For men who are committed and have demonstrated their motivation to be good fathers, it is imperative that programs be prepared and willing to assist fathers to deal with the societal and systemic barriers that present themselves. For the most part, the policies and programs of the United States have not been developed with the Latino population in mind. For families that rely on government programs, it has created a dilemma as families attempt to maintain their cultural identity while complying with the system's requirements. The voices of Latino fathers indicate that many public-welfare program requirements are at best confusing to them. In many cases, these programs create additional barriers to the fulfillment of Latino men's fatherhood responsibilities. For programs to fully understand essential values of the Latino population, it is imperative to explore the issues of cultural identity, language, the extended family system, immigration, the work ethic, self-sufficiency, and internalized oppression that impact the involvement of Latino fathers in their recovery process and their involvement with their children. Yet many of the strengths of the Latino family that assist in its survival are found within their primary cultural ties (*La Cultura Cura* [Culture Cures]). Thus, finding a balance between the dual expectations of culture and society is a major challenge for Latino fathers.

Storytelling in the *Circulo Way* has proven to a very effective approach to helping men develop a new legacy for themselves. The elders say that what we do today has an impact for seven generations. But we must first see a father to be as sacred as other human beings if we are to expect him to treat his relations that way. We must also start where fathers are developmentally. A good example of this is when we had an author sign free books for a group of fathers. As the author finished dedicating a book to one father's children, the next father stepped up. He was asked to whom he wanted the book dedicated. The father was quiet, and the author asked the names of his children. Then the father leaned over and whispered in the author's ear, "Dedicate the book to me, Antonio, because I've never had a book of my own." This experience highlights the importance of allowing a father to tell his story and give him a place to hear other men's stories before we ask him to be a father and read or tell stories to his own children. We are all on this road to healing and recovery, and in the end, we must be thankful for still being a part of the journey.

> As men prepare themselves to close the circle, we once again pray to the four directions. To give thanks to the Ancestors; *Los Hue Hues*, the Elders, we pray in the direction of the North to give us wisdom as we try to maintain the balance, rhythm, and harmony in our lives. In the direction of the West, we give thanks for and to the women who are the heart and the givers of life and to whom we give our *Palabra* to not bring harm to them again. To the East, we pray for ourselves, the men of the *Circulo*, to be able to continue to show up and support one another in an open, honest, and humble way so that we may find our true "Song" once again. To the South, we make a promise to the children to work on our baggage so that their laughter, innocence, and learning can continue. And finally, to the above and below and the center, where all relations come together, we offer prayers to all our relations, for people of all roots, so that they too may find balance, rhythm, and harmony in their lives. Aho!

Reference

Leon-Portillo, M. (1988) *HueHuetlahtolli: Testimonios de la Antigua Palabra.* Mexico City, Mexico: Comisión Nacional Conmemorativa del Centenario de do Mundos.

9

Evaluating Parenting Programs for Men Who Batter

Current Considerations and Controversies

Cris M. Sullivan

With the emergence of parenting programs for batterers comes a corresponding need for the thoughtful evaluation of such efforts. The desire to know whether these programs make a difference for families is coupled with an equally genuine concern that resources not be expended on programs that do not work. There never seems to be adequate funding for the numerous and varied programs being developed for victims as well as for perpetrators of intimate-partner abuse, and increasingly, funding decisions are being based on empirical evidence that programs are worthwhile. In light of this, it is not too early to consider how to evaluate the effectiveness of parenting programs for batterers.

At the same time, given that we are still in the very early stages of developing such programs, it is equally (if not more) important to engage in formative and process evaluations of the various parenting programs in existence. Specifically, we need to systematically examine how such programs develop across different communities, what philosophical principles guide their curricula, how participants are accepted into the program, what the program staff have determined to be desirable and realistic outcomes of the program, what specifically they are doing to attain those outcomes, and what benchmarks they are using to determine success. This will require taking a more qualitative, phenomenological approach to program evaluation. Not all programs will be guided by similar philosophies or structures, and there may not be one "gold standard" on which all programs will model themselves. Rather, it may well be that some programs will work for some men better than for others and that having multiple curricula to choose from will be beneficial to communities.

This chapter, then, is neither going to argue for one set of outcomes that all programs should accept, nor for designing evaluations that will determine one gold standard. We might or might not be ready for that in a few years, after significant program development and critical thinking have occurred across various communities (similar to the trajectory of batterer intervention program-evaluation efforts). At this point in time, however, I would suggest that we need to begin thinking about and debating the larger issues that will influence our choice of outcomes and guide our program-evaluation efforts. For example, *Why exactly are we creating these programs?* Is it to improve parenting, to increase men's access to their children, to increase men's empathy toward the woman they have been battering, to decrease their abuse, to accomplish a combination of these, or to do something else entirely? It is critical that programs be upfront and clear about their own philosophies and expectations, so that families can make informed choices about participating and so that survivors and their children can understand what they might expect (and not expect) from the abuser and program staff over time. A program with the explicit intention of increasing the access of the batterer to his children, for example, might raise red flags for survivors and domestic violence victim service programs. Such a program might be more invested in the batterer's needs and desires than in the safety and desires of the children and their mother. Similarly, a program whose intention is to improve the relationship between a father and his child (or children) would also raise some concerns. A relationship, by definition, involves more than one person. What about the rights of children who choose not to improve their relationships with their fathers? Where is their autonomy and power in this process? Another problematic example would be the program whose intended outcomes include *less* violence or *more* attentiveness to the children. How would such *improvement* be measured, and is *less* violence an appropriate outcome? Some might argue that *any* violence is unacceptable and indicates poor parenting. Similarly, *more* attentiveness is not always a good thing if such attention is controlling or manipulative. These are just a few examples of why a great deal of thought needs to go into determining the desired outcomes of these parenting programs and why mission statements and philosophies should be clearly visible within the community.

What Should a Parenting Program Accomplish?

Outcomes need to be measurable and directly tied to program activities. So what can one reasonably expect a parenting program for batterers to accomplish? Given that most programs involve one to two hours per week for a specific, and generally short, period of time, it is important not to have a too grandiose set of expectations. At the same time, the program needs to result in some significant change for it to be worthwhile. While I am not going to argue for one outcome, one measure, or one evaluation strategy that all programs should claim for their own, I present what I believe to be important guidelines for outcome development, based on limited empirical evidence to date and current promising clinical practice. Based on the assessment of numerous experts in the field (e.g., Bancroft, 2002; Bancroft & Silverman, 2002; Carrillo & Tello, 1998; Eriksson & Hester, 2001; Jaffe & Geffner, 1998; Pence & Paymar, 1993), many batterers are not just abusive to their partners but to their children as well. And any abusive behavior, regardless of toward whom it is directed, may negatively impact children in multiple ways. Given that, one focus of parenting programs should be to educate batterers that (1) family abuse in any form is unacceptable, (2) their behavior is and will be tied to their access to their children, and (3) they are responsible for all behavioral choices they make. Bancroft and Silverman (2002, pp. 180–183) have identified 12 elements (or steps, although they stress that these should not be confused with the notion of 12 steps used in recovery programs) that they believe batterers must embrace before they can be considered to be safe and responsible fathers. I present and briefly elaborate on them below:

1. *A man who batters must disclose fully the history of physical and psychological abuse toward his partner and children.* If a man who batters completes a parenting program but still refuses to admit the full extent of his prior violence and abuse, is there reason to expect that he will cease it in the future? Program staff should be greatly concerned about any batterer who continues to deny or minimize his abusive history.

2. *A man who batters must recognize that his behavior is unacceptable.* Does he still make excuses? Does he rationalize his battering behavior? This too is a sign that his abuse may continue.

3. *The man who batters must recognize that his behavior was chosen.* Once he acknowledges that all behavior is a choice, has he admitted responsibility for making different choices in the future?

4. *The man who batters must recognize and show empathy for the effects of his actions on his partner and children.* One of the reasons I have heard given for creating parenting programs for batterers is that many men who batter have an easier time empathizing with their children than with their children's mothers. Therefore, an expectation of such programs is that the batterer will increase his empathy toward his children. I would argue that this is not enough; rather, he must also show empathy for the children's mother if it is expected that he will cease his battering of her (including undermining her parenting).

5. *The man who batters must identify his pattern of controlling behaviors and entitled attitudes.* It is not enough for a man who batters to state that he understands that he has been abusive in the past. He should be able to articulate exactly *how* he has been controlling, manipulative, and deliberately hurtful in order to develop a plan for choosing not to do such things in the future.

6. *The man who batters must develop respectful behaviors and attitudes.* It is not enough for the man who batters to cease his negative behaviors. In order to be a positive parent to his children, he must learn and model respectful behaviors toward his children, their mother, and others.

7. *The man who batters must reevaluate his distorted image of his partner.* Many men who batter present a hostile and unfair image of their children's mothers. They may describe them as promiscuous, lazy, stupid, crazy, manipulative, and so forth. Until they can reassess this

impression and view their partners as multidimensional human beings, it is unlikely that they will cease their battering behavior.

8. *The man who batters must make amends both in the short term and in the long term.* Men who batter need to accept that modeling positive, nonabusive behaviors and behaving respectfully toward their children and children's mothers must be ongoing and consistent. They should also apologize for prior behavior and make amends where possible. This might involve something as concrete as paying restitution, or it might involve spending more time with the children or doing their fair share of housework. Such actions will go a long way toward building trust again.

9. *The man who batters must accept the consequences of his actions for him.* It is imperative that the man understands that his children may not immediately (or ever) forgive him for his past behaviors. No matter how much he may change in the future, he may still not get his relationship with his partner back, and his children may not regain their respect for him. This is perhaps the most difficult lesson for many batterers to accept.

10. *The man who batters must commit to not repeating abusive behavior.* If the man is not willing to verbally and publicly commit to stopping his abuse, it is not only extremely unlikely that he will change but that this has serious ramifications for his parenting abilities. One cannot simultaneously be a good parent and batter his children's mother.

11. *The man who batters must accept change as a long-term (probably lifelong) process.* Learning and engaging in violent and abusive behaviors are a long-term process, so learning nonabusive behaviors will be a long-term, if not lifetime, process as well. There is no quick fix, and such change is generally not easy.

12. *The man who batters must be willing to be accountable.* Is the man willing to admit that he should be held accountable by the system if he is abusive again? Is he willing to agree that if he batters again, he will lose access to his children? The answers to these questions will tell a staff member a great deal about the man's progress in the program.

These 12 steps have been offered as starting points for discussion. However, given that they have been found in practice to be tangible benchmarks of a man's progress toward nonabusiveness, programs should give them serious consideration as measurable outcomes of movement toward safe and responsible fatherhood.

Ideally, more extensive evaluations will also measure actual behavioral change over time rather than simply intentions and knowledge. This is methodologically complex, however, and requires obtaining information from the children's mothers (and possibly the children themselves).

The next section focuses on the major methodological considerations (including issues pertaining to design, sampling, and retention) and is then followed by a number of themes related to the research participants themselves. These include how to involve resistant abusers in evaluation efforts, how to safely recruit and retain survivors (and their children, where applicable) in evaluations, and how to maintain the confidentiality of all participants.

Ingredients of a Successful Evaluation

For the sake of simplicity, let us assume that the aforementioned 12 elements have been chosen as the desired objectives of a parenting program for batterers. The next step is to determine how to recognize whether these changes have occurred. Would the evaluator ask the man these questions directly? And, if so, how and how often? Men who batter are well known for their ability to manipulate and charm as a means of getting what they want (Bancroft, 2002; Pence & Paymar, 1993). There are legitimate fears that many men who batter simply learn to use the language they know professionals want to hear and use the phrases that they learn in intervention programs as a means of deception. Therefore, the choice of how to gather this information, and from whom, is critical.

Any evaluation of parenting programs for men who batter should include two primary ingredients. First, a highly trained professional, well educated in the tactics used by these men to obfuscate the truth, should interview the man about his understanding and acceptance of the 12 components laid out by Bancroft and Silverman (2002), which we have summarized above. Such an interview should be open-ended and conversational, giving the abuser the opportunity to fully articulate his perspective. This gives the interviewer the opportunity to listen for phrases that suggest the man has not changed as much as he is presenting (e.g., still referring to his children or their mother in possessive terms, still refusing to accept full responsibility for his actions) and also for phrases indicating that true change may be occurring. Second, it is imperative to hear from his children's mother to confirm the extent to which actual change has taken place. If the children are old enough, if they freely agree to participate, and if informed consent is obtained on their behalf from their custodial parent(s), they should be heard as well. Later in this chapter, strategies for doing this safely are discussed. As with interviewing men who batter, it is important that a highly trained professional interview the survivors and their children in order to best detect statements that may be minimizing the abuse and to detect whether the survivor or the children are frightened for their safety. An appropriately trained interviewer can also understand and respond to the ambivalence that many children feel toward their abusive fathers.

Information can also be obtained by group facilitators regarding their perspectives on the father's progress. This triangulation of data collection (i.e., obtaining data from multiple sources such as the father, mother, child, and group facilitators) gives the evaluator more confidence in the accuracy of any conclusions drawn.

Once it has been determined *what* to assess and from *whom* to gather the data, measurement tools need to be chosen or developed. There are, to date, no standardized measures that one can use to evaluate parenting programs for men who batter. It would be inappropriate to use *proxy* indicators of success, such as measures of anger management, self-esteem, or psychiatric disorder. None of these indicate whether the man has acknowledged his prior use of control and abuse, whether he now empathizes with his victims, or whether he recognizes and accepts new ways of interacting with his children and their mother. Until such measures are developed and tested for reliability and validity, parenting programs may want to rely on more qualitative, open-ended interviewing techniques by trained professionals to best examine whether desired change has occurred.

Evaluations of parenting programs for men who batter will also need to carefully attend to the issue of completion rates. As with batterer intervention programs, one would expect that there will be differential attrition from these programs, with those who complete the program possibly being more motivated to change or motivated by external factors than those who drop out. At the same time, if parenting programs are not culturally competent, one could expect to find, as with batterer intervention programs, that the completion rate of men of color will be lower than that of their white counterparts (Tolman & Edleson, 1995; Williams, 1992, 1994; Williams & Becker, 1994). Some communities are designing and implementing culturally relevant batterer parenting programs, including Alianza (the Latino Alliance for the Elimination of Domestic Violence) and Evolve (located in Connecticut and created specifically for men of color). These efforts are extremely important, as it is imperative that programs be relevant and meaningful to the men participating in them if success is to be achieved. A great deal more work must occur to ensure that culturally competent and culturally relevant research guides our programmatic efforts. Similarly, more work is needed to understand the effectiveness of batterer parenting interventions for gay and lesbian abusers, for immigrants and refugees, for those with disabilities or multiple needs, and for other traditionally marginalized groups.

It is also critical that evaluations of parenting programs for batterers be experimental wherever possible, as well as longitudinal, and thus able to assess change across time. Examining success without comparing participants with those in control groups (or at least comparison groups) can lead to erroneous conclusions. Similarly, examining outcomes only immediately following the parenting program does not tell us whether change is maintained over time. Such design components, however, are expensive and time intensive. Adequate funds are needed in order for such rigorous evaluations to be conducted.

Recruiting Men Who Batter to Participate in the Evaluation

It is standard protocol of many batterer intervention programs to mandate, as a prerequisite for being accepted into the group, that men agree to participate in intake and follow-up interviews conducted by program staff. They are also required to give the name and contact information for the partners they abused (and sometimes new partners) in order for them to be contacted periodically as well. The men participating in these programs know that any abusive behavior conveyed by themselves or their partner, or witnessed by staff, will be reported to the proper authorities. A similar protocol could exist for parenting programs designed for men who batter. While the information gained from these clinical intake and follow-up interviews and through speaking with survivors can be helpful in gauging the success of individual program participants and can be used as an imprecise form of evaluation when resources do not allow for an actual rigorous evaluation, formal and external evaluations (which include a control or at least a comparison group) are needed to judge the effectiveness of these parenting programs overall.

It is challenging to entice men who batter to agree to participate in an evaluation that involves documenting their abusive behavior, especially if they also must agree to provide information about their partners and ex-partners so that they can be invited to participate as well. This is a population that is more resistant to participating in research than most populations, and thus, they must be treated somewhat differently than the norm. While it is still imperative to gain informed consent from men who batter and to ensure that their participation in the evaluation component is voluntary, a small amount of tacit coercion may be necessary to minimize refusal rates (Gondolf, 2000). Gondolf was able to maintain a refusal rate of less than 10% in his large-scale study of men in batterer intervention programs by including evaluation measures as part of the intake and follow-up protocol already being conducted in the clinical component of the programs. While it was stressed that participating in the evaluation component of the program was voluntary, that the evaluators were not connected with the court system, and that participants could discontinue their participation in the evaluation without penalty, it is possible that some abusers felt they were expected to participate in the evaluation as part of their court order. Without this protocol, however, when Gondolf simply invited men to stay after the intake session if they wanted to hear more about the study, the refusal rate was closer to two thirds. Combining the evaluation measures with the clinical components of the program (intake and follow-up instruments) appears to be an ethical and effective way of recruiting men who batter into participating. Researchers must be careful, however, to stress the voluntary nature of participation in order to gain true informed consent.

Safely Involving Survivors and Their Children in the Evaluation

While it is imperative to verify men's accounts of their behavior toward their children and children's mothers, there are a number of safety concerns to consider when asking women (and possibly their children) to participate in such an evaluation. While there is no way to remove all risk from survivors, there are a number of strategies that can be used to maximize their safety (e.g., Dutton, et al., 2003; Gondolf, 2000; Langford, 2000; Sullivan & Cain, 2004; Sullivan, Rumptz, Campbell, Eby, & Davidson, 1996).

First, it is suggested that survivors be contacted by telephone (if they have them) to have the study explained to them by a trained staff member. Women should first be asked if this is a safe time to talk and if they would rather be contacted at another time or through another means (e.g., a different telephone, or at work). If the staff member is satisfied that the woman can freely speak, she or he should explain the purpose of the program evaluation in detail, especially including the program's attention to her safety and confidentiality, and then ask if she is willing to participate. If the survivor does not have a telephone, she should be contacted in person, if possible. Sending information about the study through the mail might endanger her if her batterer intercepts it (Gondolf, 2000).

If the evaluation also involves interviewing children, informed consent from custodial parents (usually the mothers) must first be obtained. The interviewer should discuss with the mother whether she thinks such participation would be safe for the child (e.g., will the man find out about their participation?), and it should be stressed that only children freely wishing to participate will be interviewed. Mothers also need to understand that they will not be informed of children's responses to the interview process. If the evaluation team will contact child protective services on hearing of any incident of potential child abuse and neglect, children and mothers must be fully aware of this before answering any questions. If there is any doubt about the child's understanding of this concept, then ethically, they should not participate in the evaluation.

Whenever possible, interviews should be conducted in person at a location convenient for the participants. This minimizes the risk of the abuser being present without the knowledge of the interviewer, helps the interviewer attend to body language during the interview, and is likely to build a more comfortable relationship between the interviewer and the survivor. If the interview is conducted in the survivor's home, however, it is important to first develop a strategy for explaining and ending the interview if the abuser should arrive (even if this seems extremely unlikely to the survivor). Safety planning should always be engaged in before, during, and after interviews with survivors and their children. Others have gone into a great deal more detail about this, should the reader be interested (e.g., Dutton, et al., 2003; Gondolf, 2000; Langford, 2000; Sullivan & Cain, 2004; Sullivan, et al., 1996).

Unfortunately, many men who batter interrogate their children to obtain information about their partners and ex-partners (Bancroft, 2000; McMahon & Pence, 1995; Shepard, 1992), and it is important for program evaluators to understand this and its potential impact on the research study. First, it is critical that children not feel cross-examined or badgered by the evaluation process, as this could feel similar to the batterer's interrogation techniques. Children may also be afraid of getting their fathers (or mothers) in trouble and thus might be hesitant to truthfully share incidents where they have felt fearful, threatened, or abused by them. This is understandable, and trained interviewers can relax children by (1) allowing them to speak about how things are going in their own words; (2) stating aloud that they understand that the children may have reservations about participating; (3) reminding the children that they do not have to share anything they are not comfortable sharing; and (4) explaining the concept of confidentiality in ways appropriate to the children's developmental ages.

If children will be interviewed as part of the evaluation, then similarly to their parents, the interview should be conversational and relaxed. They should also be interviewed separately from other children and from either parent so that they feel free to be completely honest. It is often helpful to begin an interview with children by asking them nonthreatening questions or by playing a brief and fun game with them. Data gathered from the children could focus on the extent to which they (1) want to have supervised, unsupervised, or no access to the abusive parent, and (2) are fearful for themselves or their nonabusive parent. It is not necessary, and might be detrimental to the children's mental health, to delve more deeply than this with them unless they want to share more.

Addressing Confidentiality Issues

Although the clinical interviews associated with batterer-focused programs are not confidential (with staff reporting to police, probation officers, or the courts when men admit to having been abusive again or if survivors note such abuse), institutional review boards (IRBs) will generally not approve evaluation studies that do not protect the confidentiality of their research participants. This can pose an ethical dilemma for external evaluators, who might be hearing about abusive behavior that has not come to the attention of program staff. A number of procedures can be put in place at the beginning of the evaluation to protect participant confidentiality while also maximizing the safety of survivors and their children.

Participant consent forms must clearly indicate the circumstances under which information received will be kept confidential. The two general exceptions to confidentiality in most states are in the cases of (1) child abuse or neglect, and (2) imminent danger to one's self or to others. States differ in their definitions and expectations regarding both, and each evaluator will need to address these issues to comply with appropriate state and federal statutes as they obtain IRB approval for their evaluation. Regardless, any exceptions to confidentiality must be clearly articulated to all research participants (including survivors and children participating in the study). The evaluators will also want to have a written protocol in place for handling safety issues. For example, if a survivor notes that she is afraid that the batterer will severely hurt her if she tells the parenting program's staff about his continued threats, the interviewer would want to brainstorm options with her and notify her of available resources in the area, such as the local shelter program. The written protocol can include standard procedures for handling severe depression, suicide ideation, threats to others, incidents of abuse that are not criminal in nature, incidents of abuse that are criminal, and fearfulness on the part of survivors or their children. Having a strong working relationship with local domestic-violence victim-service programs is extremely important as a means of creating this protocol and handling situations that occur over time. It should be noted that these crisis situations tend to be infrequent in evaluations, even in large-scale studies involving survivors (e.g., Sullivan & Bybee, 1999) or batterers (e.g., Gondolf, 2000). They do arise, however, and having a standard procedure in place for handling emergencies or ethical dilemmas is extremely important. (More detailed information about such protocols can be found in Dutton, et al., 2003; Gondolf, 2000; Sullivan, et al., 1996; and Sullivan & Cain, 2004.)

It is not easy for research staff to hear about instances of abuse that have occurred or are occurring, especially when they themselves are not at liberty to inform officials. This is true across many studies dealing with illegal or immoral behavior and needs to be handled sensitively throughout training and supervision of all staff.

Conclusions

The National Research Council (1998) identified evaluation of domestic-violence interventions as "one of the most critical needs of this field" (p. 59). Unfortunately, most of the evaluation efforts in the field to date have suffered from a variety of methodological problems, including small sample sizes and samples with limited generalizability (e.g., predominantly white samples), nonexperimental designs, cross-sectional designs that preclude identifying causal relationships, and measures lacking established validity and reliability. As evaluation efforts of parenting programs for men who batter develop and grow, it is likely that qualitative and case-study evaluations will be replaced by more rigorous, mixed-method (i.e., quantitative and qualitative) designs using valid and reliable measures. It is essential that programs and policies be guided by sound empirical evidence if we are to understand not only what works but how and why it works (or, conversely, what does not work and why it does not work). In the case of parenting programs for abusers, children's and their mothers' safety depends on it.

References

Bancroft, L. (2002). *Why does he do that? Inside the minds of angry and controlling men.* New York: P.G. Putnam's Sons.

Bancroft, L., & Silverman, J. G. (2002). *The batterer as parent: Addressing the impact of domestic violence on family dynamics.* Thousand Oaks, CA: Sage.

Carillo, R., & Tello, J. (Eds.). (1998). *Family violence and men of color: Healing the wounded male spirit.* New York: Springer.

Dutton, M. A., Holtzworth-Munroe, A., Jouriles, E., McDonald, R., Krishnan, S., McFarlane, J., et al. (2003). *Recruitment and retention in intimate partner violence research.* Washington, DC: U.S. Department of Justice, National Institute of Justice.

Eriksson, M., & Hester, M. (2001). Violent men as good-enough fathers? A look at England and Sweden. *Violence Against Women, 7*(7), 779–798.

Gondolf, E. (2000). Human subject issues in batterer program evaluation. In S. Ward & D. Finkelhor (Eds.), *Program evaluation and family violence research* (pp. 273–297). New York: Haworth Press.

Jaffe, P., & Geffner, R. (1998). Child custody disputes and domestic violence: Critical issues for mental health, social service, and legal professionals. In G. Holden, R. Geffner, & E. Jouriles (Eds.), *Children exposed to marital violence: Theory, research, and applied issues* (pp. 371–408). Washington, DC: American Psychological Association.

Langford, D. R. (2000). Developing a safety protocol in qualitative research involving battered women. *Qualitative Health Research, 10*(1), 133–142.

McMahon, M., & Pence, E. (1995). Doing more harm than good: Some cautions on visitation centers. In E. Peled, P. Jaffe, & J. Edleson (Eds.), *Ending the cycle of violence: Community responses to children of battered women* (pp. 186–206). Thousand Oaks, CA: Sage.

National Research Council (1998). *Violence in families: Assessing prevention and treatment programs.* Washington, DC: National Academy Press.

Pence, E., & Paymar, M. (1993). *Education groups for men who batter: The Duluth model.* New York: Springer.

Shepard, M. (1992). Child-visiting and domestic violence. *Child Welfare, 71*(4), 357–365.

Sullivan, C. M., & Bybee, D. I. (1999). Reducing violence using community-based advocacy for women with abusive partners. *Journal of Consulting and Clinical Psychology, 67*(1), 43–53.

Sullivan, C. M., & Cain, D. (2004). Ethical and safety considerations when obtaining information from or about battered women for research purposes. *Journal of Interpersonal Violence,19*(5), 603–618.

Sullivan, C. M., Rumptz, M. H., Campbell, R., Eby, K. K., & Davidson, W. S. (1996). Retaining participants in longitudinal community research: A comprehensive protocol. *Journal of Applied Behavioral Science, 32*(3), 262–276.

Tolman, R. M., & Edleson, J. L. (1995). Intervention for men who batter: A research review. In S. M. Stith & M. A. Straus (Eds), *Understanding partner violence: Prevalence, causes, consequences, and solutions* (pp. 163–173). Minneapolis, MN: National Council on Family Relations.

Williams, O. J. (1992). Ethnically sensitive practice to enhance treatment participation of African American men who batter. *Families in Society, 73*(10), 588–595.

Williams, O. J. (1994). Group work with African American men who batter: Toward more ethnically sensitive practice. *Journal of Comparative Family Studies, 25*(1), 91–103.

Williams, O. J., & Becker, L. R. (1994). Partner abuse programs and cultural competence: The results of a national study. *Violence and Victims, 9*(3), 287–295.

About the Contributors

Editors

Jeffrey L. Edleson, MSSW, PhD, is a Professor in the University of Minnesota School of Social Work and the Director of the Minnesota Center Against Violence and Abuse (www.mincava.umn.edu). He has published over 90 articles and seven books on domestic violence, groupwork, and program evaluation. Edleson conducted intervention research at the Domestic Abuse Project in Minneapolis over the past two decades. He has served as a consultant to the U.S. Centers for Disease Control and Prevention and to the National Council of Juvenile and Family Court Judges. Edleson is an Associate Editor of the journal *Violence Against Women* and has served on the editorial boards of several other journals. His most recent books are entitled *Domestic Violence in the Lives of Children: The Future of Research, Intervention, and Social Policy* (2001, coedited with Sandra Graham-Bermann), *Sourcebook on Violence Against Women* (2001, coedited with Claire Renzetti and Raquel Kennedy Bergen), and *Domestic Violence: Classic Papers* (2005, coedited with Raquel Kennedy Bergen and Claire Renzetti). He is developing the *Encyclopedia of Interpersonal Violence* (coedited with Claire Renzetti).

Oliver J. Williams, PhD, is the Executive Director of the Institute on Domestic Violence in the African American Community and a Professor in the School of Social Work, University of Minnesota, St. Paul. He is a practitioner as well as an academician. As a practitioner, he has worked in the field of domestic violence for more than 25 years and has provided individual, couples, and family counseling. He has been a child welfare and delinquency worker, worked in battered women's shelters, developed curricula for batterers' intervention programs and facilitated counseling groups in these programs. He has provided training across the United States and abroad on research and service-delivery surrounding partner abuse. Williams's extensive research and publications in scholarly journals and books have centered on creating effective service-delivery strategies to reduce violent behavior, as well as ethnically sensitive practice. He serves on several national advisory boards and has received numerous awards for his work addressing issues of domestic violence. Williams received a BSW from Michigan State University; a MSW. from Western Michigan University; a MPH and a PhD in Social Work from the University of Pittsburgh.

Chapter Authors

Juan Carlos Areán works as a program manager for the Family Violence Prevention Fund. He has devoted the last 15 years to engaging men across different cultures to become better fathers, intimate partners, and allies to end domestic violence and achieve gender equity. For over a decade, he worked at the Men's Resource Center of Western Massachusetts in Amherst in various capacities, including director of the Men Overcoming Violence and the Refugees and Immigrants Program. He also worked as a sexual assault prevention specialist at Harvard University. Areán is coauthor of various articles, curricula and educational tools for men, and an active trainer who has led hundreds of workshops and presentations, both nationally and internationally.

Tricia B. Bent-Goodley, PhD, is an Associate Professor at the Howard University School of Social Work. She has published in social policy, domestic violence, criminal justice, child welfare, and African American social welfare history. She is a member of the Council on Social Work Education (CSWE) Council on the Role and Status of Women in Social Work Education and the National Policy and Research Consultant for the National Association of Black Social Workers (NABSW), and she has served as the Chair and Chief Instructor of the NABSW Academy for African-centered Social Work, the Chair of the NABSW National Public Policy Institute, and the NABSW National Student Coordinator. Bent-Goodley also serves on numerous boards and local planning committees, providing expertise in advocacy efforts and research. She is the Editor of *African American Social Workers and Social Policy* and the Coeditor, with King E. Davis, of two books published by CSWE entitled *The Color of Social Policy* and *Teaching Social Policy in Social Work Education*. Bent-Goodley received her PhD from Columbia University, her MSW from the University of Pennsylvania, and her BA in Sociology from Queens College of the City University of New York. Prior to coming to Howard University, she was the director of several family violence-prevention programs in Harlem and Jamaica-Queens, New York.

Ricardo Carrillo, PhD, is in private practice as a clinical forensic psychologist. He is the Director of Training and Technical Assistance for the National Latino Alliance on Domestic Violence (Alianza) in the Latino Community (New York) and the National Compadres Network, Inc. headquartered in Santa Ana, CA. He has served as Director of Latino Mental Health for Kaweah Delta Health Care District in Visalia, CA, and is most recognized as an expert witness and international consultant in the areas of family therapy, domestic violence, cross-cultural psychology, forensic psychology, and cultural competence. He has provided leadership in the areas of program development with domestic-violence offenders, Latino mental health, and chemical-dependency populations. He attended the California School of Professional Psychology in Fresno, CA, and has taught for 10 years in professional psychology schools in the San Francisco Bay area. He maintains a private practice in Visalia, CA. He has 15 years of recovery and decends from several generations of addicts.

Claire V. Crooks, PhD, CPsych, is the Associate Director of the Centre for Prevention Science in the Centre for Addition and Mental Health (CAMH) at the University of Western Ontario in London, Ontario. She is also an Assistant Professor at the Centre for Research on Violence Against Women and Children and an Adjunct Professor in the Department of Psychology at the University of Western Ontario. Crooks is a consultant to the Centre for Children and Families in the Justice System of the London (Ontario) Family Court Clinic, where she conducts high-conflict custody assessments and victim-impact assessments with the London Custody and Access Project. She has provided testimony on understanding the intersection between domestic violence and divorce as an issue relevant to the United Nations Convention on the Rights of the Child to the Senate Committee on Human Rights for the Canadian Federal Government. Crooks is a cofounder of the Caring Dads Program, a parenting intervention for men who have maltreated their children. In addition to being an author of the program manual, she is actively involved in training, consultation, and research on the Caring Dads project.

Lonna Davis, MSW, is a Program Manager at the Family Violence Prevention Fund, a national nonprofit organization located in San Francisco, CA, dedicated to ending abuse against women and girls. In this capacity, she provides technical assistance to several national initiatives focused on the overlap of violence against women and child abuse. Prior to her current position, Davis worked for a variety of domestic-violence programs, including two shelters for battered women, the Advocacy for Women and Kids in Emergencies (AWAKE) project at Boston Children's Hospital, and the Massachusetts Department of Social Services, where she cofounded a domestic-violence program within the child-protection agency. Davis holds an MSW from Salem State College, Salem, MA.

Karen Francis, MA, has focused her research and clinical interests on family violence and violent offenders. Currently, she is conducting research to examine the characteristics of physically abusive fathers. She is also a codeveloper of a program for abusive fathers, called the Caring Dads Program. In her professional work, Francis provides consultation and training to agencies regarding intervention with high-risk populations, including adults and youth with emotional and behavioral problems and youth in conflict with the law. She has worked with both victims and perpetrators of violence and cofacilitates groups for children of divorcing parents. Francis is currently nearing completion of her PhD in Clinical Psychology at the University of Western Ontario, London, Ontario.

Betsy McAlister Groves, MSW, LICSW, is the founding Director of the Child Witness to Violence Project at Boston Medical Center and an Associate Professor of Pediatrics at Boston University School of Medicine. Her publications include a book, *Children Who See Too Much: Lessons from the Child Witness to Violence Project,* published in 2002, and numerous articles. She currently serves on the Massachusetts Governor's Commission on Domestic Violence, the National Steering Committee for the U.S. Department of Justice's Office on Violence Against Womenfunded Safe Havens Visitation Programs, and as consultant to the Massachusetts Department of Social Services, the Massachusetts Judicial Institute, the National Council of Juvenile and Family Court Judges, and the Family Violence Prevention Fund.

Peter Jaffe, PhD, CPsych, is a Professor in the Faculty of Education and the Academic Director of the Centre for Research on Violence Against Women and Children at the University of Western Ontario, London, Ontario, where he holds cross-appointments in the Departments of Psychology and Psychiatry.. He is the Director Emeritus for the Centre for Children and Families in the Justice System, London (Ontario) Family Court Clinic. Since 1997, Jaffe has been a faculty member for the National Council of Juvenile and Family Court Judges' program on Enhancing Judicial Skills in Domestic Violence Cases. He has coauthored nine books, 25 chapters, and over 75 articles related to children, families, and the justice system, including *Children of Battered Women, Working Together to End Domestic Violence,* and *Child Custody and Domestic Violence: A Call for Safety and Accountability.* He has presented workshops across the United States and Canada, as well as Australia, New Zealand, Costa Rica, and Europe, to various groups, including judges, lawyers, mental-health professionals, and educators.

Alicia F. Lieberman, PhD, is a licensed clinical psychologist in the State of California and a Professor of Medical Psychology at the University of California, San Francisco, Department of Psychiatry. She is the Director of the UCSF Child Trauma Research Project and the principal investigator of its U.S. National Institute of Mental Health-funded study of the efficacy of a relationship-based intervention with young children who witnessed domestic violence and their mothers. She is also the principal investigator of the Early Trauma Treatment Network, which is a participant in the National Childhood Traumatic Stress Initiative funded by the U.S. Substance Abuse and Mental Health Services Administration (SAMHSA). Lieberman is the author of *The Emotional Life of the Toddler* and the coauthor of three other volumes on mental health in infancy and early childhood. She was a member of the Committee on Integrating the Science of Early Childhood Development of the National Academy of Science, whose work culminated in the volume *From Neurons to Neighborhoods: The Science of Early Childhood Development.* Lieberman has written over 100 articles and book chapters and has lectured throughout the world on the subjects of attachment, infant mental health, and the impact of exposure to violence on child development.

Michele Paddon, CYC, has dedicated her career over the last 16 years to working with abused women and their children and as an advocate in working at the cross section of woman abuse and child maltreatment. During this time, while working in an abused women's shelter, she was instrumental in the development of individual and group programming for children and women. Paddon is Coordinator for both the Community Group Program for Children Exposed to Woman Abuse and the Caring Dads program, a group intervention aimed at men at risk of abusing children. She has authored a program manual for a group-program model for abused women as mothers. Additionally, Paddon has been involved as a writer for www.shelternet.ca, a national resource for abused women, for which she developed a component for children and youth. Paddon is leading the development of a model for collaborative interventions coordinated between Child Protection Services, London (Ontario) Children's Aid Society and Abusive Men's Programs, Changing Ways. Paddon is the recipient of the 2004 Frank Brennan Award.

Einat Peled, MSW, PhD, is a Senior Lecturer in the Bob Shapell School of Social Work at Tel Aviv University. Together with her students, she currently studies the areas of domestic violence and violence against women with a particular emphasis on the experiences of mothering and fathering under these circumstances. She has published widely in the areas of child witnesses of domestic violence and runaway youth. Her recent books, together with Guy Perel, are *Fathering and Violence: A Group Intervention Model for Men Who Abuse Their Partner* and *Mothering in the Shadow of Violence: A Group Intervention Model for Women Abused by Their Partner* (both in Hebrew). She is the head of the Women and Gender track in the Bob Shapell School of Social Work graduate program and an editorial executive board member of the journal *Qualitative Social Work.*

Guy Perel, MSW, has worked for the past 10 years as a counselor and a supervising social worker in centers for domestic-violence intervention and prevention across Israel. He specializes in both group and individual therapy with women abused by their partners and with abusive men. He also teaches on domestic violence, fathering, and clinical practice at the Paul Berewald School of Social Work at the Hebrew University in Jerusalem and the Bob Shapell School of Social Work at Tel Aviv University. Recently, he has coauthored, together with Einat Peled, the books *Fathering and Violence: A Group*

Intervention Model for Men Who Abuse Their Partner and *Mothering in the Shadow of Violence: A Group Intervention Model for Women Abused by Their Partner* (both in Hebrew).

Katreena Scott, PhD, CPsych, is an Assistant Professor in the Department of Human Development and Applied Psychology at the University of Toronto. Scott has authored numerous articles and book chapters on the development of violent relationships, the efficacy of service to male batterers, the effect of abuse and trauma on children, and on empirically and ethically sound policies for working with abuse perpetrators. Her interests are currently focused on two main areas: intervention strategies for hostile and resistant clients and on interventions for fathers who have been abusive in their families. She is the lead investigator on the Caring Dads: Helping Fathers Value their Children program, a new intervention program for fathers which is currently being offered in key pilot sites in Canada and the United States.

Cris M. Sullivan, PhD, is Professor of Ecological/Community Psychology at Michigan State University. She is also the Director of Evaluation for the Michigan Coalition against Domestic and Sexual Violence and the Senior Research Advisor to the National Resource Center on Domestic Violence. Sullivan has been an advocate and researcher in the movement to end violence against women since 1982. Her areas of expertise include developing and evaluating community interventions for battered women and their children and evaluating victim services. Sullivan has received numerous federal grants to support her work and has published extensively in this area. In addition to consulting for local, state, and federal organizations and initiatives, she conducts workshops on effectively advocating in the community for women with abusive partners and their children; understanding the effects of domestic violence on women and children; and evaluating victim-service agencies.

Jerry Tello is a cofounder of the National Compadres Network and the Director of the National Latino Fatherhood and Family Institute. He is an internationally recognized expert in the areas of family strengthening, community mobilization, and culturally based violence prevention/intervention issues. He has extensive experience in the treatment of victims and perpetrators of abuse and in addictive behaviors, with a specialization in working with multiethnic populations. He provides training and technical assistance to a variety of national, state, and local organizations and agencies. He began working in communities in the early 1970s and has continued to attempt to strengthen, heal, and develop children, families, and communities by building on their own internal assets. Tello is the author of a Multicultural Young Fatherhood Curriculum, *Latino Male Rites of Passage Curriculum* and Latino Parent Education Curriculum and Domestic Violence Prevention/Intervention program. He is the coeditor of *Family Violence and Men of Color* (1998, with Ricardo Carrillo) and, in April 1996, he received the Presidential Crime Victims Service award, which was presented to him by President William J. Clinton and Attorney General Janet Reno. In June 1997, he received the Ambassador of Peace Award from Rotary, International. He is presently the Director of the Sacred Circles Healing Center in Whittier, California, and a member of the Sacred Circles performance group, a group dedicated to family/community peace and healing.

Carolyn Tubbs, PhD, is an Assistant Professor in the University of Guelph (Ontario, Canada) Couple and Family Therapy Program. She has published in the areas of family-therapy research, practice and training, domestic violence, and mental health issues affecting low-income populations. She was a research scientist on the Welfare, Children and Families: A Three City-Study project, a postdoctoral fellow with the Family Research Consortium III, and a research consultant for the Institute on Domestic Violence in the African American Community. Currently, Tubbs is Research Editor for *Journal of Systemic Therapies.*

Patricia Van Horn, JD, PhD, is a licensed clinical psychologist in the State of California, Assistant Clinical Professor in the Department of Psychiatry at the University of California, San Francisco, and the Director of Training of the UCSF Child Trauma Research Project located at San Francisco General Hospital. Van Horn received her J.D. in 1970 from the University of Colorado School of Law at Boulder and her Ph.D. in 1996 from the Pacific Graduate School of Psychology in Palo Alto, CA. Her research at the Child Trauma Research Project involves investigating the efficacy of a relationship-based model for treating children under six and their caregivers in cases where the children have witnessed domestic violence or experienced other interpersonal traumas. She is coauthor of the books *Losing A Parent to Death in the Early Years: Guidelines for the treatment of Traumatic Bereavement in Infancy and Early Childhood* (with A. F. Lieberman, N. C. Compton and C. G. Ippen) and *"Don't Hit My Mommy!": A Manual of Child-Parent Psychotherapy with Young Witnesses of Family Violence* (with A. F. Lieberman).

David. A. Wolfe, PhD, holds the inaugural RBC Chair in Children's Mental Health and is a Professor of Psychiatry and Psychology at the University of Toronto and Director of the CAMH Centre for Prevention Science. He is a fellow of the American Psychological Association and past President of Division 37 (Child, Youth, and Family Services). He has broad research and clinical interests in abnormal child and adolescent psychology, with a special focus on child abuse, domestic violence, and developmental psychopathology. He has authored numerous articles on these topics, especially in relation to the impact of early childhood trauma on later development in childhood, adolescence, and early adulthood. He and Peter Jaffe are currently evaluating the "Fourth R," which is a comprehensive school-based initiative for reducing adolescent risk behaviors through the promotion of positive, nonviolent relationships. He recently received the Donald O. Hebb Award for Distinguished Contributions to Psychology as a Science from the Canadian Psychological Association and the Outstanding Career Award from the American Professional Society on the Abuse of Children. His recent books include *Child Abuse: Implications for Child Development and Psychopathology* (2nd ed., 1999); *Sex, Drugs, and Violence: A Relationships Approach to Reducing Risk* (2005, with P. Jaffe & C. Crooks), and *Abnormal Child Psychology* (3rd ed., 2005, with E. Mash).

Index

abuse, term, 47

abusive behavior. *See also* domestic violence
  committing to stop, 140
  domestic violence, 46
  Fathering After Violence (FAV) initiative, 121

abusive fathers. *See also* Caring Dads program
  community advisory committee, 113–114
  complexities of children's reactions, 69
  compromising safety of children, 108–109
  continued program evaluations, 114–115
  intervention emphasizing respect of children's mothers, 110
  intervention for diverse cultures and individual circumstances, 112–113
  programs for respectful relationships with men, 111
  programs mandating treatment, 104, 106
  training and education, 114
  views of children, 15

accepting consequences
  Fathering After Violence (FAV) initiative, 121
  men who batter, 140

access
  father-child, and domestic violence history, 41
  shared parenting assumption, 26–27

accountability. *See also* Caring Dads program
  batterer contact with children, 36

children's mothers, 108–110
communities, 113–115
guidelines for Caring Dads, 105
men who batter, 140
safety and well-being of children, 104, 106–108

acknowledging damage, Fathering After Violence (FAV) initiative, 122

acknowledgment (*conocimiento*), healing process, 133–134

African American women
  focus-group participants, 24, 26
  focus-group study of shared parenting, 23–25
  perceptions of shared parenting with batterers, 22–23, 41

alienation
  label as syndrome, 51
  Parental Alienation Syndrome, 52

allegations, domestic violence, 50–51

Alliance for Non-Custodial Parents' Rights, fathers' rights, 9

American Coalition for Fathers and Children, fathers' rights, 9

apology, men who batter, 140

Areán, Juan Carlos, about author, 150

assessment
  best interests of child, 54
  child custody, 50, 53
  collecting information, 53–54
  domestic-violence allegations, 50–56
  interventions, 61
  interviews, 54
  mental-health professionals, 52–53

assessment (*continued*)
   Parental Alienation Syndrome, 52
   requirements with violence allegations,
      52–53
   specialized needs in domestic violence
      cases, 53
assumptive beliefs, shared parenting, 26–
   27
authors, book and San Francisco meeting,
   3, 149–156

baggage issues (*cargas*), addictive
      behaviors, 132
barriers to contact, shared parenting, 38–
   39
battered mothers
   children's relationship with fathers,
      67–68
   compromising safety and stability of
      children, 108–109
   men's interference in women's
      parenting, 12
batterer intervention programs. *See also*
      Fathering After Violence (FAV);
      parenting programs for men who
      batter
   attention to fatherhood, 127–128
   cultural context, 120–121
   Family Violence Prevention Fund
      (FVPF) partner, 119
batterers. *See also* men who batter
   family court as tool, 48
   poor role models, 48
   term, 46, 47
battering, definition, 5–6
Bent-Goodley, Tricia B., about author,
   150
best interests of child
   assessing fathers in context, 45–46
   conflict and domestic violence, 46–47
   fathering intervention programs, 106–
      107
   initiating shared-parenting contact
      with former batterer, 28–29
   relevance of domestic violence to child
      custody, 47–49
biological fathers
   absence of, and nation's problems, 9
   violence, 14

blaming, Fathering After Violence (FAV)
      initiative, 121
book
   about, 4–5
   authors, 3, 149–156
   promising practices and strategies, 5
Boston Medical Center, Child Witness to
      Violence Project (CWVP), 65, 66
Brames, murder-suicide story, 19–20
Bush (G.W.) administration, 7

*Caring Dads: Helping Fathers Value Their
      Children*, 102–103
Caring Dads program
   accountability guidelines, 104, 105
   accountability to communities, 105,
      113–115
   advocating respectful relationships with
      men, 111
   battering mother compromising safety
      and stability of children, 108–109
   beginnings and philosophy, 103–104
   communicating fathering intervention
      to children, 107–108
   community advisory committee, 113–
      114
   contact with children's mothers, 109–
      110
   content, 103–104
   continued program evaluation, 114–
      115
   diverse cultures and individual
      circumstances, 112–113
   emphasizing respect to children's
      mothers, 110
   evaluating model of fatherhood, 113
   mandating men into treatment, 104,
      106
   potential benefit to children
      independent of men's progress, 106–
      107
   referring additional services, 112
   responsibility to fathers, 105, 111–113
   safety and well-being of children, 104,
      106–108
   safety of children's mothers, 105, 108–
      110
   training and education to community,
      114

Carrillo, Ricardo, about author, 150–151
Carter, Lucy Salcido, 3
certificate of good character, fathering
    intervention, 86
change, men who batter, 140
Changing Ways, Caring Dads program,
    103
character development, *La Educacion*,
    133
child abduction, 48
child abuse
    domestic violence and, 13–14, 102
    family violence, 50–51
child custody
    domestic violence recognition, 55
    intervention, 56–59
    relevance of domestic violence, 47–49
    research, 59–60
    specialized assessment in domestic
        violence case, 53
childhood, experience of parenting in,
    93–94
child maltreatment, 47
child outcomes, domestic violence, 22
child-protection services, excluding
    fathers, 102
children. *See also* best interests of child
    accountability to safety and well-being
        of, 104, 106–108
    appraisals of violence and conflict in
        home, 70
    attention on, and fatherhood, 128
    benefits of fathering intervention, 106–
        107
    common bond for estranged parents,
        21
    communicating fathers' involvement in
        intervention, 107–108
    coparents communicating about, 34
    coparents communicating with, 35
    developmental needs and initiating
        contact, 28–29
    fathers through their children's eyes,
        14–15
    feelings conflicting with mother's, 70
    impact of violent man's behavior, 13–
        14, 71, 94, 97, 139
    involvement in adult domestic
        violence, 11–12

motivation for men to change, 72
    reactions to abusive fathers, 69
    rejecting parent post-separation, 51–52
    relationship to violent adult, 14
    reversing long-term effects of domestic
        violence, 128
    safe contact with fathers, 71
    safe involvement in program
        evaluations, 144–145
    targets of domestic violence, 15
    views of abusive fathers, 15
children's developmental needs
    initiating shared-parenting contact
        with former batterer, 28–29
    parallel with life-course process, 40–41
children's lives, impact of domestic
    violence, 4–5
children's mothers. *See also* fathers'
    involvement in children's treatment
    parenting program evaluation, 141–142
children's treatment
    involvement of fathers, 80–82
child support, initiating contact with
    former batterer, 30
Child Trauma Research Project (CTRP)
    clinical program, 65, 66–67
    discussions regarding father
        involvement, 73
child visitations, post-separation violence
    by men who batter, 12–13
Child Witness to Violence Project
    (CWVP)
    clinical program, 65, 66
    discussions regarding father
        involvement, 73
    Family Violence Prevention Fund
        (FVPF) partner, 119
    surveying contact with fathers, 68–69
The Circle (*Circulo*). *See also* Latino
    fathers in recovery
    learning to father, 131, 132
    storytelling in *Circulo Way*, 135–136
clinical programs
    Child Trauma Research Project
        (CTRP), 65, 66–67
    Child Witness to Violence Project
        (CWVP), 65, 66
    decision-making paradigm for
        involving fathers, 74

clinical programs (*continued*)
  goals of interventions, 67
  hearing voices of mothers and children,
    67–70
clinician's perspective, father's behavior, 80
cognitive behavioral treatment, Israeli
    domestic-violence centers, 91
Common Purpose, Family Violence
    Prevention Fund (FVPF) partner,
    119
communication
  coparents informing children, 35
  coparents strengthening, about
    children, 34
  fathers' involvement in intervention,
    107–108
community, accountability of Caring
    Dads to, 113–115
community advisory committee, abusive
    fathers, 113–114
community development, domestic
    violence, 60–62
completion rates, batterer intervention
    programs, 142
compliance, violent parent and court
    orders, 74–76
confidentiality, program evaluations,
    145–146
conflict
  children's appraisal of, in home, 70
  custody interventions in domestic
    violence, 57
  domestic violence and, 46–47
  relational dimension in shared
    parenting, 21
  term, 46, 47
Conflict Tactics Scale, intimate-partner
    violence, 47
connection, yearning by men who batter,
    89
consensus, shared parenting, 40–41
consequences. *See* accepting consequences
contact with former batterer. *See also*
    shared parenting
  accountability components, 36
  barriers, 38–39
  best interest of child, 29–30
  child mental health and emotional
    security, 31–32

children's developmental needs, 28–29
child support, 30
court services and officials, 37–38
emotional manipulation, 36–37
enforcement components, 38
facilitators of contact, 31–32, 35–38
guardian ad litem, 37
impact of time, 39–40
initiating shared-parenting contacts,
    28–31
parameters of contact, 30–31
structural components, 36–38
terminating shared-parenting, 39
continued program evaluation, abusive
    fathers, 114–115
control
  behavior patterns of men who batter,
    139
  perpetual litigation, 48
  violent fathers and courts, 71
cooperation, relational dimension in
    shared parenting, 21
coparenting
  clear expectations, 34–35
  communication about children, 34
  encouraging positive parenting, 35
  father's recommendations, 34–35
  informing children, 35
  objective third party, 35
couple relationship, separation from
    father-child relationship, 29–30
court orders, compliance of violent
    parent, 74–76
court systems
  facilitators of contact, 37–38
  fathers' rights groups, 9–10
  perpetrators of domestic violence, 58–
    59
  tool of batterers, 48, 71
coyote spirit, Latino fathers in recovery,
    132
criminal-justice response, domestic
    violence, 45
Crooks, Claire V., about author, 151
cultural background, father involvement,
    77
cultural diversity. *See also* Latino fathers
    in recovery
  intervention programs, 112–113

culture, batterer intervention programs, 120–121

custodial role, common wisdom in divorce field, 50

danger, intervention with men who batter, 85–86

data collection, 53–54

David and Lucile Packard Foundation, 3

Davis, Lonna, about author, 151

denial, Fathering After Violence (FAV) initiative, 121

destiny (*destino*), fathers in recovery, 134–135

developmental needs
    child, parallel with life-course process, 40–41
    children's, and initiating contact, 28–29

dignity (*dignidad*), healing process, 133–134

domestic violence. *See also* violence
    assessment, 50–56
    assessment following allegations of, 61–62
    battering, 6
    cases entering formal court system, 49–50
    child abuse and, 13–14, 102
    child custody, specialized assessment needs, 53
    children involvement in adult, 11–12
    clinical issues, 49–59
    conflict and, 46–47
    conflicting claims of progress, 55
    coordination between programs, 128–129
    differentiated custody interventions, 57
    fatherhood movements, 10–11
    first wave of public policy, 45
    intervention, 56–59, 61
    legislation and community development, 60–62
    mediation practices, 55–56
    overlap with child maltreatment, 47
    range of outcomes without formal court system, 49
    relationship between child outcomes and, 22

    relevance to child custody, 47–49
    research, 59–60
    reversing effects on children, 128
    risk of homicide, 48
    scarcity of research on fathering and, 11–15
    shared parenting and history of, 21–23, 41, 42
    shortcomings within court system, 58–59
    targeting children, 15
    term, 46
    victims undermining parenting role, 48
    visitation and child custody, 48–49

domestic violence survivors, 144–145

Dorchester Community Roundtable, Family Violence Prevention Fund (FVPF) partner, 119, 125–126

duality in practice, 89–90

dynamic psychotherapy, 93–94

dysfunctional families, 8–9

Edleson, Jeffrey L., about the editor, 149

education, abusive fathers, 114

La Educacion, character development, 133

"El Amor de Este Hijo" ("The Love of this Son"), 133

EMERGE batterer intervention program, Family Violence Prevention Fund (FVPF) partner, 119

emotional manipulation, 36–37

emotional protection, 41

emotional security, children's, 29

empathy, for partner and children, 139

empathy exercise, Fathering After Violence (FAV) initiative, 123–124

employment training, 8

enforcement, contact with former batterer, 38

evaluation. *See* parenting programs for men who batter

exercises
    batterer intervention groups, 123–125
    empathy exercise, 123–124
    Michael's story exercise, 124–125
    modeling exercise, 124

expectations, coparenting recommendation, 34–35

family
   coordination of domestic violence
      programs, 128–129
   fathers' views of role in, 32–33
   involvement in other systems, 79–80
family court
   perpetrators of domestic violence, 58–59
   tool of batterers, 48
family-systems theory, 23–24
family violence
   level, 76–77
   safety of victims, 119–120
Family Violence Prevention Fund
      (FVPF). *See also* Fathering After
      Violence (FAV)
   Fathering After Violence (FAV)
      initiative, 118
   focus groups, 118
   service for families, 102–103
father-child accessibility, 41
father-child relationship
   importance, 87–88
   separation from couple relationship,
      29–30
fatherhood advocates, 6–7
fatherhood movements
   domestic violence, 10–11
   term, 7
fathering
   attention on children and, 128
   generative, 87–88
   scarcity of research on, and domestic
      violence, 11–15
   supporting men's capacity to father, 86
Fathering After Violence (FAV)
   attention on children and fathering, 128
   attention to fatherhood, 127–128
   consortium of Boston-based providers,
      119
   cultural context, 120–121
   empathy exercise, 123–124
   examining impact, 125–127
   exercises, 123–125
   Family Violence Prevention Fund
      (FVPF), 118
   framework to end violence against
      women, 119
   goal, 118–119
   lessons learned, 127–130

   Michael's story exercise, 124–125, 126
   modeling exercise, 124
   overview, 118–120
   program development, 121–123
   reparative framework, 121–122, 129
   safety of victims, 119–120
   staff training, 125
   stopping the violence, 129–130
   tools, 128
fathering experience, 93–94
fathering intervention
   analysis of daily events, 96
   being father, 96
   children and impact of violence, 97
   closure sessions, 97
   context, 90–91
   duality challenge, 89–90
   dynamic psychotherapy, 93–94
   feminist issue, 91–92
   goals, 94–95
   justification and importance, 87–89
   parenting skills, 96
   parents' parenting, 96
   phenomenology, 92–93
   problematic and dangerous, 85–86
   structure, 95–97
   supporting capacity to father, 86
   theoretical premises for safe and
      effective, 91–94
father-involvement programs, 7–8
Fatherless America, Blankenhorn, 8
fathers. *See also* Caring Dads program;
      men who batter
   assessing, in child's best interest, 45–46
   being a father, 96
   children's safe contact with, 71
   exclusion from child–protection
      strategies, 102
   interference in women's parenting, 12
   literature on, 88
   mandated treatment programs, 76
   responsibility to, 105, 111–113
   rights in light of violence, 33
   social movements involving, 6–11
   understanding impact on children, 128
   view of their role in family, 32–33
   views about involvement with children,
      78–79
   view through children's eyes, 14–15

father's behavior, clinician's view, 80
fathers in recovery. *See* Latino fathers in
    recovery
fathers' involvement in children's
    treatment
    children's appraisals of violence and
        conflict, 70
    children's reactions to abusive fathers,
        69
    clinical programs, 65–67
    clinician's perspective on father's
        behavior, 80
    cultural context within family, 77
    decision-making paradigm, 74
    hearing battered women's ideas and
        wishes, 67–70
    involvement in mandated treatment
        programs, 76
    involvement in other systems, 79–80
    key questions, 73–80
    level of violence in family, 76–77
    men who batter as parents, 71–73
    thoughts and desires of family
        members, 78–79
    violent parent compliance with court
        orders, 74–76
fathers' rights group, 9–10
fathers' voices, 32
father violence, 71
female-headed households, 8–9
female-initiated violence, 50
feminist issue, fathering intervention as,
    91–92
financial resources, barrier to contact, 38–
    39
focus groups, Family Violence Prevention
    Fund (FVPF), 118
focus-study group
    access, 26, 27
    assumptive beliefs, 26–27
    conditions for shared parenting, 28
    data collection and analysis, 24–25
    emergent themes, 26–31
    informing perspectives, 23–24
    participants, 24, 26
    safety, 26–28
    shared parenting, 23–25
Francis, Karen, about author, 151–152
funding, parenting programs, 138

generative fathering, concept, 87–88
goals, interventions with fathers, 94–95
group intervention, Caring Dads
    program, 103
Groves, Betsy McAlister, about author,
    152
guardian *ad litem*, 37

harassment, perpetual litigation, 48
healing process, Latino fathers in
    recovery, 133–135
high conflict cases, intervention, 57
homicide, 48
human-ecological theory, 23–24
humanistic approach, 93

importance, of fathering intervention,
    87–89
individual circumstances, intervention
    programs, 112–113
informed consent, interviewing children,
    144
Institute for American Values,
    responsible-fatherhood group, 8
integration (*integracion*), healing process,
    133, 134
interventions. *See also* Caring Dads
    program; Fathering After Violence
    (FAV); fathering intervention with
    men who batter
    Caring Dads program, 103
    child-custody and visitation, 56–59
    custody, 57
    domestic violence, 45, 61
    goals for, with fathers, 94–95
    goals of, with children exposed to
        violence, 67
    potential to benefit children, 106–107
    structure of, with fathers, 95–97
interviews
    assessment with alleged domestic
        violence, 54
    parenting program evaluations, 144–145
intimacy, yearning by men who batter, 89
Israeli community center
    mothering and fathering intervention,
        95
    parenting group-intervention model,
        90–91

Jaffe, Peter, about author, 152
justification
    Fathering After Violence (FAV)
        initiative, 121
    fathering intervention with men who
        batter, 87–89

kidnapping, structural visitation, 36–37

Latino fathers in recovery
    acknowledgment (*conocimiento*), 133–
        134
    baggage issues (*cargas*), 132
    The Circle (*El Circulo*), 131
    coyote spirit, 132
    dignity (*dignidad*), 133–134
    integration (*integracion*), 133, 134
    lessons of childhood (*La Educacion*),
        133
    love (*cariño*), 133, 134
    "The Love of this Son" (*El Amor de
        Este Hijo*), 133
    movement (*movimento*), 133, 135
    process of healing and development,
        133–135
    respect (*respeto*), 133, 134
    storytelling in *El Circulo* (The Circle),
        135–136
    Teachings of the Elders (*Hue Hues*),
        133
    trust (*confianza*), 133, 134–135
    understanding (*entendimento*), 133, 134
legislation, domestic violence, 60–62
Lieberman, Alicia F., about author, 152–
    153
life-course perspective, 23
listening, Fathering After Violence (FAV)
    initiative, 122
literature, fathers who abuse partners, 88
litigation, control and harassment, 48
long-term change, 140
love (*cariño*), healing process, 133, 134
"The Love of this Son" ("*El Amor de Este
    Hijo*"), 133

male controlling interactive violence, 50
mandated treatment programs
    fathers, 76
    identifying and encouraging, 104, 106

manipulation, facilitators of contact, 36–
    37
marriage promotion, G. W. Bush
    administration, 7
measurement, parenting program
    evaluations, 138, 142
mediation practices, 55–56
mental health, children's, and initiating
    contact, 29
mental health professionals, assessments,
    52–53
men who batter. *See also* Caring Dads
    program; fathering intervention with
    men who batter; parenting programs
    for men who batter
    African American women's perceptions
        of shared parenting with, 22–23
    compromising safety and stability of
        children, 108–109
    definition, 5–6
    direct parenting intervention, 72–73
    empathy for partner and children, 139
    making amends, 140
    parenting group-intervention model
        with, 90–91
    parenting styles, 11–12
    as parents, 71–73
    post-separation violence by, 12–13
    recruiting, for parenting program
        evaluation, 143
    steps to be safe, responsible fathers,
        139–140
    term, 46
Michael's story exercise, Fathering After
    Violence (FAV) initiative, 124–125,
    126
model, parenting group-intervention, 90–
    91
Model Code, evaluating application, 56
modeling constructive behavior
    Fathering After Violence (FAV)
        initiative, 121
modeling exercise, Fathering After
    Violence (FAV) initiative, 124
mother-child relationship, Caring Dads
    program emphasizing respect, 110
mothers
    accountability to safety of children's,
        105, 108–110

children's relationship with fathers, 67–68
empathy by men who batter, 139
feelings conflicting with children's, 70
gatekeepers in children's healing, 68
outreach to, of abusive men's children, 109–110
parenting program evaluation, 141–142
parenting programming for children's fathers, 127
safe involvement in program evaluations, 144–145
views about father's involvement, 78–79
mothers' parenting
  Fathering After Violence (FAV) initiative, 122
  men's interference, 12
movement (*movimiento*), healing process, 133, 135
murder-suicide, Brames, 19–20

National Congress for Fathers and Families, 9
National Council of Juvenile and Family Court Judges (NCJFCJ)
  application of Model Code, 56
  children's and women's safety, 116
  community accountability, 113–115
  domestic violence, 60
  service for families, 102–103
National Family Violence Survey of 1985, co-occurring maltreatment, 13–14
National Fatherhood Initiative (NFI), responsible-fatherhood group, 8–9

objective third party, coparenting recommendation, 35
ongoing/episodic male battering, 50
outcomes, parenting program evaluation, 138–141
outreach, mothers of abusive men's children, 109–110

Paddon, Michele, about author, 153
Parental Alienation Syndrome, assessment, 52

parenting
  childhood-rooted experience, 93–94
  fathers' voices on, 32
  mothers wanting, for children's fathers, 127
parenting context
  history of domestic violence, 21–23
  relationship dissolution, 20
  shared parenting, 20–23
parenting intervention. *See also* Caring Dads program
  men who batter, 72–73
parenting programs for men who batter
  completion rates, 142
  confidentiality issues, 145–146
  desired outcomes, 138–141
  elements of safe, responsible fathers, 139–140
  formative and process evaluations, 137
  funding, 137
  ingredients for successful evaluation, 141–142
  issues influencing program-evaluation efforts, 137–138
  measurement, 138, 142
  recruiting batterer to participate in evaluation, 143
  safely involving survivors and children in evaluation, 144–145
parenting role, 48
parenting skills, interventions with fathers, 96
parenting styles, perpetrators, 11–12
parents
  children rejecting, post-separation, 51–52
  men who batter as, 71–73
parents' parenting, interventions with fathers, 96
passive-aggressive behavior, 36–37
patience, Fathering After Violence (FAV) initiative, 122
peer-group support programs, low-income fathers, 8
Peled, Einat, about author, 153
Perel, Guy, about author, 153–154
perpetrators
  domestic violence and children, 15
  litigation as control and harassment, 48
  parenting styles, 11–12

phenomenological approach, 92–93
philosophy, Caring Dads program, 103–
    104
physical abuse, domestic violence and,
    13–14
physical protection, safety, 41
positive parenting, coparents
    encouraging, 35
post-separation violence, 12–13
program development, Fathering After
    Violence (FAV) initiative, 121–
    123
psychotherapy, parenting experience,
    93–94
psychosis/paranoia, 50
public-welfare programs, Latino fathers,
    135

recovery. See Latino fathers in recovery
recruiting, men who batter for program
    evaluation, 143
relational dimensions, shared parenting,
    21
relationship dissolution, rate and causes,
    20
reparative framework
    Fathering After Violence (FAV)
        initiative, 121–122
    men and children, 129
    relationship of children and fathers,
        124–125, 126
research
    domestic violence, 59–60
    fathering after violence, 129
    fathering and domestic violence, 11–
        15
    fathers through their children's eyes,
        14–15
    impact of violent man's behavior on
        child, 13–14
    men's interference in women's
        parenting, 12
    parenting styles of perpetrators, 11–12
    post-separation violence by men who
        batter, 12–13
respect (respeto), healing process, 133,
    134
respect for fathers, Caring Dads program,
    111

responsibility, fathers, 105, 111–113
responsible fatherhood, G. W. Bush
    administration, 7
responsible-fatherhood groups, 8–9
risk assessment, domestic violence and
    homicide, 48
role-inadequacy perspective, fathering
    intervention with men who batter,
    87
role in family, fathers' view, 32–33
role models, 48
Roxbury Comprehensive Community
    Health Service, Family Violence
    Prevention Fund (FVPF) partner,
    119

safety
    accountability to, and well-being of
        children, 104, 106–108
    accountability to, of children's
        mothers, 105, 108–110
    African American couples and domestic
        violence history, 41
    barrier to contact, 38
    Caring Dads program, 105
    consideration of children's and
        women's, 116
    domestic violence after separation,
        48–49
    Family Violence Prevention Fund
        (FVPF) priority, 119–120
    fathering intervention, 92
    mother and child, 41–42
    physical and emotional protection,
        41
    shared parenting assumption, 26–27
San Francisco General Hospital, Child
    Trauma Research Project (CTRP),
    65, 66–67
San Francisco Safe Start, 72
Scott, Katreena, about author, 154
self-reflection, 94
separation
    abuse continuation, 47
    children rejecting parent after, 51–
        52
    homicide and domestic violence, 48
separation/divorce trauma, 50
services, problems in providing, 58

shared parenting. *See also* contact with
    former batterer
  access, 27–28
  African American women's perceptions
    of, 22–23
  assumptions, 26–27
  Brames' murder-suicide story, 19–20
  child mental health and emotional
    security, 29–30
  conditions for, 28
  contact logistics, 31–32, 35–40
  data collection and analysis, 24–25
  domestic violence, 56–57
  facilitators of contact, 31–32, 35–38
  fathering interventions, 94
  fathers' recommendations on
    coparenting, 34–35
  focus-group study, 23–25
  history of domestic violence, 21–23
  impact of time, 39–40
  informing perspectives, 23–24
  initiating contacts, 28–31
  parameters of contact, 30–31
  relational dimensions, 21
  relationship dissolution, 20–21
  safety, 27–28
  terminating contacts, 39
social movements
  fatherhood movements and domestic
    violence, 10–11
  father-involvement programs, 7–8
  fathers' rights groups, 9–10
  involving fathers, 6–11
  responsible-fatherhood groups, 8–9
spousal abuse
  allegations, 51
  family violence, 50–51
staff training, 125
stepfathers, violence, 14
storytelling, Latino fathers, 131–132,
    135–136
structural components, facilitating
    contact with former batterer, 36–38
structure, intervention with fathers, 95–97
Sullivan, Cris M., about author, 154
support
  fathering intervention with men who
    batter, 87
  men's capacity to father, 86

survivors, 144–145
symbolic interaction, 23
syndrome, alienation as, 51

teachings of elders (*Hue Hues*), Latino
    fathers in recovery, 133
Tello, Jerry, about author, 154–155
termination, shared-parenting contacts,
    39
third party, coparenting
    recommendation, 35
threats of harm, facilitators of contact,
    36–37
time, impact on shared parenting, 39–40
trained professional, parenting program
    evaluation, 141–142
training
  abusive fathers, 114
  batterer intervention program staff,
    125
training programs, domestic violence, 60–
    61
treatment
  domestic violence, 45
  mandating men into, 104, 106
treatment programs, mandated, 76
triangulation, 21
trust (*confianza*), healing process, 133,
    134–135
Tubbs, Carolyn, about author, 155

understanding (*entendimento*), healing
    process, 133, 134

validation, Fathering After Violence
    (FAV) initiative, 122
Van Horn, Patricia, about author, 155
violence. *See also* domestic violence;
    Fathering After Violence (FAV)
  children's appraisal of, 70
  co-occurring maltreatment, 13–14
  fathers' rights in light of, 30
  fathers' voices on, 32
  impact on children, 13–14, 71, 94, 97
  interventions with children exposed to,
    67
  level in family, 76–77
  post-separation, 12–13
  programs for stopping, 129–130

violent men, understanding, 89
violent parent, 74–76
visitation
    facilitators of contact, 36–37
    intervention, 56–59
    recommendations for domestic
        violence, 55
visitation disputes, 48–49

well-being, accountability for, of children,
    104, 106–108

Williams, Oliver J., about editor, 149–
    150
Wolfe, David A., about author, 155–156
women
    fathers' rights groups, 9–10
    safe involvement in program
        evaluations, 144–145
women's parenting, men's interference,
    12

yearning, understanding violent men, 89